Working Time Around the World

John Maynard Keynes once made the bold prediction that the three-hour work day would prevail for his grandchildren's generation. Seventy years later, the question of working time is as pertinent as it was at the inception of the 40-hour week. Not until now, however, has there been a global comparative analysis of working time laws, policies and actual working hours. Despite a century-long optimism about reduced working hours and some progress in legal measures limiting working hours, this book demonstrates that differences in actual working hours between industrialized and developing countries remain considerable – without any clear sign of hours being reduced. This study aims to offer some suggestions about how this gap can begin to be closed.

Lee, McCann and Messenger trace the theoretical background of the concept of working time before examining recent trends in working time laws in developing countries and countries in transition. The study then shifts its focus to developments in selected countries, considering both broad trends in working time at a national level and the structure and dynamics underlying these trends. The authors provide a remarkable set of policy suggestions that preserve health and safety, are 'family-friendly', promote gender equality, enhance productivity and facilitate workers' choice and influence over their working hours.

This book will be of great interest to policy-makers engaged with working conditions or health and safety, labour market experts, trade union leaders and workers' organizations, as well as academics and researchers in the fields of industrial relations, labour economics and labour law.

Sangheon Lee, **Deirdre McCann** and **Jon C. Messenger** are Research and Senior Officers for the Conditions of Work and Employment Programme at the International Labour Office in Geneva. Jon Messenger is the editor of and Sangheon Lee and Deirdre McCann are contributors to *Working Time and Workers' Preferences in Industrialized Countries*, also published by Routledge.

Routledge Studies in the Modern World Economy

Interest Rates and Budget Deficits
A study of the advanced economies
Kanhaya L. Gupta and Bakhtiar Moazzami

World Trade after the Uruguay Round
Prospects and policy options for the twenty-first century
Edited by Harald Sander and András Inotai

The Flow Analysis of Labour Markets
Edited by Ronald Schettkat

Inflation and Unemployment
Contributions to a new macroeconomic approach
Edited by Alvaro Cencini and Mauro Baranzini

Macroeconomic Dimensions of Public Finance
Essays in honour of Vito Tanzi
Edited by Mario I. Blejer and Teresa M. Ter-Minassian

Fiscal Policy and Economic Reforms
Essays in honour of Vito Tanzi
Edited by Mario I. Blejer and Teresa M. Ter-Minassian

Competition Policy in the Global Economy
Modalities for co-operation
Edited by Leonard Waverman, William S. Comanor and Akira Goto

Working in the Macro Economy
A study of the US labor market
Martin F. J. Prachowny

How Does Privatization Work?
Edited by Anthony Bennett

The Economics and Politics of International Trade
Freedom and trade: volume II
Edited by Gary Cook

The Legal and Moral Aspects of International Trade
Freedom and trade: volume III
Edited by Asif Qureshi, Hillel Steiner and Geraint Parry

Capital Markets and Corporate Governance in Japan, Germany and the United States
Organizational response to market inefficiencies
Helmut M. Dietl

Competition and Trade Policies
Coherence or conflict
Edited by Einar Hope

Rice
The primary commodity
A. J. H. Latham

Trade, Theory and Econometrics
Essays in honour of John S. Chipman
Edited by James C. Moore, Raymond Riezman and James R. Melvin

Who Benefits from Privatisation?
Edited by Moazzem Hossain and Justin Malbon

Towards a Fair Global Labour Market
Avoiding the new slave trade
Ozay Mehmet, Errol Mendes and Robert Sinding

Models of Futures Markets
Edited by Barry Goss

Venture Capital Investment
An agency analysis of UK practice
Gavin C. Reid

Macroeconomic Forecasting
A sociological appraisal
Robert Evans

Multimedia and Regional Economic Restructuring
Edited by Hans-Joachim Braczyk, Gerhard Fuchs and Hans-Georg Wolf

The New Industrial Geography
Regions, regulation and institutions
Edited by Trevor J. Barnes and Meric S. Gertler

The Employment Impact of Innovation
Evidence and policy
Edited by Marco Vivarelli and Mario Pianta

International Health Care Reform
A legal, economic and political analysis
Colleen Flood

Competition Policy Analysis
Edited by Einar Hope

Culture and Enterprise
The development, representation and
morality of business
Don Lavoie and Emily Chamlee-Wright

Global Financial Crises and Reforms
Cases and caveats
B. N. Ghosh

Geography of Production and Economic Integration
Miroslav N. Jovanović

Technology, Trade and Growth in OECD Countries
Does specialisation matter?
Valentina Meliciani

Post-Industrial Labour Markets
Profiles of North America and
Scandinavia
Edited by Thomas P. Boje and Bengt Furaker

Capital Flows without Crisis
Reconciling capital mobility and economic
stability
Edited by Dipak Dasgupta, Marc Uzan and Dominic Wilson

International Trade and National Welfare
Murray C. Kemp

Global Trading Systems at Crossroads
A post-Seattle perspective
Dilip K. Das

The Economics and Management of Technological Diversification
Edited by John Cantwell, Alfonso Gambardella and Ove Granstrand

Before and Beyond EMU
Historical lessons and future
prospects
Edited by Patrick Crowley

Fiscal Decentralization
Ehtisham Ahmad and Vito Tanzi

Regionalisation of Globalised Innovation
Locations for advanced industrial
development and disparities in
participation
Edited by Ulrich Hilpert

Gold and the Modern World Economy
Edited by Moon Joong Tcha

Global Economic Institutions
Willem Molle

Global Governance and Financial Crises
Edited by Meghnad Desai and Yahia Said

Linking Local and Global Economies
The ties that bind
Edited by Carlo Pietrobelli and Arni Sverrisson

Tax Systems and Tax Reforms in Europe
Edited by Luigi Bernardi and Paola Profeta

Trade Liberalization and APEC
Edited by Jiro Okamoto

Fiscal Deficits in the Pacific Region
Edited by Akira Kohsaka

Financial Globalization and the Emerging Market Economies
Dilip K. Das

International Labor Mobility
Unemployment and increasing returns to
scale
Bharati Basu

Good Governance in the Era of Global Neoliberalism
Conflict and depolitization in Latin
America, Eastern Europe, Asia and Africa
Edited by Jolle Demmers, Alex E. Fernández Jilberto and Barbara Hogenboom

The International Trade System
Alice Landau

International Perspectives on Temporary Work and Workers
Edited by John Burgess and Julia Connell

Working Time and Workers' Preferences in Industrialized Countries
Finding the balance
Edited by Jon C. Messenger

Tax Systems and Tax Reforms in New EU Members
Edited by Luigi Bernardi, Mark Chandler and Luca Gandullia

Globalization and the Nation State
The impact of the IMF and the World Bank
Edited by Gustav Ranis, James Vreeland and Stephen Kosak

Macroeconomic Policies and Poverty Reduction
Edited by Ashoka Mody and Catherine Pattillo

Regional Monetary Policy
Carlos J. Rodríguez-Fuentez

Trade and Migration in the Modern World
Carl Mosk

Globalisation and the Labour Market
Trade, technology and less-skilled workers in Europe and the United States
Edited by Robert Anderton, Paul Brenton and John Whalley

Financial Crises
Socio-economic causes and institutional context
Brenda Spotton Visano

Globalization and Self Determination
Is the nation-state under siege?
Edited by David R. Cameron, Gustav Ranis and Annalisa Zinn

Developing Countries and the Doha Development Round of the WTO
Edited by Pitou van Dijck and Gerrit Faber

Immigrant Enterprise in Europe and the USA
Prodromos Panayiotopoulos

Solving the Riddle of Globalization and Development
Edited by Manuel Agosín, David Bloom, George Chapelier and Jagdish Saigal

Foreign Direct Investment and the World Economy
Ashoka Mody

The World Economy
A global analysis
Horst Siebert

Production Organizations in Japanese Economic Development
Edited by Tetsuji Okazaki

The Economics of Language
International analyses
Edited by Barry R. Chiswick and Paul W. Miller

Street Entrepreneurs
People, place and politics in local and global perspective
Edited by John Cross and Alfonso Morales

Global Challenges and Local Responses
The East Asian experience
Edited by Jang-Sup Shin

Globalization and Regional Integration
The origins, development and impact of the single European aviation market
Alan Dobson

Russia Moves into the Global Economy: Breaking Out
John M. Letiche

The European Economy in an American Mirror
Barry Eichengreen, Michael Landesmann and Dieter Stiefel

Working Time Around the World
Trends in working hours, laws and policies in a global comparative perspective
Sangheon Lee, Deirdre McCann and Jon C. Messenger

Working Time Around the World

Trends in working hours, laws and policies in a global comparative perspective

Sangheon Lee, Deirdre McCann and Jon C. Messenger

LONDON AND NEW YORK

First published 2007
by Routledge
2 Park Square, Milton Park, Abingdon, Oxon OX14 4RN

Simultaneously published in the USA and Canada
by Routledge
270 Madison Ave, New York, NY 10016

Published in Switzerland in 2007 by the
International Labour Office
1211 Geneva 22, Switzerland
www.ilo.org/publns
ISBN: 978–92–2–119311–1

Routledge is an imprint of the Taylor & Francis Group, an informa business

Typeset in Times by
Book Now Ltd, London
Printed and bound in Great Britain by
TJ International Ltd, Padstow, Cornwall

British Library Cataloguing in Publication Data
A catalogue record for this book is available from the British Library

Library of Congress Cataloging in Publication Data
Lee, Sang-Heon.
Working time around the world: trends in working hours, laws and policies in
a global comparative perspective/Sangheon Lee, Deirdre McCann and Jon
C. Messenger.
     p. cm.
Includes bibliographical references and index.
1. Hours of labor. 2. Hours of labor–Law and legislation. 3. Labor laws and
legislation. 4. Hours of labor–Cross-cultural studies. I. McCann, Deirdre M.
II. Messenger, Jon C. (Jon Carleton), 1960– III. Title.

HD5106.L44 2007
331.25'7–dc22   2007004840

ISBN10: 0–415–43937–X (hbk)
ISBN10: 0–203–94521–2 (ebk)

ISBN13: 978–0–415–43937–4 (hbk)
ISBN13: 978–0–203–94521–6 (ebk)

Contents

List of figures		x
List of tables		xi
List of boxes		xii
List of authors		xiii
Foreword		xv
Acknowledgements		xvii

1 Introduction 1
1.1 Background and issues 1
1.2 Information sources 4
1.3 Structure of the book 5

2 Legal progress towards reducing working hours 7
2.1 Introduction 7
2.2 Working hours limits: international standards 8
2.3 National working hours limits: 1967–2005 9
    2.3.1 Limits on normal hours 11
    2.3.2 Other limits 18
2.4 Conclusions 20

3 Global trends in actual working hours 22
3.1 Introduction 22
3.2 Historical developments: a century-long progress 24
3.3 Average weekly hours 27
3.4 Beyond average hours: patterns and variations in individual working hours 33
3.5 Excessive hours (I): non-observance 36
    3.5.1 Defining excessive hours 36
    3.5.2 Observance of statutory norms and 'effective working-hour regulation index' 38
3.6 Excessive hours (II): working longer than 48 hours 45
    3.6.1 Global estimates 53

3.7 Short hours and underemployment   55
    3.7.1 Short hours   55
    3.7.2 Time-related underemployment   58
3.8 Distribution of working hours: bifurcation and double
    challenges   60
3.9 Conclusions   62

4 Gender, age and working time   64
4.1 Introduction   64
4.2 Differences in male and female labour market participation 65
    4.2.1 Temporal constraints on availability   66
    4.2.2 Patterns of hours   67
4.3 Work schedules and family responsibilities   69
4.4 Working time flexibility   74
    4.4.1 Policies and programmes   74
    4.4.2 Workers' attitudes towards flexibility   75
4.5 Working time and age: variable hours of work over the
    life course   78
    4.5.1 Patterns of hours over the life course   79
    4.5.2 Part-time work   81
4.6 Conclusions   83

5 Tertiarization, informalization and working time   86
5.1 Introduction   86
5.2 The rise of the service sector across the world   87
5.3 Working hours in the service sector   89
5.4 Work schedules in the service sector   96
    5.4.1 Shift work   96
    5.4.2 Night work   98
    5.4.3 Weekend work   99
    5.4.4 Other flexible working time arrangements   100
5.5 The 'informalization' of national economies   101
5.6 Working time in the informal economy: self-employment
    as a proxy measure   103
    5.6.1 Industrialized countries   105
    5.6.2 Developing countries   113
    5.6.3 Transition countries   114
5.7 Conclusions   118

6 Working time issues in developing countries   120
6.1 Introduction   120
6.2 Reducing working hours   121
    6.2.1 Time or money: working time and wages   121
    6.2.2 Working time, productivity and work organization 123
6.3 Working time flexibility   124

6.3.1 Hours averaging   125
6.3.2 Flexibilization and weekly rest periods   127
6.3.3 Part-time work and other 'non-standard' working time
      arrangements   128
6.3.4 Worker-oriented flexibility   130
6.3.5 The extent of flexible working time arrangements   131
6.4 Work–family and gender equality   132
6.5 Policy and practice: enforcement, exclusion and the informal
    economy   134
6.6 Conclusions   137

7 Summary and implications for policy   138
7.1 Summary of main findings   138
7.2 Implications for policy in developing and transition countries 141
      7.2.1 Towards decent working time   141
      7.2.2 Healthy working time   143
      7.2.3 'Family-friendly' working time   146
      7.2.4 Gender equality through working time   147
      7.2.5 Productive working time   149
      7.2.6 Choice and influence over working time   151
7.3 Concluding remarks   153

Notes   155
Bibliography   161
Statistical annex   168
Index   214

Figures

3.1 Historical trend in annual working hours in selected countries (1879–2000)　25

3.2 Weekly working hours versus incomes　33

3.3 Different types of working-hour distributions: illustrative examples　35

3.4 Observance rate and income by statutory working-hour standards　39

3.5 Effective working-hour regulation index (ERI) and national income　44

3.6 The ratification of Conventions Nos 1 and 30 and the share of workers who are working more than 48 hours per week　53

3.7 Incidence of short hours by national income　58

3.8 The distribution of working hours in the Republic of Korea (2004)　61

3.9 Working-hour bifurcation in selected countries: double challenges　62

4.1 Average weekly hours of work by age group (percentage, 2000)　80

4.2 Share of workers working short hours by age group (percentage, 2000)　82

5.1 Informal employment in non-agricultural employment by gender (1994–2000)　102

5.2 Wage employment and self-employment in non-agricultural informal employment by gender (1994–2000)　103

5.3 Usual versus actual working hours in the informal economy (the Republic of Moldova, 2003)　116

Tables

2.1   Weekly normal hours limits (1967)   13
2.2   Weekly normal hours limits (1984)   14
2.3   Weekly normal hours limits (1995)   15
2.4   Weekly normal hours limits (2005)   16
2.5   Minimum annual leave periods (2005)   19
3.1   Changes in working hours and paid leave (1956–2004) in selected countries   26
3.2   Average weekly working hours in manufacturing (1995–2004)   28
3.3   Statutory hours, observance and effective working-hour regulation index   40
3.4   Incidence of long working hours   46
3.5   The proportion of workers with shorter hours   56
3.6   Time-related underemployment (2001, percentage of total employment)   59
4.1   Changes in global labour market indicators by gender (1993–2003)   66
4.2   Proportion of workers working long hours, by gender (2004–5)   70
4.3   Proportion of workers working short hours, by gender (2004–5)   72
4.4   Working time and work–family balance in selected countries: coefficients matrix (2002)   76
5.1   Share of total employment in the service sector in selected countries   88
5.2   Average weekly working hours in manufacturing versus services in selected countries (2002)   90
5.3   Average weekly working hours in services (by subsector, 2002)   91
5.4   Proportion of workers working part-time hours in service subsectors (2000)   96
5.5a   Distribution of working hours for the self-employed by gender (industrialized countries)   106
5.5b   Distribution of working hours for the self-employed by gender (developing countries)   108
5.5c   Distribution of working hours for the self-employed by gender (transition countries)   110
6.1   Working hours, earnings and benefits (Mexico, 2000)   122

Boxes

2.1 The ILO Database of Working Time Laws 11

3.1 ILO data collection on the distribution of employed persons by their hours of work 36

3.2 Global estimates for workers working longer than 48 hours 54

4.1 Role reversal: longer hours of paid work for women in the Philippines 68

4.2 Plantation work and family responsibilities in Kenya 73

4.3 Long hours among retirement-age workers in Mexico 83

5.1 Excessive hours of work in the security industry: a global phenomenon 94

5.2 Extended opening hours in the retail trade: the case of Malaysia 97

5.3 The increasing fragmentation of working time: the case of split shifts in Peru 99

5.4 Very long hours and low pay: the case of domestic workers 115

5.5 Work schedules in the informal economy: everything depends on the volume of work 117

Authors

Sangheon Lee is an economist and Senior Research Officer with the International Labour Office (ILO) Conditions of Work and Employment Programme in Geneva. He specializes in analysing and monitoring changes in the quality of employment and has published widely on various aspects of employment conditions. He is currently editing a book on *Globalization and Changes in Employment Conditions in East Asia and the Pacific* (Chandos and ILO). He holds a PhD in economics from Cambridge University.

Deirdre McCann is a labour lawyer and Research Officer with the International Labour Office (ILO) Conditions of Work and Employment Programme in Geneva. Her research focuses on the legal aspects of working conditions, and she has published on working time, non-standard work and the reconciliation of work and family life. She is currently completing a book on *Regulating Flexible Work* (Oxford University Press, forthcoming). She holds a DPhil in law from the University of Oxford.

Jon C. Messenger is a Senior Research Officer with the International Labour Office (ILO) Conditions of Work and Employment Programme, Geneva, with the lead responsibility for its sub-programme on working time and work organization. He specializes in policy-focused research on working time and work organization, with a special interest in issues relating to temporal and spatial flexibility, gender and the informal economy. His most recent publication is *Decent Working Time: New trends, new issues* (with Jean-Yves Boulin, Michel Lallement and François Michon (Geneva, ILO, 2006)). Prior to joining the ILO, he worked at the US Department of Labor in Washington, DC for 15 years, where he served as Team Leader for Research on employment and training.

Foreword

Almost a century has passed since the adoption of the first international labour standard on working hours, which stipulates the principle of the eight-hour day and 48-hour week, and 70 years since the 40-hour week was adopted as the standard to which countries should aspire. Reading the documents that record the debates surrounding the adoption of these working time standards, one is struck by the optimism of the government, employer and worker participants regarding the possibility of shorter hours. One may recall that the great economist of the time, John Maynard Keynes, made a cheerful prediction during the economic depression that a three-hour workday would prevail for the generation of his grandchildren. One may wonder, then, how much progress has since been made and what can be done to make further progress towards making such predictions a reality.

This book, *Working Time Around the World*, takes up this historical perspective in the context of global economic integration and the Decent Work Agenda, and offers useful insights on these questions based on a number of unique information sources. As is well known, working time has been controversial and has accrued great social importance in many industrialized countries, but a systematic study that embraces both developing and industrialized countries has been surprisingly lacking. This is certainly unfortunate, given the widely shared belief that the disparity in working hours between these two groups of countries is considerable. The authors of the book, Sangheon Lee, Deirdre McCann and Jon Messenger, have made an important step forward in filling this knowledge gap, relying on the data they have collected for a number of years from legal texts, statistical surveys and national studies.

Their findings are mixed. They provide some good news concerning the progress made in the regulation of maximum working hours in developing and transition countries, although regional differences are substantial. Other findings are definitely worrying: despite progress in some measures, a substantial number of workers – estimated by the authors at about 22 per cent of the workers in the world – are still working more than 48 hours per week, while another significant proportion are basically underemployed, suffering from shorter hours. New policy challenges have emerged in many developing and transition countries, as demographic factors such as the feminization and ageing of the workforce have impacted on working hours. In addition, this book shows that informalization and tertiarization (service sector expansion) have intensified, such that working time is becoming increasingly diversified among individual workers.

What, then, can be done? The authors offer an impressive set of policy suggestions for ILO constituents and other interested organizations, based on five inter-connected criteria for Decent Working Time, by advocating working time arrangements that: preserve health and safety; are 'family-friendly'; promote gender equality; enhance productivity; and facilitate workers' choice and influence over their working hours. In doing that, they have expressed strong reservations about the single-minded deregulatory approach towards working time often recommended by influential international financial organizations, as being potentially counter-productive and risking undesirable social outcomes.

While the policy elements and principles that the authors lay out in this book are certainly necessary for developing and implementing better and more balanced policies on working time, it is obvious that they do not attempt to provide a 'ready-made' policy prescription. They clearly recognize that in developing working time policies, great attention needs to be paid to the needs and circumstances of individual countries, such as their level of economic development, industrial relations and legal systems, and cultural and social traditions. As readers will find out, these policy elements require social dialogue for a successful result: no social dialogue, no gains.

In light of the policy challenges outlined in this book, it is clear that we need global research and global action. As a recent book on working time, *La France et le temps de travail* (Fridenson and Reynaud, eds, 2004), reminds us, the ILO has been the locus of working time debates since its inception, especially with regard to the relationship between working time, health and safety, and job creation. These debates have developed, however, to incorporate additional policy goals, most notably those of ensuring that working hours allow workers adequate time to devote to their families and other elements of their lives. The role of the ILO, however, appears to have lost its momentum over the last two decades, with the most intense debates being conducted at the European level. However, we believe that this book makes a case that the ILO should restore its traditional role in working time debates, and take coordinated action to ensure decent working time for workers around the world.

François Eyraud
Executive Director
ILO Turin Centre

Manuel Tomei
Director
ILO Conditions of Work and Employment Programme

Acknowledgements

This report is the product of a seven-year long effort that received invaluable contributions and support from numerous people around the world. First, this report benefited considerably from a series of country studies, and we are very much grateful to the authors of these studies for their high-quality research: A. Maharramov (Azerbaijan), J. Saboia (Brazil), M. Echeverría (Chile), X. Zeng and his colleagues (China), J. Berkovský, J. Řehák and their colleagues (Czech Republic), P. Galasi (Hungary), O. Taylor (Jamaica), J. Yoon (Republic of Korea), S. Nagaraj (Malaysia), N. Richards (Mauritius), B. Esponda (Mexico), L. Aparicio Valdez (Peru), T. Chetvernina and her colleagues (Russian Federation), A. Ndiaye (Senegal), and Y. Alouane and his colleagues (Tunisia).

We are also most grateful to the team of researchers who carried out work on the ILO's Database of Working Time Laws (www.ilo.org/travdatabase): Mariela Dyrberg, Kristine Falciola, Christina Holmgren, Ingrid Sipi-Johnson, Olivier Mabilat, Corinne McCausland, Pernilla Melin, Esther Peeren, Helena Perez, Matteo Sasso and Anna-Christina Winterstein. Our appreciation is also due for the continuing efforts of the ILO's International Labour Standards Department to collect and make available labour legislation from around the world in the NATLEX Database (www.ilo.org/natlex), and in particular for the work of Oliver Liang and Claire Marchand.

A special word of thanks goes out to the national statistical agencies who kindly participated in the ILO special survey on working hours between 2004 and 2005. We were impressed by the high response rate and even more so by the high quality of the data, especially as, owing to the unique and demanding nature of this survey, in many cases these agencies had to prepare re-estimations from their raw data sets. We are also grateful to our colleagues in the ILO Bureau of Statistics, especially Bob Pember, who was extremely supportive throughout the entire survey process. We are also thankful for the considerable support from our colleagues in the ILO field offices in assisting us to initiate the country studies. Thanks also go to Andi Kabili and Sungmee Woo for their excellent work in data entry and preliminary analysis of the survey data.

This report was immeasurably improved by the comments and guidance from our peer reviewers, Thomas Haipeter, Georges Politakis and Jin Ho Yoon, as well as by the comments and insights of Dominique Anxo, Peter Auer, Janine Berg, Iain Campbell, Colette Fagan, Najati Ghosheh, Enrique Fernández Macías, Michelle Gallant, Lonnie Golden, David Kucera, Michele Jankanish, Steffen Lehndorff, Jillian Murray, Jouko Nätti, Alena Nesporova, Peter Peek and Barbara Pocock.

We would also like to express our appreciation to several individuals from the International Labour Office, especially François Eyraud, the current Executive Director, the ILO Turin Centre, and former Director of the Conditions of Work and Employment Programme, for his support and encouragement throughout the many years of research and writing for this publication. We would like to thank William Salter and our other colleagues in the Conditions of Work and Employment Programme, whose support over the years has been critical in completing this project. We are also grateful to Ariel Golan and his team, Hiep Nguyen and their colleagues in the ILO Library for both their invaluable contributions to this report and their continuing support for ILO research.

Finally, we are particularly grateful to our long-time colleague Mariela Dyrberg, who deserves special thanks for all of her assistance with the preparation of the manuscript, as well as compiling a comprehensive set of references for the report.

1 Introduction

The eight-hour day, implying the 48-hour week, was a key demand of the working class all over the world before the ILO was established ... To the workers, the extension and generalized application of the eight-hour day represented a reform which no other could equal in value – a chance to share in the distribution of the new wealth created by modern industry and to receive that share in the form of spare time. More generally, the need to safeguard the health and well-being of workers was recognized; over-long hours had been shown to be harmful to economic efficiency as well as to material and moral welfare of the workers and to be incompatible with political democracy. Finally, there was a feeling in many quarters that international standards relating to hours of work might be a useful means of limiting the possibilities of unfair competition. In reflection of this trend of world opinion, the adoption of the eight-hour day and 48-hour week was a prime objective of the ILO.

(ILO 1958: 3)

1.1 Background and issues

The first ILO Convention, the Hours of Work (Industry) Convention, 1919 (No. 1), which established the principle of '8 hours a day and 48 hours a week' for the manufacturing sector, is expected to celebrate its centennial anniversary at the end of the next decade. The main motivations underlying the adoption of this Convention are well captured in the quotation above, although it appears that a complex set of factors played out at that time so that, in retrospect, it is not entirely clear which of these are dominant.[1] Following Convention No. 1, numerous working time Conventions were subsequently adopted: the Hours of Work (Commerce and Offices) Convention, 1930 (No. 30) extended the 48-hour working week to workers in commerce and offices in 1930, and the Forty-Hour Week Convention, 1935 (No. 47) established a new standard of the 40-hour working week in 1935 at a time when the world was devastated by economic crisis and war. The principle of a minimum of one-day weekly rest was introduced in the Weekly Rest (Industry) Convention, 1921 (No. 14) and the Weekly

Rest (Commerce and Offices) Convention, 1957 (No. 106). Conventions concerning night work and holidays with pay also followed.

How much progress, then, has been made in working time, especially in relation to the centennial wisdom of a 48-hour working week?[2] In light of the economic growth that we have witnessed in many parts of the world in the twentieth century, one might assume that this wisdom has now become a well-rooted reality. In addition, it appears that statutory normal hours of work have been reduced gradually from 48 hours to 40 hours in a large number of countries (ILO 2005d; McCann 2005), which can be considered as a historical achievement in the last century. This is all good news for international working time standards.

However, others may argue that the 48-hour working week and the 40-hour working week are no more than 'paper tigers', as they are stipulated in the law but their enforcement in practice is weak. A day cannot pass without hearing complaints about long working hours in developing countries such as China, but surprisingly also in some industrialized countries as well (Lee 2004). Concerns are often expressed in phrases such as 'time squeeze', 'time poverty' and '*karoshi*' (death from overwork). Yet, how much do we know about long hours in these countries? To our surprise, despite such frequent coverage of long working hours in developing countries, the paucity of reliable data makes it difficult to know about the exact extent to which workers are working long hours, say more than 48 hours per week. In a sense, there is a mismatch between our concerns and our knowledge about working time in the developing world. Thus, a more systematic data collection and analysis is called for.

In fact, surveys have been undertaken to gauge the extent to which such principles have been adopted, and the results have been reported to the International Labour Conference. Yet, due to the nature of this exercise, the focus has been on national laws and practice, with little information on actual patterns of working hours. The most recent survey attempted to capture actual working time practice around the world, pointing out that 'the overall picture is still far from clear, due to in part to the non-submission of reports and to the lack of comprehensive statistical data' (ILO 2005d: 23).

More generally, it should also be noted that the existing body of literature on working time is heavily biased towards industrialized countries, particularly Europe (e.g. Bosch *et al.*, eds, 1993; Golden and Figart, eds, 2000; O'Reilly *et al.*, eds, 2000; Houseman and Nakamura, eds, 2001; Wong and Picot, eds, 2001; Messenger, ed., 2004; Boulin *et al.*, eds, 2006). Therefore, our knowledge is very limited regarding developing and transition countries, with the likely exception of new EU Member States (see, for example, European Foundation 2006). 'Global' debates on working time, for instance concerning working time flexibility, often lack practical importance or relevance for developing countries, mainly due to the large gaps between developing and industrialized countries in terms of working time developments. As traditional sources of working time flexibility (such as overtime) are readily available in these countries and informal employment is widespread, it is quite conceivable that incentives for new types of working time flexibility may not be very strong. Again, this question begs for a closer and more empirically based scrutiny.

At the same time, however, there is increasing concern about working time regulations and their negative impact on the labour market in developing countries. Indeed, there is a recent but nonetheless widely quoted view that developing countries tend to have more 'rigid' regulations on working hours and paid leave than many developed countries. For instance, the World Bank argued in a recent report that:

> Regulation affecting working hours and paid leave can involve similar tradeoffs [between providing high levels of protection for workers enjoying regular employment and expanding protection and opportunities to a broader group of workers]. Many developing countries have adopted far-reaching regulations on these subjects – in some cases going beyond what is on the books in most developed countries. Even among countries at similar stages of development, the differences in regulations can be large, with significant effects on labor costs and on the ability of firms to accommodate fluctuations in demand.
>
> (World Bank 2004: 145)

If this statement is accurate, then the logical future policy direction regarding working time should be deregulation and flexibilization. How convincing is this argument? First, questions can be raised about the method of determining the supposed 'rigidity' of working time regulations, which is basically incompatible with international working time standards (Lee and McCann 2007). Second, consideration should be given to the fact that little is known about enforcement gaps in developing countries and how they are related to economic and labour market performance. Without these, it is extremely difficult to evaluate the deregulation argument. Specifically, how large is the enforcement gap and how different is it across countries?

In addition, the overall working time picture can be rather complicated as we move down to individual workers working in different conditions. For instance, it is often reported in industrialized countries that long working hours are a male phenomenon while short hours are a female one. This gender-related variation can be further complicated in countries with significant informal employment where workers appear to be more diversified. Here again, we need data and analysis to examine the extent of working-hour diversification. Although work–family balance does not appear as a big social issue in developing countries, this does not mean that the difficulties of workers with family responsibilities are fewer. While in industrialized countries this issue tends to be increasingly handled through flexible working time arrangements (e.g. part-time work, flexi-time), developing countries tend to rely more on gender-biased informal employment as a coping strategy or on extended family support. To the best of our knowledge, this diversification of working hours by gender and employment status (formal/informal) has never been considered in a global context.

This book is aimed at investigating working time around the world by addressing these and other issues. The available sources of information on working time in developing and transition countries, such as legal texts, statistical data and case studies, are examined to give a contemporary picture of working time in these countries in an accurate and balanced way. While we cannot claim that we have been able to provide satisfactory answers to all of these issues, we do believe that this report offers useful information and analysis, offering valuable insights regarding the issues at hand and some important policy implications.

1.2 Information sources

Given the paucity of information and data, which has made it difficult to carry out a global review of working time, it is worthwhile mentioning the information sources used in this book. Major information sources are of three types.

First, the ILO's Database of Working Time Laws allows us to undertake a comprehensive analysis of working time regulations around the world.[3] This database provides searchable information on the laws of more than 100 countries, covering a broad range of subjects such as weekly and daily hours limits, rest periods, holidays, and flexible working time arrangements (see Box 2.1 in Chapter 2).

Second, in order to fill our knowledge gap concerning developing countries, a series of 15 country studies has been carried out based on a standard research framework. The selection of countries for such studies was based on geographical and strategic importance: whether working time issues have been debated as a social concern; or if changes in working time policy (including legal changes) have been recently introduced. In some cases where working time data are scant (e.g. China), new data collection through small-scale surveys was undertaken. A list of these country study reports is provided in the Bibliography.

Finally, to complement the existing ILO data on average weekly working hours, data on the distribution of weekly working hours (the number of workers in specified categories defined according to the number of weekly working hours) were collected from national statistics. An ILO questionnaire, which provides a standard tabular format for reporting, was sent to national statistical agencies, and a total of 60 countries kindly participated in the survey. The data that we received were carefully entered in a single standardized database, which will be made publicly available (see Box 3.1 in Chapter 3 and also the Statistical annex).

We believe that this study benefits greatly from these information sources, which are probably more comprehensive and more reliable than those previously available, although we also note that more should be done to capture working time developments in developing countries (see Chapter 7).

1.3 Structure of the book

The remainder of this report is structured as follows: Chapter 2 will focus on international trends towards reducing working hours. It will review the development of legal hours limits in the international standards and national laws over the latter part of the twentieth century to the present, incorporating an examination of the policy objectives underlying these initiatives. The chapter will identify an overall global trend towards shorter hours (i.e. the 40-hour working week), with considerable regional variations.

Following an overview of regulatory frameworks, Chapter 3 turns to the actual working hours that workers are working, reviewing both recent trends in average working hours and the distribution of working hours. The extent of long working hours, defined as more than 48 hours per week, is examined and a global estimate is provided. The gap between law and reality is measured based on the concepts of 'observance' and 'effective regulation'. The chapter also includes a discussion of the incidence of short hours among workers.

Chapter 4 introduces an important thematic issue, 'gender, age and working time', reflecting the diversification of the global workforce along the lines of gender and age. In this chapter we investigate gender gaps in working hours and working time arrangements and their implications. In addition, we discuss the question of how working time flexibility is related to workers' feelings about over-work and address the work–family balance, based on the available evidence. Similar questions will be asked about age and its implications.

In Chapter 5 we turn to the issues of 'tertiarization' (the expanding service sector) and informalization, which have gained increasing importance in recent years in both industrialized and developing countries. Given the widespread assumption that these changes have led to the diversification of working time, this chapter examines actual working hours in the service sector and its component subsectors in these countries. It also analyses newly available information on working time in the informal economy from the ILO questionnaire in order to study how patterns of working hours in the informal economy vary within a country and across countries. The primary focus of these latter discussions will be the self-employed, who account for the largest share of informal employment and for whom data are most readily available.[4]

In order to present a more vivid picture of trends in working time, in Chapter 6 we illustrate dominant trends in working time policies with a rich set of country examples. On initiatives to reduce working hours, we explore two of the primary factors that influence the impact of these policies, the relationship between working hours and wages, and the recourse to overtime as a way of increasing productivity. Focusing on developing and transition countries, we show that working time 'flexibility', although often mentioned in policy documents, is not widespread in practice in these countries. In particular, limited attention has so far been paid to 'employee-oriented' forms of flexibility, including those that benefit workers with family responsibilities. Finally, we return to the questions raised in Chapter 2 about the often limited influence of working time policies on workplace practice, and outline a number of the factors that contribute towards this divergence.

Chapter 7 concludes, summarizing the main findings of the previous chapters, and based on these, outlining policy suggestions for consideration by governments and the social partners. The recommendations are made within the 'decent working time' framework developed in *Working Time and Workers' Preferences in Industrialized Countries* (Messenger, ed., 2004), a previous study of working time in industrialized countries.

2 Legal progress towards reducing working hours

2.1 Introduction

Hours of work feature prominently in expert and public debates about working conditions and workers' lives in developing countries. In these debates the concern is being voiced that, as one element of poor working conditions, many workers are being required to work long and disruptive hours to the detriment of their health, families and lives outside of work. These concerns extend to the role of the law in improving working conditions. Discussions on the impact of globalization, in particular, incorporate a focus on its consequences for labour laws, including those that limit working hours and structure their scheduling. These fears about the future of legal regulation take different forms. It is pointed out, for example, that globalization has the potential to unleash destructive regulatory competition, resulting in a levelling-down of the protections found in labour laws, including those on working hours. In contrast, an alternative scenario does not foresee the weakening of national legal norms. Instead, it suggests that the standards embodied in legislative texts are having little influence on actual working conditions in developing countries; in the case of working time, that long and inconvenient hours could be widespread even in countries in which the legal standards are exemplary.

Evaluating these predictions has so far been difficult due to a lack of data (Lee and McCann 2007). In assessing countries' legal standards, for example, researchers have been compelled to take into account the ratification of the international standards, rather than the content of domestic legislation. And where national legal measures have been drawn on, it has not been possible to compare their standards with actual working hours, in order to assess their influence on workplace practice. This and the following chapter take steps to address these deficiencies with respect to one of the central elements of working time laws – limits on working hours. In particular, they focus on the limits on the number of hours that can be worked over the period of a week, although rights to annual leave are also briefly reviewed.

Weekly hours limits are working time law's primary method of preventing consistent or regular long hours. Where influential, these limits play the most significant role in determining the volume of hours worked each week. As such, they make a substantial contribution towards preserving health and safety and permitting workers to strike an acceptable balance between paid work, domestic and caring labour and other aspects of their lives. However, these legal standards are significant not solely in that they represent the limits within which working time arrangements should be designed. They also represent the standards that governments uphold as acceptable working hours for their citizens. Even where they are not widely adhered to in practice, then, they are best viewed as embodying a national aspiration for working hours.

The objective of this chapter is to asses the evolution of hours limits, their current status and the policy objectives that underlie them. By focusing on national laws, it permits an assessment of whether there has been a process of convergence in weekly hours limits towards an international 'floor' of legal standards on acceptable hours. To this end, Section 2.2 provides background on the historical development of the international standards on working hours limits, while Section 2.3 reviews the historical trends at national level, the current extent and nature of hours limits and the debates being conducted on policy directions in limiting working hours.

2.2 Working hours limits: international standards

The reduction of working hours was one of the original objectives of labour law. The primary technique towards achieving this goal, mandating of limits on the hours that can be worked in each day or week, was first reflected in laws enacted in European countries in the mid-nineteenth century to reduce the working hours of children (ILO 1967). These early, more limited, measures were followed by laws that addressed the working hours of adults, which spread across Europe, resulting in a ten-hour daily limit being relatively widespread in this region by the start of World War I. While this was the high point of progress in Europe, however, two pioneer countries, New Zealand and the United States, had adopted a 48-hour week at the beginning of the century. Soon after the end of the war, this standard had spread to most European and a number of Latin American countries, including Mexico and Uruguay (ILO 1967). When union campaigns for global standards on working hours culminated in their inclusion in the Preamble to the ILO's Constitution and its first standard, the Hours of Work (Industry) Convention, 1919 (No. 1), it was the eight-hour day and 48-hour week that were included (see Murray 2001). And in 1930, the international limits were extended to cover all but agricultural workers by the adoption of the Hours of Work (Commerce and Offices) Convention, 1930 (No. 30).

The significance of this initial standard of the 48-hour week is that it is the legal standard closest to the point beyond which regular work becomes unhealthy, which is identified in the health literature as 50 hours (see, for example, Spurgeon 2003). Indeed, the preservation of workers' health was a primary strand in the adoption of this standard from its inception, and remains a prominent rationale of policies aimed at keeping working time within this limit. Health and safety was not, however, the sole objective underlying the 48-hour week. Other goals were reflected, for example, in the debates around the adoption of Convention No. 1, in which, although health and safety concerns were voiced, the dominant rationale was to ensure adequate non-work, or 'leisure', time for workers.[1]

The 48-hour limit did not, however, remain the only standard to be adopted at the national or international levels. By the 1920s, a number of industries in Europe and the United States had introduced a 40-hour week (ILO 1967). And during the depression of the following decade, when hours reductions first came to be identified as having the potential to promote employment, it was embodied in a new international instrument, the Forty-Hour Week Convention, 1935 (No. 47), which refers to the hardship caused by widespread unemployment and requires measures to reduce working hours towards this standard. The 40-hour limit has not been viewed solely as stimulating employment, however, but has been recognized as contributing to a broader range of objectives, including, in recent years, towards advancing work–life balance. It has gradually become the vision of acceptable working hours in many jurisdictions, and at the international level it was reinforced in the substantially different economic context of the early 1960s, when it was expressed as 'a social standard to be reached by stages if necessary' in the Reduction of Hours of Work Recommendation, 1962 (No. 116).

Finally, in reviewing the evolution of working hours limits it is also useful to recall that the concern for the limitation of working hours is not confined to labour law, but that it has also been identified as a human right. The right to limits on working hours is included in the human rights instruments that emerged in the wake of World War II, in which it is expressed in less concrete terms than in the ILO standards. The Universal Declaration of Human Rights recognizes a right to rest and leisure that encompasses a 'reasonable limitation' of working hours;[2] and the International Covenant on Economic, Social and Cultural Rights includes working hours limits as elements of the right to just and favourable working conditions.[3] Working time limits are also included in more recent regional human rights instruments: in the Revised European Social Charter 1996,[4] Charter of Fundamental Rights of the European Union[5] and the Protocol of San Salvador[6] (McCann 2008).

2.3 National working hours limits: 1967–2005

As we saw in the previous section, by the mid-twentieth century two primary standards were available for limiting weekly working hours, the 48-hour limit of the earliest international instruments and the more recent objective of the 40-hour week. This section concentrates on the evolution of national working hours limits over the latter part of the twentieth century to the present day, focusing, in particular, on the balance between each of these two limits. It is, then, primarily concerned with limits on weekly hours, the most significant method of limiting working hours. This is not to say, however, that the limits on daily hours that have been enacted in most countries across the world are irrelevant. These can also be of great value, in particular towards preventing workplace accidents and allowing workers adequate time to devote to their unpaid work and leisure on a regular basis, and are discussed in more detail in Chapter 6. More relevant to avoiding consistently long hours are limits on overtime work and entitlements to minimum periods of weekly rest and annual leave, which are briefly reviewed in this section.

The concern of this chapter is statutory regulation, rather than working time norms that are established through collective bargaining. Collective agreements can be a significant element of working time regulation and have often been the driving force behind regulatory innovation, generating approaches later transferred to legislative measures. In a number of European countries they are the dominant regulatory technique. In developing and transition countries, however, although collective agreements are influential in certain sectors and can offer innovative examples of best practice, collective bargaining is a less significant regulatory tool, and legislation has long been the dominant technique in the field of working time (ILO 1967, 2005d). Moreover, although the laws reviewed in this section are confined to provisions in legislation, it is worth noting that in a number of countries, particularly in Latin America[7] and Central and Eastern Europe,[8] these measures reiterate hours limits that are embodied in their constitutions.

There has always been a substantial degree of uniformity in the techniques used to regulate working time. The international standards and legislation in the vast majority of countries share a similar structure, in that they specify a limit on the number of hours that can be worked before overtime payments are to be made, plus additional limits on overtime hours. Their similarity makes it possible to compare most of the main elements of working time legislation from across the world, including weekly hours limits, and this work has been carried out periodically by the ILO. The historical data on statutory limits included in this section are drawn from such analyses, from 1967, 1984 and 1995 (ILO 1967, 1984, 1995). The most recent information, which is reviewed in more detail, covers the legislation in force in 102 countries in 2005, and is drawn from research conducted for the ILO's Database of Working Time Laws (see Box 2.1) (see also Botero *et al.* 2004; ILO 2005d).

Tables 2.1–2.4 present national hours limits, using comparative country data from the four research periods. Although there is some variation in the coverage of the countries included in these tables, it is sufficiently consistent to offer a broad picture of the evolution of working hours limits. In these tables, working hours limits are largely categorized into the three central groupings of 40 hours, 41–46 hours and 48 hours. The developing countries are categorized by region, to make it possible not only to identify global developments in working time legislation, but to single out trends among developing countries and highlight differences and similarities among regions.

These data, then, make it possible to track the development of this element of working time regulation during the years in which concerns have emerged about the impact of economic globalization on employment and social policy, including its potential to undermine labour laws. The following analysis is intended to clarify the development of this form of legal protection, and, in particular, to evaluate whether there has in fact been any levelling-down of standards on the duration of working hours. It also contributes data on the legal measures necessary to analyse their influence in practice, an analysis which is carried out in the following chapter.

Box 2.1 The ILO Database of Working Time Laws

By the early years of this century, the available information on working time laws, especially those of developing countries, was inadequate. Although comparisons of legislation and collective agreements in European Union countries were available, developments in other regions, and therefore the global picture, were unclear.

In response to this knowledge gap, the International Labour Office's Conditions of Work and Employment Programme began in 2004 to compile and translate national working time legislation and to include summaries of their content in an online Database of Working Time Laws.

This database is the most comprehensive available source of information on national working time laws.[9] It covers the legislation of more than 100 countries and extends to all the main elements of working regulation, including: hours limits; overtime work; rest periods; annual leave and public holidays; night work; part-time work; and rights for individual workers to change their working hours. The database can be searched for comprehensive information on individual countries or used to make comparisons between countries or regions.

The Database of Working Time Laws is available at www.ilo.org/travdatabase.

2.3.1 Limits on normal hours

As we have seen in Section 2.2, although national working time laws favoured the 48-hour limit at the end of World War I, by 1935 the 40-hour limit was embodied in some national laws and had found a place among the international standards that was confirmed in 1962. By the time of the ILO's first comprehensive review of national working time laws in 1967, a trend towards the 40-hour limit was also evident in national measures (ILO 1967). Only 35 of the 93 countries included in the 1967 survey had a statutory 48-hour working week, and the rest had adopted lower limits. Table 2.1 highlights the regional differences at this time in the countries covered by this chapter. As can be seen, the 40-hour limit was influential in a number of industrialized countries, and also present in a significant number of countries in Africa. In Latin America, however, the 48-hour limit was virtually uniform. It was also prominent in Asia, although a number of countries, including India, did not specify an hours limit applicable across the entire labour force.

This trend towards lower limits continued over the next two decades, and by 1984 the influence of the 40-hour limit was beginning to approach that of the 48-hour week (ILO 1984) (see Table 2.2). Again, however, the 48-hour limit continued to be strong in Latin America, and, to a lesser degree, in Asia. A number of significant reductions took place in these regions over the following decade, as can be seen in Table 2.3. In Brazil, for example, statutory hours were reduced to 44 hours in 1988, in a shift away from the 48-hour limit that had been in place since 1934; the Republic of Korea made the same transition in 1989; and China adopted a 40-hour week in 1995 (ILO 1995).

With respect to current working hours limits, Table 2.4 confirms that the 40-hour week is the most prevalent standard. Almost half of the countries covered by the 2005 research have enacted a limit of 40 hours or less; and among the others, the intermediate limits (41–46 hours) and the 48-hour week are of almost equal significance. Moreover, a comparison of Tables 2.3 and 2.4 offers no evidence of any weakening of the standards found in statutory texts, at least in the form of the introduction of higher basic limits (measures that permit these limits to be averaged over periods of longer than a week are discussed in Chapter 6). The only shift in weekly limits has been towards their reduction in 16 of the countries covered by this chapter (Algeria, the Bahamas, Belgium, Bulgaria, Chad, Chile, the Czech Republic, Egypt, Italy, Mongolia, Morocco, the Netherlands, the Republic of Korea, Portugal, Rwanda and Slovenia).

The experience of those countries in which hours reductions have been introduced during the last decade confirms the continuing relevance of the traditional policy objectives of working time law. Chile, for example, offers a recent illustration of hours reductions being tied to the goal of job creation, an approach familiar, among industrialized countries, in France and Germany. When the 48-hour limit that had been in force in Chile since 1924 was reduced to 45 hours in 2005, the overarching objective was to create jobs (Echeverría 2002). In the Republic of Korea, too, the debate around reducing the 44-hour limit that began in the wake of the economic crisis in 1997 was centred initially on tackling unemployment (Yoon 2001; Lee 2003). The Republic of Korea also illustrates the use of policy objectives of a more recent vintage. As the economy recovered, the goals envisioned for the hours

Table 2.1 Weekly normal hours limits (1967)

	No universal statutory limit	35–39 hours	40 hours	41–46 hours	48 hours	More than 48 hours
Industrialized countries	Australia, Denmark, Ireland, United Kingdom		Canada, Finland, France, New Zealand, United States	Belgium, Luxembourg (commerce and offices), Norway, Portugal (offices), Sweden, Switzerland	Austria, Germany, Italy, Japan, Luxembourg (industry), Netherlands, Portugal (industry and commerce), Spain	
Africa	Kenya, Nigeria, United Republic of Tanzania		Algeria, Cameroon, Chad, Gabon, Ivory Coast, Mali, Mauritania, Niger, Senegal		Congo (Kinshasa), Morocco, Tunisia	
Asia	India, Malaysia, Pakistan	Singapore (offices)		Singapore (industry and commerce)	China, Philippines, Thailand	
Caribbean	Jamaica			Cuba, Dominican Republic	Haiti	
Central and Eastern Europe				Bulgaria, Czechoslovakia, USSR	Romania	
Latin America				Guatemala, Uruguay (commerce), Venezuela (commerce and offices)	Argentina, Bolivia, Brazil, Chile, Colombia, Costa Rica, Mexico, Nicaragua, Panama, Peru, Uruguay (industry), Venezuela (industry)	

Source: ILO 1967.

Table 2.2 Weekly normal hours limits (1984)

	No universal statutory limit	35–39 hours	40 hours	41–46 hours	48 hours	More than 48 hours
Industrialized countries	Australia, Denmark, United Kingdom	France	Austria, Belgium, Canada, Finland, Luxembourg, New Zealand, Norway, Spain, Sweden, United States	Portugal (offices), Switzerland (industrial and white collar)	Germany, Ireland, Italy, Japan, Netherlands, Portugal (industry and commerce)	Switzerland (all other workers)
Africa	Seychelles		Benin, Cameroon, Chad, Congo, Djibouti, Gabon, Ivory Coast, Madagascar, Mali, Mauritania, Niger, Nigeria, Senegal, Togo	Algeria, Angola, Burundi, Cape Verde, Rwanda, United Republic of Tanzania	Guinea-Bissau, Morocco, Mozambique	
Asia	India, Pakistan, Viet Nam		Indonesia	Mongolia, Singapore	China, Lao People's Democratic Republic, Malaysia, Philippines, Thailand (industry)	Thailand (commerce)
Caribbean	Grenada, Jamaica			Cuba, Dominican Republic	Bahamas, Haiti	
Central and Eastern Europe				Bulgaria, Czechoslovakia, Romania, USSR		
Latin America	Belize		Ecuador	El Salvador, Honduras, Uruguay (commerce), Venezuela (commerce and offices)	Argentina, Bolivia, Brazil, Chile, Colombia, Costa Rica, Guatemala, Mexico, Nicaragua, Panama, Paraguay, Peru, Uruguay (industry), Venezuela (industry)	
Middle East					Egypt, Jordan, Lebanon	

Source: ILO 1984.

Table 2.3 Weekly normal hours limits (1995)

	No universal statutory limit	35–39 hours	40 hours	41–46 hours	48 hours	More than 48 hours
Industrialized countries	Australia, Denmark, Germany, United Kingdom	France	Austria, Belgium, Canada, Finland, Japan, Luxembourg, New Zealand, Norway, Spain, Sweden, United States	Portugal, Switzerland (workers in industrial enterprises, offices, technical posts and sales staff in large commercial enterprises)	Ireland, Italy, Netherlands	Switzerland (all other workers)
Africa	Nigeria, Seychelles		Benin, Burkina Faso, Cameroon, Chad, Congo, Côte d'Ivoire, Djibouti, Gabon, Madagascar, Mali, Mauritania, Niger, Senegal, Togo	Algeria, Angola, Burundi, Cape Verde, Guinea-Bissau, Namibia, Rwanda, South Africa, United Republic of Tanzania	Morocco, Mozambique, Tunisia	Kenya
Asia	India, Pakistan		China, Indonesia	Republic of Korea, Mongolia, Singapore	Cambodia, Lao People's Democratic Republic, Malaysia, Philippines, Thailand (industry), Viet Nam	Thailand (commerce)
Caribbean	Jamaica			Cuba, Dominican Republic	Bahamas, Haiti	
Central and Eastern Europe	Romania		Latvia, Russian Federation	Bulgaria, Czech Republic, Slovenia		
Latin America			Ecuador	Belize, Brazil, El Salvador, Honduras, Uruguay (commerce), Venezuela	Argentina, Bolivia, Chile, Colombia, Costa Rica, Guatemala, Mexico, Nicaragua, Panama, Paraguay, Peru, Uruguay (industry)	
Middle East					Egypt, Jordan, Lebanon	

Source: ILO 1995.

Table 2.4 Weekly normal hours limits (2005)

	No universal statutory limit	35–39 hours	40 hours	41–46 hours	48 hours	More than 48 hours
Industrialized countries	Australia, Denmark, Germany, Ireland, United Kingdom (48 hour limit on total hours)	Belgium, France	Austria, Canada, Finland, Italy, Japan, Luxembourg, Netherlands, New Zealand, Norway, Portugal, Spain, Sweden, United States	Switzerland (workers in industrial enterprises, offices, technical posts and sales staff in large commercial enterprises)		Switzerland (all other workers)
Africa	Nigeria, Seychelles	Chad	Algeria, Benin, Burkina Faso, Cameroon, Congo, Côte d'Ivoire, Djibouti, Gabon, Madagascar, Mali, Mauritania, Niger, Rwanda, Senegal, Togo	Angola, Burundi, Cape Verde, Democratic Republic of the Congo, Guinea-Bissau, Morocco, Namibia, South Africa, United Republic of Tanzania	Mozambique, Tunisia	Kenya
Asia	India, Pakistan		China, Indonesia, Republic of Korea, Mongolia	Singapore	Cambodia, Lao People's Democratic Republic, Malaysia, Philippines, Thailand, Viet Nam	
Caribbean	Jamaica, Grenada		Bahamas	Cuba, Dominican Republic	Haiti	
Central and Eastern Europe			Bulgaria, Czech Republic, Estonia, Latvia, Lithuania, the former Yugoslav Republic of Macedonia, Romania, Russian Federation, Slovakia, Slovenia			
Latin America			Ecuador	Belize, Brazil, Chile, El Salvador, Honduras, Uruguay (commerce), Venezuela	Argentina, Bolivia, Colombia, Costa Rica, Guatemala, Mexico, Nicaragua, Panama, Paraguay, Peru, Uruguay (industry)	
Middle East		Egypt			Jordan, Lebanon	

Source: ILO Database of Working Time Laws (www.ilo.org/travdatabase).

reduction shifted towards improving work–family reconciliation and quality of life (Lee 2003).

These hours reductions in Chile and the Republic of Korea also highlight a technique available to governments to ensure that firms can bring themselves in line with reduced statutory limits on their entry into force. In both countries, the lower limit did not take immediate effect: the 45-hour limit was introduced in legislation in Chile in 2001 but its entry into force was delayed for four years, while in the Republic of Korea the new 40-hour limit is being phased-in according to firm size over the period from 2004 to 2011. Such phased approaches are intended to allow employers time to take the steps needed to reduce hours, such as introducing new forms of work organization or conducting negotiations with unions.

Despite the overall shift towards lower hours limits in recent years, the 48-hour week remains the legal standard in a significant number of countries. This can be seen from the regional picture presented in Table 2.4. All the industrialized countries that have a normal hours limit mandate a basic working week of 40 hours or less, with the exception of Switzerland with respect to certain workers. The 40-hour limit is also present in all of the Central and Eastern European countries covered by this chapter. And almost half of the African countries have adopted a 40-hour or shorter working week, while only three have limits above 46 hours. In contrast, Latin America remains the outlier with respect to hours limits. Most countries in this region have a 48-hour week and all the others, except Ecuador, are in the intermediate range. And only partial progress has been made towards firmer limits in Asia, where the hours reduction in the Republic of Korea has highlighted a polarization between lower and higher limits. Six of the 11 Asian countries with a general hours limit have a 48-hour standard. The others legislate a 40-hour week, with the exception of Singapore, which has adopted a 44-hour limit. Also of some significance in this region is the absence of a generally applicable weekly statutory limit on working hours in India and Pakistan.[10]

This is not to say, however, that interest in hours reductions is entirely absent in countries in which statutory limits remain high, and vigorous debates have taken place in a number of countries in which the statutory limits ultimately remained unchanged. This was the case in Brazil, for example, where a reduction in the working week was suggested as a method of tackling unemployment during the economic transition of the 1990s (Saboia 2002). Although in more recent years the intensification of international competition and the opening up of the Brazilian economy have seen proposals on hours reductions eclipsed by initiatives to promote working time flexibility, they remain a feature of the employment relations landscape. The three Brazilian trade union confederations, for example, have forged a consensus on the need for a lower limit, and hours reductions have featured in a number of collective agreements in recent years.

2.3.2 Other limits

Although this chapter is mainly concerned with limits on normal weekly hours, other measures also play a role in restricting working hours and are therefore worth briefly reviewing. Prominent among these are limits on overtime work. The international standards require that overtime be subject to a limit, without indicating a specific level. The ILO's Committee of Experts on the Application of Conventions and Recommendations, however, requires that such limits be reasonable and in line with the goals of averting fatigue and ensuring that workers have sufficient time to spend on their lives beyond paid work (ILO 2005d). At national level, legislation generally contains specific limits on overtime, usually on a daily, weekly or annual basis or as a combination of these limits. Depending on the extent of recourse to overtime work in individual countries, these caps on overtime hours can represent the effective limit on weekly hours, a point that is returned to in Chapter 3.

Rights to minimum periods of weekly rest also operate in conjunction with normal hours limits to curb weekly hours. A longstanding element of working time law, a right to at least 24 consecutive hours of rest each week, has been present in the international standards since the Weekly Rest (Industry) Convention, 1921 (No. 14) and was extended to cover more workers by the Weekly Rest (Commerce and Offices) Convention, 1957 (No. 106). Weekly rest is perhaps the most universally accepted element of working time law, and almost all countries mandate at least one rest day. Moreover, reductions in working hours can be achieved by extending weekly rest periods, an approach that has a history of being adopted to reach the 40-hour limit (ILO 1967). This technique remains relevant, and can be used to reduce hours even where the reductions are carried out by lowering weekly hours limits. The shift to the 40-hour week in the Republic of Korea, for example, is widely referred to in the policy debates as the introduction of a 'five-day week', since this is the method through which it is expected to be realized in practice.

Provisions targeted at weekly hours are not the only measures that can contribute towards reducing working hours. Ensuring a more extensive period of rest during the year is also vital towards advancing well-being and allowing workers sufficient periods of time away from their jobs, including time to devote to their families. To this end, a right to a period of annual leave is available at the international level, in the shape of the right to at least three working weeks of paid holiday contained in the Holidays with Pay Convention (Revised), 1970 (No. 132). Annual leave entitlements are also present in almost all countries. As Table 2.5 indicates, the most widespread entitlement is to leave of 20–23 days.[11] There is substantial variation in minimum leave periods across different regions, however, from the lower limits in Latin America, the Caribbean and Asia to the more extensive leave periods in operation across Europe and in Africa.

Table 2.5 Minimum annual leave periods (2005)

	No universal statutory minimum	Less than 10 days (including no provision)	10–14 days	15–19 days	20–23 days	24–25 days
Industrialized countries	Australia, United States		Canada, Japan	New Zealand	Belgium, Germany, Ireland, Italy, Netherlands, Norway, Portugal, Spain, Switzerland, United Kingdom	Austria, Denmark, Finland, France, Luxembourg, Sweden
Africa		Nigeria, United Republic of Tanzania (Zanzibar)	Democratic Republic of the Congo, Tunisia	Angola, Burundi, Cameroon, Cape Verde, Mauritania, Morocco, Mozambique, Rwanda, Seychelles, South Africa	Algeria, Benin, Burkina Faso, Chad, Congo, Côte d'Ivoire, Djibouti, Guinea-Bissau, Madagascar, Mali, Namibia, Niger, Senegal, United Republic of Tanzania (mainland Tanzania), Togo, Zimbabwe	Gabon, Madagascar
Asia	India, Pakistan	Malaysia, Philippines, Singapore, Thailand	Indonesia, Republic of Korea, Lao People's Democratic Republic, Mongolia, Viet Nam	Cambodia		
Caribbean			Bahamas, Dominican Republic, Grenada, Haiti, Jamaica		Cuba	
Central and Eastern Europe					Bulgaria, Czech Republic, Estonia, Latvia, Lithuania, the former Yugoslav Republic of Macedonia, Russian Federation, Romania, Slovakia, Slovenia	
Latin America		Bolivia, Honduras, Mexico	Argentina, Belize, Chile, Colombia, Costa Rica, Ecuador, El Salvador, Guatemala, Nicaragua, Paraguay, Venezuela		Brazil, Panama, Peru, Uruguay	
Middle East			Jordan	Lebanon	Egypt	

Source: ILO Database of Working Time Laws (www.ilo.org/travdatabase).

In recent years, attention has been directed in some countries to the possibility of reducing annual hours by extending leave periods. In Mexico, for example, there has been some concern that the current five-day annual leave period is insufficient for full rest and recovery, and proposals have been tabled to increase it to up to 15 days (Esponda 2001). In other jurisdictions, the crucial issue is not the length of the leave period, but rather the extent to which the available leave is being taken up in practice. In the Republic of Korea, for example, during the period when workers were entitled to up to 32 days of various forms of leave each year, they have been found to have taken an average of only 8.4 days per year, and 38 per cent took none at all (Yoon 2001). And even though a relatively short minimum leave period of 14 days is specified in the Chinese working time legislation, the number of days actually taken is estimated to be around half of this entitlement (Zeng *et al.* 2005).

2.4 Conclusions

This chapter has examined the evolution of statutory limits on working hours during the latter part of the twentieth century, their current status and the policy approaches that underlie them. In doing so, it has identified a broad convergence towards a 40-hour limit on weekly working hours. The research reviewed from the period from 1967 to 1995 revealed a gradual progress towards 40 hours, while over the last decade the vast majority of governments retained their existing statutory working hours limits and the few changes were towards the enactment of shorter hours limits. As a result, the evidence from 2005 confirms that the 40-hour limit is now the dominant standard.

This development in statutory working hours limits is of some significance. In particular, it shows no evidence of deregulatory trends in weekly working hours limits, countering any assumption that countries have embarked on a race towards long hours and suggesting that such a 'race to the bottom' in legal standards cannot be considered inevitable. The chapter has also, however, highlighted significant regional differences in progress towards limiting working hours, and, in particular, the continuing dominance of the 48-hour week in Latin America and uneven progress towards shorter hours in Asia. The concern about these and other countries that retain long hours limits is returned to in Chapter 7 and addressed in the set of suggestions for working time policy outlined in that chapter.

Moreover, the convergence in the legal standards does not necessarily entail that the emerging international floor evolving in these measures is being widely observed in practice. This highlights the fear about the role of working hours laws in the era of globalization identified in the opening section of this chapter, namely that exemplary textual standards may be widely flouted in practice. This is among the primary questions that need to be addressed by transition and developing countries, as well as a number of industrialized countries. The following chapter explores this issue further, through an analysis of the relationship between legal standards and actual working hours.

3 Global trends in actual working hours

3.1 Introduction

We have seen variations in the regulation of working hours, especially in terms of normal statutory weekly working hours. Yet such standards do not always materialize in practice, and indeed it is not uncommon that substantial gaps exist between what is written in law and what is actually happening at the workplace. Therefore, in order to get an accurate picture of working time, working time regulation needs to be understood in relation to actual working time patterns.

This does not deny that working time regulation is an important determinant of actual working hours. The point is that its impacts vary considerably depending on many other individual and institutional factors, as well as economic factors. One well-known economic understanding is that with higher income workers tend to have a higher demand for 'leisure', and thus gaps between law and actual practice will be reduced as the economy grows. As will be shown later, there is some truth in this statement, but the relationship is surprisingly weak (Bienefeld 1972; Anxo 1999). In general, it is known that the actual outcomes of such reduction are dependent on the *capabilities* of workers and employers to maximize net benefits through the reduction of working hours (White 1987). Obviously, union strength is an important factor in reducing gaps between regulation and practice. Moreover, especially in developing countries, working time regulation suffers from substantial gaps in the influence or 'observance' of the legislation so that the proportion of workers benefiting from the regulation is typically low. Therefore, it is not easy to establish the extent to which existing or new regulations can affect actual working hours in practice in different countries.

The importance of making the regulatory standard of working time *effective* in practice is well illustrated in the Reduction of Hours of Work Recommendation, 1962 (No. 116) which establishes the principle of a 40-hour week as a 'social standard'. To pursue this goal in a realistic manner, the Recommendation suggests taking into account:

- The level of economic development attained and the extent to which the country is in a position to bring about a reduction in hours of work

without reducing total production or productivity, endangering its economic growth, the development of new industries or its competitive position in international trade, and without creating inflationary pressures which would ultimately reduce the real income of workers;
- The progress achieved and which it is possible to achieve in raising productivity by the application of modern technology, automation and management techniques;
- The need in the case of countries still in the process of development for improving the standards of living of their peoples; and
- The preferences of employers' and workers' organizations in the different branches of activity concerned as to the manner in which the reduction in working hours might be brought about.

Given the possible gaps between law and reality and the importance of narrowing such gaps, this chapter aims to examine how many hours workers are actually working, thus providing a global picture, probably for the first time in working time research, about 'the hours we are working'. In doing so, it is intended to show the scale of the global challenge ahead in the area of working hours. For this, a new comprehensive data set which has been collected from national statistical offices concerning 'number of employed by hours of work' is used extensively (see Box 3.1).

The rest of the chapter is constructed as follows: after briefly reviewing the historical developments in working hours in the industrialized world, in which the speed of working-hour reduction has been contrasting and uneven, this chapter examines changes in weekly working hours around the world focusing on the manufacturing sector. We then shift to individual working hours to see how working hours vary among individual workers. Different types of working-hour distributions will be discussed, followed by an investigation of long and short working hours. As long working hours are a relative concept, two different methods are used to examine this issue. Based on the concept of 'observance of working time laws', we estimate the proportion of workers who are working at or below the statutory normal hours of work. The resulting 'observance rate' is examined in relation to the levels of statutory hours and economic development in order to see if there is any systematic pattern that can be identified from the available data. We also estimate the proportion of workers who are working more than 48 hours per week, the standard stipulated in Conventions Nos 1 and 30 and which is also known as a threshold beyond which potentially negative physical and mental effects could begin to occur. This chapter attempts to provide a global estimate of long hours, which to our knowledge has never been done in working time research before. In the case of short hours, the focus will be placed on underemployment, or more specifically time-related underemployment. The simultaneous presence of short and long hours (i.e. bifurcation of working hours) in developing countries will also be briefly discussed. The chapter will conclude with a brief summary of its key findings.

3.2 Historical developments: a century-long progress

It is widely believed that the advent of industrial capitalism was accompanied by the emergence of the modern concept of time and increases in working hours (Thompson 1967; Phelps Brown and Browne 1968; Schor 1992; see also Lee and McCann 2006). The dominant concept of working time in early industrialization was based on the perception that hours spent outside work were seen simply as 'lost' time, which meant in practice the subordination of workers' lives to production demands. The logical result of this perspective was the extension of working hours, often to the physical maximum, and the policy concern was how to secure *minimum* hours of work to discipline workers and maintain production levels.

Such an extension of working hours in many parts of Europe was achieved through the widespread adoption of the 12-hour day and the reduction of holidays. Their negative consequences on health and productivity were slowly recognized, and the importance of guaranteeing 'free time' or 'leisure' for workers was gradually acknowledged. As a result, working hours began to be progressively reduced from as early as the 1830s, notably through legal interventions (Phelps Brown and Browne 1968; Bourdieu and Reynaud 2006). In the late nineteenth century, the idea for the eight-hour day gathered increasing support, and its positive impacts on productivity (i.e. the eight-hour day pays for itself) were reported in various pioneering experiments, which were eloquently summarized by John Rea in his then well-known book *Eight Hours for Work* (Rae 1894). In this process, the role of trade unions, as well as that of 'enlightened' employers, was critical in that they successfully drew attention to the 'social' costs of long hours and mobilized political pressures for the reduction of working hours. All this eventually paved a way to the adoption of the first international labour convention in 1919, the Hours of Work (Industry) Convention, 1919 (No. 1), which stipulates the principle of 'eight hours a day and 48 hours a week'. Such progress was accompanied by the recognition of the economic value of leisure, echoed in Henry Ford's remark that 'a workman would have little use for an automobile if he had to be in the shops from dawn until dusk' (Ford 1926: 614).

Unfortunately, it is not entirely clear how much progress has been made since in reducing actual working hours in different parts of the world, mainly due to the lack of reliable historical, global data on working hours. While there is no question that working hours were reduced considerably during the twentieth century, the scale of the working-hour reductions and their cross-country variations have yet to be understood. Nonetheless, some estimates are available for industrialized countries. Maddison (1995) estimated annual working hours for the period between 1870 and 1992 in Europe, North America and Australia, which shows that annual working hours in these countries were about 2,900 hours in 1870 and then gradually declined, such that working hours in 1992 had been almost halved. The overall trend is a consistent and homogenous decline in annual working hours throughout the twentieth century.

A more realistic estimate of annual working hours is provided by Huberman (2002), who takes into account differences in weekly working hours, paid leave and public holidays. As Figure 3.1 shows, working hours in industrialized countries were reduced dramatically in the last century. In the Netherlands, for example, workers worked 3,285 hours per year in 1870 but only 1,347 hours in 2000. Interestingly, this reduction of working hours coincided with economic progress: the period of severe economic turbulence between 1929 and 1950 was accompanied by fluctuations in working hours, sometimes involving an upward trend. Other periods such as post-World War I and post-World War II are largely characterized by progressive reductions in working hours.

However, this overall historical development masks variations across countries in terms of the speed or intensity of working-hour reductions. In 1870, the Netherlands, Germany and France had very long working hours which exceeded 3,000 hours per year, while the United States, the United Kingdom and Australia were enjoying much shorter hours (less than 3,000 hours per year). As Figure 3.1 demonstrates, a catching-up process began in the early 1900s, and there was a strong sign of convergence in the 1920s when annual working hours were dispersed in a narrow range between 2,213 (the United Kingdom) and 2,371 (the Netherlands). Even after fluctuations during World War II, working hours showed a small difference among these

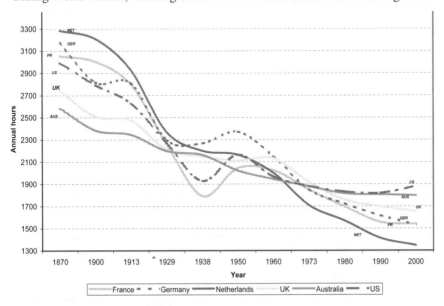

Figure 3.1 Historical trend in annual working hours in selected countries (1870–2000)

Source: Huberman 2002.

countries. It appears that a diverging trend came into force in the 1970s and since then the direction of working-hour changes has been reversed in some countries such as the United States. As a result, the country rankings in annual working hours has changed completely so that the Netherlands had the shortest hours in 2000, while Australia, the United States and the United Kingdom now have relatively long average working hours by the standard of industrialized countries.

Such contrasting developments are also illustrated in Table 3.1, which compares weekly working hours and paid annual leave over the last five decades in six industrialized countries. Due to data constraints, only the textile industry is considered for actual weekly working hours. First, a huge reduction of weekly working hours was achieved in Finland (from 44.8 to 37.1 hours), France (from 43 to 35 hours), Germany (from 48.6 to 38.3 hours) and the Netherlands (from 45.2–48.0 to 38.4 hours). It is also these countries which witnessed considerable increases in paid annual leave. Moreover, it should be noted that the length of paid leave specified in Table 3.1 is the statutory minimum and that collective agreements tend to provide more days of annual leave than required in the law.[1]

Table 3.1 Changes in working hours and paid leave (1956–2004) in selected countries

	Actual working hours in the textile industry		Annual holidays with pay (statutory)	
	1956	*2000–2004*	*1956*	*2004*
Finland	44.8	37.1	3 weeks	20 working days (4 weeks)
France	43	35	3 weeks	25 working days (5 weeks)
Germany (West)	48.6	38.3	12 days	24 working days (about 5 weeks)
Netherlands	45.2–48.0	38.4	12 days[a]	20 working days (4 weeks)
UK	48.3	41.2	6 days or 2 weeks[a]	20 working days (4 weeks)
US	39.6	40.8[b]	1 week[a]	8.9–19.2 days[c]

Sources: ILO 1958; ILO Labour Statistics Database; ILO Conditions of Work and Employment Database.

Notes
a Collective agreements.
b Manufacturing sector.
c The figures refer to 'paid vacation days' in medium and large private sector firms in the US, in which paid leave normally increases according to the length of service. For example, average US workers were given 8.9 days' annual leave after one year of service with a company with a particular company. The length of annual leave was increased on average to 19.2 days after 25 years of service.

One important implication which can be drawn here is that developments in working hours are far more complex than is normally understood. Economic development and income growth matter in reducing working hours, but the speed at which the reduction is achieved is very different across countries. In some cases working hours can increase despite economic and income growth. European experience in fact indicates that the institutional framework in the country and union strength are far more important in determining working hours (e.g. Lehndorff 2000). Trade unions in Europe have tended to put an emphasis on shorter hours to protect workers' health, increasingly to maintain or create jobs, and more recently to address work–life balance. By contrast, overall such efforts have not generally been strong in Anglo-Saxon countries. Yet, a more complicated picture emerges when we consider other parts of the world, especially developing countries and transition economies.

3.3 Average weekly hours

With these historical developments in industrialized countries as a backdrop, then, what is the situation in other countries? How many hours are workers working around the world? Given the tendency towards lower standard hours, as discussed in Chapter 2, is there any trend towards shorter hours? How large are the gaps between countries, particularly between developing and industrialized countries? Are they increasing or being narrowed? To address these questions, Table 3.2 provides average weekly working hours for the last ten years in the 44 countries and territories for which data are available in the ILO statistical database. In addition to questionable data quality for some countries, the marked difference in industrial structures across countries makes it difficult to make international comparisons. For this reason, only the manufacturing sector is considered in this table,[2] while complex developments in the service sector, often characterized by diversification and individualization, will be discussed in Chapter 5.

As Table 3.2 shows, average weekly working hours in selected countries largely range between 35 and 45 hours, but a significant number of developing countries have longer weekly working hours, often exceeding 48 hours (e.g. Costa Rica, El Salvador, Peru, Philippines, Thailand, and Turkey). Most high-income countries are enjoying relatively short working hours, with the notable exception of some Asian countries such as Singapore and the Republic of Korea, where the average worker in the manufacturing sector is working more than 48 hours per week.

As regards changes in weekly working hours during the period between 1995 and 2004, the trend is rather mixed. First, average working hours are stable in many countries (e.g. Australia, Austria, Cyprus, Finland, Hungary, Iceland, Israel, New Zealand, Norway, Spain, Switzerland and the United Kingdom). Most of these countries belong to the industrialized world, so it confirms the widespread belief that working hours in this part of the world

Table 3.2 Average weekly working hours in manufacturing (1995–2004)

Country[a]	Source[b]	Type of working hours[c]	Worker coverage[d]	Gender	1995	1996	1997	1998	1999	2000	2001	2002	2003	2004
Argentina	BA	I	TE	All	45.1	46.3	46.5	46.5	45.8	45.4	44.6	42.6		
	BA	I	TE	M	46.8	47.9	48.0	48.2	47.9	47.6	47.0	45.4		
	BA	I	TE	F	40.0	40.8	41.3	40.5	39.0	38.8	37.8	34.5		
	BA	I	EM	All		46.4	47.1	46.8	46.4	46.1	45.4	44.1		
	BA	I	EM	M		47.4	48.1	47.9	47.6	47.6	47.1	45.9		
	BA	I	EM	F		42.8	43.3	42.6	41.8	40.7	39.7	37.5		
Australia	BA	I	EM	All	38.8	38.7	38.6	38.6	38.9	38.6	38.6	38.5	38.5	
	BA	I	EM	M	41.0	40.8	40.7	40.6	40.9	40.7	40.9	40.6	40.6	
	BA	I	EM	F	32.6	32.9	32.7	32.9	33.3	32.9	32.3	32.9	33.0	
Austria	BA	I	EM	All	36.1	36.6	36.9	35.8	36.7	36.6	36.5	36.8	36.9	
	BA	I	EM	M	37.2	37.5	38.0	36.7	37.8	37.7	37.6	38.0	38.1	
	BA	I	EM	F	32.8	33.8	33.7	31.5	33.3	33.2	33.5	33.1	33.1	
Belgium	DA	I	SE	All	38.4	38.4	38.3							
	DA	II	EM	All					36.9					
	DA	II	EM	M					37.0					
	DA	II	EM	F					36.5					
Bermuda	CA	I	EM	All								34.0	29.0	
	CA	I	EM	M								36.0	30.0	
	CA	I	EM	F								31.0	26.0	
Bulgaria	CA	I	EM	All						33.0	33.0			
Costa Rica	BA	I	TE	All	48.5	49.3	49.2	49.4	49.1	48.9	49.0	50.0	49.0	50.0
	BA	I	TE	M	49.6	50.5	50.1	50.5	50.5	49.6	51.0	51.0	50.0	51.0
	BA	I	TE	F	46.4	46.2	46.8	46.7	45.8	47.2	47.0	47.0	47.0	46.0
	BA	I	EM	All							49.8		49.0	
	BA	I	EM	M							51.0		50.0	
	BA	I	EM	F							47.4		47.0	
Cyprus	DA	II	EM	All		40.5	40.2	39.9	40.5	40.2	40.5	40.0		
	DA	II	EM	M		41.7	40.8	40.5	41.1	40.5	40.9	40.3		
	DA	II	EM	F		38.9	39.3	39.1	39.6	39.9	39.8	39.5		

Country													
	DA	II	WE	All		40.6	40.1	39.8	40.5	40.4	40.6	39.7	
	DA	II	WE	M		42.6	41.0	40.6	41.5	40.7	41.4	40.2	
	DA	II	WE	F		38.4	39.0	38.8	39.3	40.1	39.2	38.8	
Czech Republic	DA	I	WE	All	40.4	40.5	40.9	40.8	41.0	40.7	40.7	40.7	
El Salvador	DA	I	WE	All							45.0	52.0	46.0
	DA	I	WE	M							46.0	51.0	47.0
	DA	I	WE	F							45.0	54.0	46.0
Estonia	DA	I	EM	All	33.1	33.1	33.6	33.0	33.8	33.9	33.8	34.0	
Finland	BA	I	EM	All	38.0	38.1	39.6	38.4	38.1	38.0	37.8	37.6	37.5
	BA	I	EM	M	38.7	38.9	40.4	39.1	38.6	38.7	38.5	38.2	38.1
	BA	I	EM	F	36.2	36.3	37.8	36.6	36.7	36.2	36.3	36.4	36.0
France	BA	I	EM	All	37.07	36.61	37.54	37.41	37.6	36.32	35.65	35.31	
	BA	I	EM	M	37.9	37.31	38.26	37.93	38.12	36.9	36.27	35.81	
	BA	I	EM	F	34.91	34.78	35.61	35.98	36.2	34.67	33.89	33.88	
Greece	BA	I	TE	All	42.0	42.0	42.0	42.0	42.0	43.0	42.0	42.0	
	BA	I	TE	M	43.0	43.0	43.0	43.0	43.0	43.0	43.0	43.0	
	BA	I	TE	F	40.0	40.0	39.0	40.0	40.0	41.0	40.0	40.0	
Hong Kong, China	BA	I	TE	All	43.7	45.0	43.8	44.0	45.0	45.3	45.4	45.6	45.4
	BA	I	TE	M	45.3	46.6	45.2	45.5	46.7	46.8	47.1	47.4	47.1
	BA	I	TE	F	41.1	42.3	41.4	41.4	42.0	42.4	42.3	42.6	42.3
Hungary	DA	I	WE	All	33.8	34.0	34.2	34.3	34.4	34.4	33.8	33.9	34.0
Iceland	BA	I	EM	All	42.9	43.0	42.7	41.4	42.7	43.5	43.5	42.3	
	BA	I	EM	M	48.5	47.3	47.1	47.5	47.2	47.5	47.2	45.4	
	BA	I	EM	F	33.8	35.5	34.7	31.3	33.4	34.1	35.1	35.9	
Ireland	BA	I	TE	All	40.4	40.8	40.6	40.2	39.9	39.5	39.6	39.4	39.2
	BA	I	TE	M	41.9	42.2	41.9	41.7	41.3	40.9	41.0	40.9	40.7
	BA	I	TE	F	37.4	37.9	37.7	37.2	37.1	36.7	36.4	36.2	36.0
Israel	BA	I	TE	All	41.7	41.8	42.1	42.0	41.6	42.6	41.5	42.2	41.9
	BA	I	TE	M	43.7	43.9	43.8	43.8	43.6	44.5	43.3	43.9	43.7
	BA	I	TE	F	36.6	36.8	37.6	37.4	36.8	37.7	36.8	37.7	37.2
Italy	BA	I	TE	All	40.7	40.5	40.5	40.5	40.6	40.5	40.5	39.4	39.2
	BA	I	TE	M	41.7	41.5	41.5	41.6	41.6	41.6	41.7	40.5	40.4
	BA	I	TE	F	38.2	37.9	38.0	38.0	38.1	37.9	37.8	36.7	36.4
Japan	BA	I	TE	All									43.1
	BA	I	TE	M									46.4

Table 3.2 Continued

Country[a]	Source[b]	Type of working hours[c]	Worker coverage[d]	Gender	1995	1996	1997	1998	1999	2000	2001	2002	2003	2004
	BA	I	TE	F									36.6	
	BA	I	EM	All									43.6	
	BA	I	EM	M									46.5	
	BA	I	EM	F									37.5	
Korea, Republic of	DA	I	EM	All	49.2	48.4	47.8	46.1	50.1	49.3	48.3			
	DA	I	EM	M	49.5	48.6	48.0	46.1	49.8	49.2	48.3			
	DA	I	EM	F	48.6	47.9	47.4	46.1	50.7	49.8	48.4			
Lithuania	CA	II	EM	All		38.6	38.6	38.6	38.8	38.6	38.6	38.6		
Malta	BA	I	TE	All						41.0	40.0	40.0	38.7	
	BA	I	TE	M						42.0	41.0	40.9	39.6	
	BA	I	TE	F						39.0	38.0	38.4	36.2	
Mexico	BA	I	EM	All	45.4	45.5	46.2	45.0	45.4	44.4	43.9	45.1	44.4	
	BA	I	EM	M	46.5	46.4	47.4	45.9	46.5	45.6	45.1	46.1	45.4	
	BA	I	EM	F	42.5	43.2	43.3	43.0	43.2	42.1	41.7	43.2	42.6	
Moldova, Republic of	CA	I	EM	All		22.2	22.8	22.7	22.7	24.4	26.6	27.7	29.7	
Netherlands	DA	II	EM	All	37.0	36.7	36.5	36.4	36.1	36.0				
	DA	II	EM	M	38.2	38.1	37.9	37.9	37.7	37.6				
	DA	II	EM	F	31.6	31.2	30.8	30.6	30.2	30.1				
New Zealand	BA	I	EM	All			37.3	37.4	38.1	37.0	37.4	37.9	38.0	
	BA	I	EM	M			39.7	39.7	40.4	39.1	39.7	40.0	39.8	
	BA	I	EM	F			31.8	31.9	32.7	32.0	31.7	32.4	33.2	
Norway	BA	I	EM	All		36.8	36.7	36.6	36.6	36.5	36.5	36.7	36.3	
	BA	I	EM	M		38.5	38.4	38.3	38.3	38.0	38.0	38.1	37.8	
	BA	I	EM	F		31.8	31.6	31.1	31.6	32.2	31.9	32.2	31.8	
Peru	DA	II	WE	All	43.0	49.2	47.7	48.5	49.6	49.1	49.3			
	DA	II	WE	M	43.0									
	DA	II	WE	F	44.0									
Philippines	DB	I	WE	All		48.3	48.5	48.4						
	DB	I	WE	M		48.7	48.5	48.6						
	DB	I	WE	F		47.9	48.5	48.2						

Country													
Portugal	DA	II	EM	All					39.3				
Portugal	DA	II	EM	M					39.4				
Portugal	DA	II	EM	F					39.2				
San Marino	E	I	EM	All	38.5	39.5	39.1	38.6	38.8			40.3	38.4
Singapore	CA	II	EM	All					49.2	49.8	48.6	48.9	49.0
Slovenia	BA	I	EM	All	40.7	40.4	40.1	40.4	40.5	40.3	34.9	36.0	36.7
Slovenia	BA	I	EM	M	40.9	40.8	40.4	40.7	40.7	40.5	35.8	37.5	38.0
Slovenia	BA	I	EM	F	40.3	39.8	39.6	40.0	40.1	40.2	33.7	33.7	34.7
South Africa	DA	II	EM	All						42.7	43.0		
Spain	BA	I	TE	All	36.7	37.1	37.1	37.1		36.1	36.3	36.0	36.0
Spain	BA	I	TE	M	37.3	37.8	37.8	37.7		36.9	37.0	36.7	36.8
Spain	BA	I	TE	F	34.7	34.8	35.0	34.9		34.0	34.1	33.9	33.5
Sweden	BA	I	TE	All							38.2	37.9	37.5
Sweden	BA	I	TE	M							39.3	39.0	38.5
Sweden	BA	I	TE	F							34.7	34.6	34.3
Sweden	BA	I	EM	All							37.8	37.5	37.1
Sweden	BA	I	EM	M							38.9	38.5	38.0
Sweden	BA	I	EM	F							34.6	34.5	34.1
Switzerland	FA	II	EM	All	41.4	41.4	41.4	41.4	41.3	41.3	41.2	41.2	41.2
Thailand	DA	II	EM	All	49.4	49.4	49.1	50.5	50.1				
Turkey	BA	I	TE	All						51.3	51.4	51.9	52.2
Turkey	BA	I	TE	M						52.6	52.6	53.1	53.3
Turkey	BA	I	TE	F						46.0	46.5	47.4	47.8
United Kingdom	DA	II	EM	All	42.2	41.9	42.0	41.8	41.4	41.4			
United Kingdom	DA	II	EM	M	43.0	42.7	42.8	42.6	42.0	42.0			
United Kingdom	DA	II	EM	F	39.4	39.3	39.2	39.2	39.0	38.9			
United States	DA	II	WE	All	41.6	41.6	42.0	41.7	41.7	41.6	40.7	40.9	
Uruguay	DB	I	WE	All	39.4	39.4							

Sources: ILO Labour Statistics Database (http://laborsta.ilo.org/applv8/data/isic3e.html); ISIC Revision 3 – D.

Notes

a For Austria and Slovakia weekly averages are calculated from monthly averages (divided by 4.35).

b BA – labour force survey; CA – labour-related establishment census; DA – labour-related establishment survey; E – official estimates; FA – insurance records.

c I – hours actually worked; II – hours paid for.

d TE – total employment; EM – employees; WE – wage earners; SE – salaried employees.

have not decreased on a notable scale, probably not since the late 1970s (Lehndorff 2000). Of course, one important exception to this pattern is France which experienced about a two-hour reduction between 1995 and 2002. It is expected that working hours have recently been further reduced, thanks to the 35-hour law. Slovenia has also witnessed a large-scale reduction of working hours (by four hours) during the last ten years. Argentina is another country which recorded a continued decline in working hours in the 1990s, but interestingly enough, such reduction came mostly from women workers who are typically working less than 35 hours per week. In 2004, it is estimated that the majority of women workers (56.0 per cent) were working less than 35 hours, compared with 20.3 per cent for male workers.

By contrast, working hours have increased in a significant minority of countries and territories such as Costa Rica, Hong Kong (China), and most strikingly Peru (by almost six hours). In the case of Peru, the increase in average working hours appears to be due to the significant increase in extremely long working hours (e.g. 60 hours: see Table 3.4 and Statistical annex), and indeed in the 1990s in the manufacturing sector companies shifted from a 45-hour system to a 48-hour rotating shift system (Aparicio Valdez 2001).

One common assumption concerning such cross-country variations is that the length of working time is negatively correlated with income level. The extent to which this assumption is well grounded on a global scale, however, is not easy to know, particularly due to the lack of reliable data on wages and working hours. Nonetheless, Figure 3.2 provides a useful illustration of the relationship between working hours and income. When average weekly hours in Table 3.2 are plotted against gross national income per capita (GNI) expressed in US dollars, there is a negative correlation, indicating that shorter weekly hours are associated with higher average incomes (coefficient = –0.497 significant at the 0.01 level). Yet, it should be noted that this result masks differences between low- and high-income countries. When the sample is split into two groups of countries – low- and high-income countries (income threshold is US$15,000) – only low-income countries show a stronger, significant correlation (coefficient = –0.587) but, as hinted at in the previous section, the sign of the correlation coefficient reverses for high-income countries, though it is not significant (coefficient = 0.017). The difference between these two groups of countries is highlighted by two dotted circles in Figure 3.2. Thus, it appears that economic growth matters in reducing working hours until a certain point beyond which the impact of income on working hours becomes unclear and other factors must be playing a role. This finding is largely in line with the historical developments illustrated in the previous section.

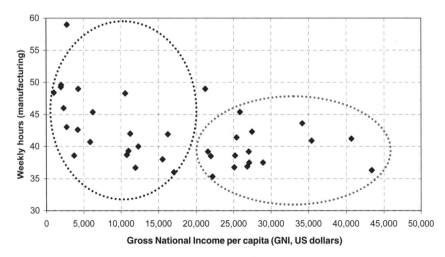

Figure 3.2 Weekly working hours versus incomes

Sources: ILO Labour Statistics Database for Working Hours and World Bank Database for GNI.

3.4 Beyond average hours: patterns and variations in individual working hours

Average working hours tell only part of the story, however. If the focus is on total labour supply in the economy, average working hours could be used as a good indicator. However, when it comes to working hours as a key component of working life (which underlines working time regulations), average working hours could potentially be misleading, depending on the distribution of those hours. If working hours among individual workers are so diversified that average hours are relevant for only a small number of workers, great caution should be taken in using these average figures.[3]

This aspect has recently attracted much interest in industrialized countries where average working hours do not differ considerably but the distribution of working hours is markedly different (Anxo and O'Reilly 2000; Lee 2004; ILO 2005a). For example, the overall stability observed for industrialized countries in Table 3.2 in fact masks changes in the distribution of working hours, especially towards diversification or even bifurcation (Lee 2004). It is known that such distributions are closely associated with the incidence of part-time work and also with the regulatory framework for working time. For instance, the exceptional reduction of working hours in the Netherlands over recent decades was achieved through a huge increase in the use of part-time work. Great attention has also been given to the way in which different levels of regulations (state, industry, enterprise and individual) are articulated in structuring working time. This regulatory framework can be called a working time regime (see Anxo and O'Reilly 2000). The relative strength of legal intervention and collective bargaining is generally the key element of working time regimes.

As far as industrialized countries are concerned, four types of working time regimes and their corresponding distributional patterns are found. First, where working time is effectively regulated by a strong statutory intervention and part-time work is not widely accepted as an alternative to full-time work, the distribution of working hours is a highly concentrated one around the statutory standard hours (see Figure 3.3A). The standard hours are so dominant that both part-time work and long working hours among employees are relatively rare. The best example of this type of regime is found in France.

Second, collective agreements play a dominant role in determining working hours, while statutory maximum hours provide a safeguard for unorganized workers. In this case, working hours can vary depending on collective agreements, thereby allowing for multiple peaks in the distribution of working hours (see Figure 3.3B). Germany and Austria provide good examples of this type of regime. When a national-level agreement is reached for all workers and there is only one universal standard for working hours (e.g. Denmark), then the distribution pattern will be similar to the first type.

Two variations on these two basic types come from the extent of part-time work and the effectiveness of statutory regulations. When statutory regulation is effective and part-time work is common, the distribution of working hours will look like Figure 3.3C (e.g. Belgium). By contrast, when statutory regulation is not particularly effective (and collective agreements on working hours are rather fragmented) and part-time work is widespread, the overall distribution of working hours will be close to a uniform distribution without having a well-defined peak (Figure 3.3D). In this type of regime, there is a significant proportion of workers who are working more than the statutory standard hours. The well-known examples of this type include the United Kingdom and Japan (see Lee 2004).

In the case of other parts of the world, however, there are two further variations on the distribution of working hours, especially in reference to types C and D. First, in many developing countries (and even in some developed countries) the effectiveness of statutory standard hours is very much limited, such that non-compliance or non-observance and/or overtime work are the norm in these countries (see the next section about the concept of observance).[4] As Figure 3.3E demonstrates, most workers are working more than the statutory normal hours. One of the well-known examples is the Republic of Korea, in which the extension of working hours through overtime is largely 'institutionalized' and various counter-policy measures including the reduction of the statutory working hours have been introduced (Yoon 2001). The Korean case will be revisited later in this chapter (Section 3.8). It is also interesting to note that the United States falls within this category, as the majority of workers are working more than the statutory hours (currently 40 hours per week). In the United States, there is no upper limit

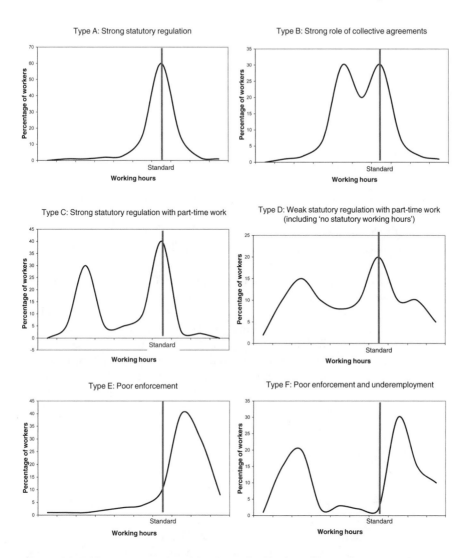

Figure 3.3 Different types of working-hour distributions: illustrative examples

on overtime hours (thus, no maximum limit), which clearly undermines the effectiveness of the legislation.

In addition, if this situation is compounded by a lack of sufficient work, there is then a group of overworked workers along with a group of workers who are working very short hours and therefore cannot earn a decent income (hence, underemployment). In this case, the distribution of working hours will look like Figure 3.3F. It is expected that such a bifurcation of hours is common in developing countries, especially among low-income countries.

Despite the potentially important policy implications of these latter two types of working time regimes (Figure 3.3E and F), little is known about the distribution of working hours in developing countries, mainly due to the lack of a relevant data set. In order to overcome this barrier, the ILO carried out data collection through national statistical agencies in 2005 (see Box 3.1). The rest of this chapter will be based on these data.

Box 3.1 ILO data collection on the distribution of employed persons by their hours of work

In light of the need for more detailed data on working hours, especially with regard to variations in hours among different workers, the ILO sent out a questionnaire to national statistical agencies around the world in order to collect new statistics on the distribution of employed persons by weekly working hours.

To ensure comparability, it was recommended that data from household-based labour force surveys be used. Whenever possible, national statistical agencies were asked to report on the size of the employed population according to their weekly working hours, preferably usual hours of work. The working-hour bands recommended were 1–15 hours; 15–24 hours; 25–34 hours; 35 hours; 36–39 hours; 40 hours; 41–47 hours; 48 hours; 49–59 hours; 60 hours or more. This breakdown is more detailed than that illustrated in the 'Resolution concerning statistics of hours of work adopted by the tenth International Conference of Labour Statisticians' (1962, paragraph 16).

In addition, national statistical agencies were asked to report by gender, employment status (self-employed and paid employees), and age group (youth and adults). In order to make comparisons over time, they were also asked to report for: (i) the most recent year for which these data are available; (ii) a year as close as possible to 1995; and (iii) a year as close as possible to 2000. A total of 62 countries provided data, and their relevance and accuracy were examined. A brief summary of these data is provided in the Statistical annex and a full data set is available to the public at the ILO website.

3.5 Excessive hours (I): non-observance

3.5.1 Defining excessive hours

When working hours and their impact on workers are discussed, the focus tends to be placed on the extent of long working hours. As discussed in the previous chapters, most working time regulations have been enacted with a particular emphasis on reducing long working hours for the safety and health of workers, among other objectives. However, it is not easy to know the extent to which long working hours are undertaken, especially from an international perspective. The key reason is that the concept of long working hours is a relative one, depending on how many hours can be seen as long enough to cause concerns.

There appears to be three ways of examining long hours:

- Hours exceeding the statutory normal hours: this highlights the fact that the statutory normal hours determine a socially acceptable level of working hours – 'observance' (see below).
- Hours exceeding the maximum hours of work beyond which negative consequences on workers are known to be visible: the effects on health and safety are crucial here.
- Hours exceeding those which workers prefer to work: this reflects the idea that whether or not working hours are 'long' needs to be determined by taking into account whether or not workers would like to maintain or reduce, or even increase, their working hours. This is closely related to the concept of 'inadequate employment related to excessive hours' which, according to the 1998 resolution of the International Conference of Labour Statisticians, refers to 'a situation where persons in employment wanted or sought to work fewer hours than they did during the reference period, either in the same job or in another job, with a corresponding reduction of income'.

The third method has gained more importance in research and policy debates in the industrialized world (see Fagan 2004; Lee 2004; Lee and McCann 2006). There is evidence that the longer workers work, the stronger their demand for shorter hours, but the intensity of this relationship varies considerably across countries. Moreover, the survey results are very sensitive to the wording of questions and response options (Altman and Golden 2005).

Available data about 'inadequate employment related to excessive hours' are again limited for developing countries. Some studies indicate that the incidence may not be high, as most workers are working long hours for higher earnings, especially when the hourly wage rate is low. In the Philippines, for example, more than 90 per cent of those workers who are working more than 48 hours per week are doing so in order to earn more (Mehran 2005). This implies that most workers who work long hours would not like to reduce their hours while earning less, so 'inadequate employment related to excessive hours' would not be so common as in industrialized countries. In any case, the paucity of data does not allow any systematic analysis of this issue in the context of developing countries, and therefore, the first two methods ('hours exceeding the statutory normal hours' and 'hours exceeding the maximum hours of work beyond which negative consequences on workers are known to be visible') are used in this chapter.

3.5.2 Observance of statutory norms and 'effective working-hour regulation index'[5]

As discussed in the previous chapter, the vast majority of countries have statutory normal hours of work beyond which an overtime premium payment should be made under the law. However, we have already seen that the impact of these measures varies considerably across countries, and in some countries their role as a standard is not preserved because the majority of workers are working longer than the standard hours. In this regard, we can draw on the notion of the 'observance' of statutory working time regulation to indicate the extent to which actual hours are in line with the statutory standard (for details, see Lee and McCann 2007). In other words, the notion of 'observance' refers to whether the statutory standard is *de facto* a socially accepted standard for working hours. This concept is intended to be broader than more conventional notions of the 'enforcement' of national laws in that it captures the enforcement of the standards through the state labour inspectorate or through court decisions in individual cases and also takes into account the other ways in which laws can have an effect on practice, in particular through becoming a cultural norm that is influential even when not strongly enforced (Browne *et al.* 2002). This approach is particularly important, given the call for deregulation in developing countries, as discussed in Chapter 1.

Table 3.3A shows estimates for the proportion of paid *employees* who are working at or below the statutory standard hours in each country, which we term the 'observance rate'. Note that only employees are considered, as the self-employed and family workers are often not covered by working time regulations and labour law in general. A total of 48 countries are considered, excluding those that do not have statutory normal hours (e.g. Germany and the United Kingdom, which provide for a limit only on maximum hours (including overtime)). In response to the concern that regulations should reflect 'local realities' (see World Bank 2004), gross national income per capita is also considered, and statutory standards categorized into three groups ('40 hours or less', '41 to 47 hours'[6] and '48 hours'). Some descriptive statistics are provided in Table 3.3B and scatter diagrams are shown in Figure 3.4.

Table 3.3 and Figure 3.4 reveal, first, that higher statutory hours limits (i.e. less stringent standards) are largely associated with lower national income per capita. While the mean GNI per capita is much lower in countries with higher hours limits, it is statistically significant only for the '48 hours' group (see Table 3.3B). Overall, then, it would be overstated to suggest that working time regulation in developing countries is unnecessarily 'rigid', in the sense of containing overly strict weekly hours limits. Second, it is apparent from Figure 3.4 that, overall, a significant proportion of employees are working more than the statutory normal hours limits, and that in some countries this proportion exceeds 40 per cent of the workforce (i.e. the

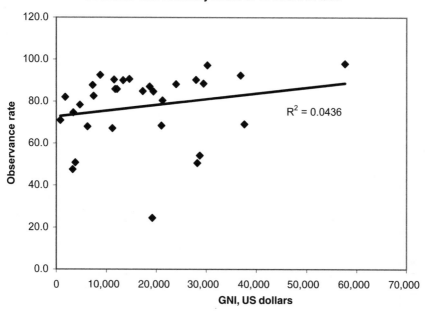

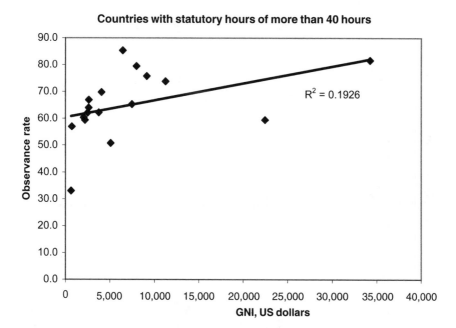

Figure 3.4 Observance rate and income by statutory working-hour standards

Source: see Box 3.1.

Table 3.3 Statutory hours, observance and effective working-hour regulation index

Panel A

	Legal normal hours	Observance rates			Normalized values (for 'both' only)		
		Both	Female	Male	Statutory-hour strictness (0–10)	Observance degree (0–10)	Effective regulation index (0–10)
Albania	40	78.4	81.2	76.5	6.2	7.8	7.0
Armenia	40	50.9	65.1	38.1	6.2	5.1	5.6
Azerbaijan	40	74.6	82.9	68.9	6.2	7.5	6.8
Bolivia	48	62.1	79.6	54.6	0.0	6.2	3.1
Bulgaria	40	87.8	88.6	87.0	6.2	8.8	7.5
Canada	40	88.5	94.8	82.5	6.2	8.9	7.5
Croatia	40	67.1	81.0	66.5	6.2	6.7	6.4
Cyprus	40	80.5	78.9	81.9	6.2	8.0	7.1
Czech Republic	40	84.8	91.2	79.3	6.2	8.5	7.3
Estonia	40	85.9	89.4	82.2	6.2	8.6	7.4
Ethiopia	48	57.0	56.9	57.0	0.0	5.7	2.8
Finland	40	90.3	94.2	86.3	6.2	9.0	7.6
France	35	50.7	62.3	40.1	10.0	5.1	7.5
Georgia	41	66.9	78.9	54.9	5.4	6.7	6.0
Guatemala	48	69.8	76.9	66.5	0.0	7.0	3.5
Honduras	44	64.0	64.5	63.7	3.1	6.4	4.7
Hungary	40	90.7	94.1	87.5	6.2	9.1	7.6
Indonesia	40	47.6	56.0	43.9	6.2	4.8	5.5
Israel	43	59.5	77.3	43.1	3.8	5.9	4.9
Japan	40	54.2	73.3	41.0	6.2	5.4	5.8
Korea, Republic of	40	24.5	33.0	19.1	6.2	2.4	4.3

Lithuania	40	90.3	93.0	87.7	6.2	9.0	7.6
Luxembourg	40	98.0	98.0	98.0	6.2	9.8	8.0
Macedonia, FYR	40	68.0	68.4	67.8	6.2	6.8	6.5
Madagascar	40	70.9	78.4	66.8	6.2	7.1	6.6
Mauritius	45	73.8	80.3	70.4	2.3	7.4	4.8
Mexico	48	75.8	87.8	69.2	0.0	7.6	3.8
Moldova, Republic of	40	82.1	85.1	78.5	6.2	8.2	7.2
Netherlands	40	97.2	98.9	95.7	6.2	9.7	7.9
New Zealand	40	68.5	83.3	53.9	6.2	6.8	6.5
Norway	40	92.4	96.2	88.9	6.2	9.2	7.7
Pakistan	48	60.4	77.9	57.5	0.0	6.0	3.0
Panama	48	85.4	87.9	83.7	0.0	8.5	4.3
Peru	48	50.8	NA	NA	0.0	5.1	2.5
Poland	40	85.9	92.5	80.2	6.2	8.6	7.4
Portugal	40	87.1	91.1	83.5	6.2	8.7	7.4
Romania	40	82.6	84.8	80.7	6.2	8.3	7.2
Russian Federation	40	92.5	94.6	90.4	6.2	9.3	7.7
Slovakia	40	90.0	94.3	86.2	6.2	9.0	7.6
Slovenia	40	84.7	87.9	81.6	6.2	8.5	7.3
Spain	40	88.2	92.5	85.2	6.2	8.8	7.5
Sri Lanka	45	62.2	70.0	58.9	2.3	6.2	4.3
Switzerland	45	81.6	92.7	72.6	2.3	8.2	5.2
Tanzania, United Rep. of	45	33.1	NA	NA	2.3	3.3	2.8
Thailand	48	65.3	68.8	62.7	0.0	6.5	3.3
United States	40	69.1	76.5	62.6	6.2	6.9	6.5
Uruguay	48	79.5	89.7	71.7	0.0	7.9	4.0
Zimbabwe	48	59.4	57.5	60.2	0.0	5.9	3.0
Total							
Mean	42.1	73.1	81.0	69.9	4.5	7.3	5.9
Standard deviation	3.5	16.6	13.6	17.3	2.7	1.7	1.7

Source: see Box 3.1.

Table 3.3 Continued

Panel B

Statutory hours	No. of countries	GNI per capita		Observance rate		Correlations between GNI and observance	
		Mean	Standard error	Mean	Standard error	Coefficients	Significance
[40 hours or less]	31	17398.7	2312.3	77.5	17.1	0.209	0.260
41 to 47 hours	7	11074.3	4809.6	63.0	15.2	0.577	0.175
48 hours	10	4754.0*	916.6	66.5	10.9	0.657*	0.039
Total	48	13482.1	1797.8	73.1	16.6	0.362*	0.012

Source: see Box 3.1.

Notes
[ ] Refers to the reference group.
* Significant at 0.05 level.

observance rate is less than 60 per cent). This result could be taken to imply that the standard hours are not 'standard' in practice. Third, however, it is interesting to note that observance rates are relatively low in those countries that have higher statutory limits, and it can thus be said that low-income countries have lower observance rates *despite (not because of)* higher statutory hours limits (or in effect, laxer standards). In short, concerns about the rigidity of working time laws in developing countries are not well grounded. If our findings regarding statutory weekly hours limits hold true for other elements of labour regulation, any widespread assumption about low compliance with labour standards in developing countries due to their 'strictness' would need to be reassessed (e.g. World Bank 2004: 145–46). Finally, when it comes to low-income countries, the relationship between statutory hours, national income and observance rates is much weaker and remains unclear.

In light of the need to examine both *de jure* and *de facto* regulation in establishing indicators, we have made a preliminary attempt to establish such an indicator for working hours. This 'effective regulation' index for working hours (ERI) was established by averaging the normalized values of statutory hours and observance rates, which range between 0 (the weakest regulation) and 10 (the strongest regulation), in order to capture both the strength of the limit and the extent to which it is observed.[7] The results are provided in the final column of Table 3.3A. This index can be seen in contrast to the World Bank's 'rigidity of hours' index, which was developed solely from national working time legislation and implies that developing countries tend to have more 'rigid' regulations on working hours (see Lee and McCann 2007 for a critique of this index).

It should be noted, from the outset, that an aggregate index, even when other methods such as non-linear combination are used, has implicit assumptions which could create bias in the analysis. In our simple method, it is assumed that the length of statutory hours and the observance rate are *equally* important in determining the effectiveness of regulation in a particular country. What this means in practice is revealed by comparing the Republic of Korea and Panama: both have the same level of regulation (ERI = 4.3) yet the Republic of Korea has a much lower statutory hours limit (40 hours) and lower observance rate (24 per cent), while Panama's higher statutory limit (48 hours) attracts a higher observance rate (85 per cent).[8] While it is conceivable to introduce other more sophisticated methods (e.g. a well-grounded weighting scheme), reliable guidance for such methods is not currently available, mainly due to the paucity of data and analysis on the regulation of working time in developing countries.[9]

With this caveat, let us turn to the index. Among the countries considered in Table 3.3A, Ethiopia, Peru and the United Republic of Tanzania have the weakest regulation according to this index, while Luxembourg and the Netherlands lead the group of countries with the strongest regulation. Geographical divisions are clearly present: Europe (including transition economies) tends to have strong regulation, while Africa, Asia and Latin America are, overall, characterized by weak regulation. How, then, is economic development associated with the ERI: that is, is effective regulation associated with economic growth, at least with respect to weekly hours? A positive correlation is conceivable if the benefits of economic growth can be translated into either shorter statutory hours or a higher observance rate (e.g. through strengthening labour inspection), or both. As Figure 3.5 shows, there is a positive correlation between the index and GNI per capita (significant at the 0.01 level). Yet, once again, when the sample is separated into two groups of countries by income level (exactly half of the sample have GNI of less than US$10,000), there is no correlation within each group (see the dotted circles in Figure 3.5). For instance, Albania and Peru have a similar income level (around US$5,000), but contrasting ERI levels (7.0 and 2.5 respectively). Finally, and probably not surprisingly, it is noteworthy that the ERI does not have any significant correlation with the World Bank index mentioned above.

This finding should not be seen as surprising, given the evidence of variations between countries in the way that different components of working time regulation are articulated with related labour market institutions. Among high-income countries, it is relatively well established that the impact of statutory working time regulation differs depending on the working time regimes within which they are articulated (see Lee 2004). If collective negotiations are well organized and the coverage of collective agreements is extensive, working time law tends to represent a minimum standard, with the result that collectively agreed normal hours tend to be lower than the statutory standard. In this case, the latter represents the upper limit on actual working hours. In some other countries, however, where legal

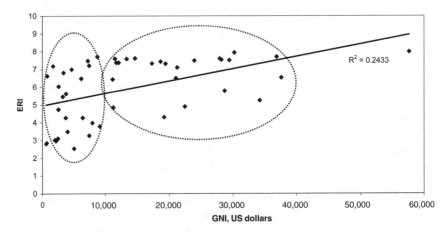

Figure 3.5 Effective working-hour regulation index (ERI) and national income

Source: see Box 3.1.

interventions are minimized, the incidence of long working hours is relatively high and therefore the statutory standard is often a lower limit on actual working hours. Another factor which is worth mentioning is that in some industrialized countries, working time laws lack an upper limit on overtime hours or allows for individual opt-outs from that limit, so that its ability to curb long hours is effectively limited (e.g. New Zealand, the United Kingdom and the United States).

3.6 Excessive hours (II): working longer than 48 hours

Another way of measuring the extent of long hours is to see how many workers are exposed to potential safety and health risks relating to long working hours. This concern underlies most statutory regulations on working time as well as relevant international standards (see Chapter 2). For example, the EU Working Time Directive of 1993 states in its preamble that 'the improvement of workers' safety, hygiene and health at work is an objective which should not be subordinated to purely economic considerations'. Of course, the probability of such risks can vary depending on how the hours are organized, the nature of work, and the characteristics of individual workers, but there is evidence that working hours longer than 48–50 hours per week could expose workers to potential health risks (see e.g. Spurgeon 2003). In light of this, the EU Directive stipulates 48 hours as the maximum working hours which includes overtime hours, while leaving the determination of normal standard hours to its Member States. Similarly, the Hours of Work (Industry) Convention, 1919 (No. 1) which stipulates 48 hours as normal working hours (hence excluding overtime hours) was originally intended to limit working hours to 48 hours by also restraining overtime hours.

Taking into account these concerns, a threshold of 48 hours is used across countries in determining long hours. The results are presented in Table 3.4. First, insofar as total employment is concerned, cross-country variations are considerable. Countries in which the incidence of long hours is low include the Russian Federation (3.2 per cent, the threshold of 50 hours is used), the Republic of Moldova (4.9 per cent), Norway (5.3 per cent) and the Netherlands (7.0 per cent), whereas more than 40 per cent of all employees are reported to work more than 48 hours per week in a few countries such as Ethiopia (41.2 per cent), Indonesia (51.2 per cent: the threshold of +45 hours is used), the Republic of Korea (49.5 per cent), Pakistan (44.4 per cent in 2003), and Thailand (46.7 per cent in 2000). This confirms the widely shared view that long working hours are common in the Asian region, especially among the so-called East Asian Tigers (e.g. the Republic of Korea) and South Eastern Dragons (e.g. Indonesia and Thailand). As a recent report noted, '[w]hile rapid economic growth and productivity gains have contributed to rising real wages in some Asian developing countries, the benefits of growth have not translated into shorter hours' (ILO 2005b: 23). Despite the

Table 3.4 Incidence of long working hours

	Gender	Total employment			Paid employees			Hour cutoff	Age
		1995	2000	2004–5	1995	2000	2004–5		
Albania	Both		7.7**			6.0**		49+	15+
	F		5.9***			3.7***			
	M		9.3**			7.4**			
Argentina	Both			28.4			24.7	49+	25+
	F			16.0			12.0		
	M			37.4			35.3		
Armenia	Both		27.2**	29.9		19.7**	24.2	49+	25+
	F		18.6**	17.1		10.4**	12.3		
	M		34.8**	40.1		29.4**	34.9		
Australia	Both	22.0	21.0	20.4	17.6	18.4	17.7	50+	25+
	F	9.4	9.7	9.2	7.5	8.3	7.8		
	M	29.3	29.6	29.1	25.4	26.6	26.1		
Azerbaijan	Both			10.6***			8.8***	51+	25+
	F			5.3***			3.5***		
	M			14.4***			12.5***		
Bolivia	Both		37.7			37.9		49+	15+
	F		33.6			20.4			
	M		40.9			45.4			
Bulgaria	Both			6.5			4.1	49+	15+
	F			5.0			3.4		
	M			7.8			4.7		
Canada	Both	14.7	11.3	10.6	9.6	5.6	5.0	49+	25+
	F	6.9	5.0	4.6	4.6	2.3	2.0		
	M	21.0	16.5	15.7	14.1	8.7	8.0		
Croatia	Both		13.2**	11.9		9.3**	9.9	49+	15+
	F		8.8**	4.6		2.1**	0.0		
	M		17.1**	16.3		12.5**	12.3		

Country	Sex								
Cyprus	Both		16.1	14.6		8.7	6.3	49+	25+
	F		8.3	6.0		5.6	3.3		
	M		21.5	21.2		11.3	9.0		
Czech Republic	Both	17.5	19.4	17.7	10.1	11.3	9.3	48.5+	25+
	F	8.8	9.4	7.2	4.9	5.1	3.9		
	M	24.4	27.1	25.6	14.6	16.5	14.1		
Estonia	Both	18.5	13.6	9.8***	16.2	10.8	7.4***	49+	15+
	F	12.8	9.5	6.0****	11.5	7.8	4.5****		
	M	23.8	17.6	13.5****	20.9	13.8	10.3****		
Ethiopia	Both			41.2			43.2	49+	10+
	F			37.3			43.2		
	M			44.2			43.1		
Finland	Both	10.5	11.4	9.7	3.4	5.1	4.5	49+	25+
	F	5.7	6.1	5.3	1.9	2.7	2.4		
	M	15.0	16.2	13.7	5.1	7.5	6.6		
France	Both	11.9	10.5	14.7	6.7	6.1	8.6	49+	25+
	F	6.4	5.7	7.9	3.4	3.4	4.9		
	M	16.7	14.8	20.4	9.6	8.5	11.9		
Georgia	Both			12.0			13.9	51+	25+
	F			8.2			7.7		
	M			15.7			18.8		
Greece	Both	21.2	18.8	18.3	6.7	6.6	6.7	49+	25+
	F	14.4	12.9	11.3	3.4	4.1	4.3		
	M	25.0	22.3	22.6	8.7	8.2	8.3		
Guatemala	Both			28.5			30.2	49+	25-60
	F			23.0			23.1		
	M			31.4			33.5		
Honduras	Both	35.0*	32.3**		39.3*	36.0**		49+	10+
	F	33.6*	32.4***		39.0*	35.5***			
	M	35.7*	32.2**		39.5*	36.3***			
Hungary	Both	11.2	10.1	7.3	7.3	7.1	5.1	49+	25+
	F	5.5	4.8	3.3	3.4	3.2	2.3		
	M	16.2	15.0	11.0	11.1	11.0	7.9		

Table 3.4 Continued

	Gender	Total employment			Paid employees			Hour cutoff	Age
		1995	2000	2004-5	1995	2000	2004-5		
Indonesia	Both	46.9*	49.1	51.2***	52.6*	53.4	53.0***	45+	15+
	F	36.1*	40.0	42.0***	42.9*	45.2	44.7***		
	M	52.0*	53.6	55.1***	56.8*	57.4	56.6***		
Ireland	Both		14.7	11.6		7.3	5.5	49+	25+
	F		4.6	3.0		2.7	1.8		
	M		22.2	18.4		11.4	8.9		
Israel	Both	27.5	26.6	25.5	24.3	23.9	23.2	50+	25+
	F	9.8	10.5	11.0	9.0	9.8	10.1		
	M	40.2	39.8	37.7	36.4	36.5	35.3		
Japan	Both	28.8	17.4	17.7	27.2	16.7	17.0	49+	15+
	F	15.8	8.3	8.3	13.1	7.0	7.2		
	M	37.6	24.3	25.1	36.2	23.9	24.7		
Korea, Republic of	Both		56.3	49.5		54.0	45.7	49+	25+
	F		48.8	42.6		43.8	36.4		
	M		61.1	54.0		60.0	51.6		
Lithuania	Both		8.2	4.6		5.7	3.2	49+	25+
	F		6.2	3.1		4.1	2.1		
	M		10.2	5.9		7.5	4.4		
Luxembourg	Both	9.3	6.7	4.2	4.0	3.4	0.9	49+	15+
	F	6.5	2.8	2.4	2.6	1.1	0.4		
	M	11.0	9.3	5.5	4.8	5.0	1.2		
Macao	Both	41.0*	41.9	39.1				50+	14+
	F	38.2*	40.2	35.4					
	M	43.3*	43.4	42.4					
Macedonia, FYR	Both		16.6	18.7***		7.9	7.1***	49+	15+
	F		14.4	14.8***		5.3	4.6***		
	M		17.9	21.4***		9.6	8.8***		

Madagascar	Both	16.7**				22.6**		49+	15+
	F	14.9**				16.0**			
	M	18.3**				26.4**			
Malta	Both	10.3		9.4		7.7	5.3	49+	15+
	F	0.0		2.5		0.0	0.0		
	M	13.8		12.4		10.4	7.2		
Mauritius	Both	22.1		22.1		19.9	20.6	49+	25+
	F	17.0		16.4		16.4	16.0		
	M	24.4		24.8		21.6	23.0		
Mexico	Both	26.7	30.8	26.2	28.4	23.8	24.2	49+	25+
	F	15.8	18.1	16.2	13.5	12.0	12.2		
	M	32.3	36.8	31.8	35.2	29.8	30.8		
Moldova, Republic of	Both	6.0		4.9		3.9	3.9	48+	25+
	F	4.2		3.5		2.7	2.8		
	M	7.8		6.4		5.1	5.1		
Netherlands	Both	8.1	8.5*	7.0	1.9*	2.0	1.4	49+	15+
	F	2.3	2.5*	1.7	0.5*	0.5	0.3		
	M	12.3	12.5*	11.0	2.8*	3.1	2.2		
New Zealand	Both	23.6	22.6	23.6	16.6	17.8	16.4	49+	25+
	F	10.8	9.4	10.8	6.7	8.5	7.8		
	M	34.0	32.9	34.0	25.5	26.8	24.9		
Norway	Both	6.0	7.2*	5.3	4.5*	3.6	3.3	49+	16+
	F	1.9	2.2*	1.8	1.3*	1.2	1.2		
	M	9.5	11.5*	8.4	7.4*	5.9	5.4		
Pakistan	Both	44.4***		44.4***			39.6***	49+	10+
	F	14.4***		14.4***			22.1***		
	M	50.9***		50.9***			42.5***		
Panama	Both	15.3	15.7	17.3	13.6	11.9	14.6	49+	15+
	F	12.0	13.1	13.0	11.9	9.8	12.1		
	M	17.2	17.2	19.9	14.6	13.3	16.3		
Peru	Both	47.1**		50.9		46.0**	49.2	48+	25+
	F								
	M								

Table 3.4 Continued

	Gender	Total employment			Paid employees			Hour cutoff	Age
		1995	2000	2004–5	1995	2000	2004–5		
Poland	Both	16.5	18.0	19.3	12.7	13.0	14.1	50+	15+
	F	9.0	10.3	11.1	6.8	7.2	7.5		
	M	22.7	24.0	25.8	17.7	17.8	19.8		
Portugal	Both		11.5	10.6		5.8	5.2	49+	15+
	F		8.3	7.1		3.6	2.8		
	M		14.0	13.6		7.6	7.4		
Romania	Both	17.1*	16.8	18.2	11.6*	14.6	16.6	46+	15+
	F	14.5*	13.5	14.7	9.8*	13.1	14.3		
	M	19.1*	19.6	21.2	12.9*	15.9	18.6		
Russian Federation	Both	1.6	3.5**	3.2	1.4	2.7**	2.5	51+	25+
	F	0.8	2.1***	1.8	0.7	1.5***	1.4		
	M	2.4	4.9**	4.5	2.0	3.9	3.6		
Slovakia	Both			9.2			5.3	50+	15+
	F			4.1			2.9		
	M			13.4			7.4		
Slovenia	Both	30.2	22.8	20.6	22.4	15.7	15.2	41+	25+
	F	27.3	19.7	16.1	22.0	13.9	12.2		
	M	33.1	25.5	24.5	24.9	17.7	18.6		
Spain	Both	13.0	13.4	12.1	5.5	6.4	6.0	49+	25+
	F	8.4	7.3	6.4	2.5	2.9	3.0		
	M	15.3	16.9	15.7	7.1	8.5	8.0		
Sri Lanka	Both	24.0*	25.2	26.7***	22.9*	23.2	25.3***	49+	25+
	F	15.0*	16.1	17.2***	15.0*	15.9	17.6***		
	M	27.8*	29.5	30.8***	26.4*	26.6	28.7***		

								49+	25+
Switzerland	Both	18.5*	19.6	19.2	14.7*	16.1	16.6	49+	25+
	F	7.9*	7.8	7.8	5.6*	6.0	6.4		
	M	26.4*	28.7	28.4	21.6*	24.1	25.0		
Tanzania, United Republic of	Both		30.0			66.9		50+	10+
	F								
	M								
Thailand	Both	51.8	46.7		43.8	34.7		50+	15+
	F	47.9	42.3		39.8	31.2			
	M	54.6	50.1		46.4	37.3			
United Kingdom	Both		25.9	25.7***		25.0	24.9***	49+	25+
	F		12.4	13.5***		12.1	13.1***		
	M		35.4	34.5***		34.3	33.5***		
United States	Both	19.9	19.9	18.1	18.6	18.9	17.3	49+	16+
	F	11.2	11.8	10.8	10.4	11.2	10.2		
	M	27.1	26.7	24.3	25.7	25.7	23.5		
Uruguay	Both	25.5	25.3	22.1	20.5	20.7	18.3	49+	25+
	F	16.2	14.7	13.8	10.3	11.0	9.8		
	M	33.7	33.4	28.6	28.3	29.2	25.9		
Zimbabwe	Both		29.2			40.6		49+	15+
	F		24.2			42.5			
	M		33.7			39.9			

Source: see Box 3.1.

Note
* 1996 figure; ** 2001 figure; *** 2003 figure.

persistence of cross-country variations, the dominant trend in many countries is the overall decrease in the incidence of long working hours, with some notable exceptions such as Armenia, Indonesia, Panama, Peru and Poland.

It is well known that the self-employed tend to work longer hours than paid employees. This is the case in many countries considered in Table 3.4, although data for the self-employed are not reported here due to space limitations (see the Statistical annex). Countries such as Cyprus, the Czech Republic, Macedonia, the Netherlands and Spain show a striking difference in the incidence of long hours between the self-employed and paid employees. In the Netherlands, for example, the incidence of long hours is so low (1.4 per cent) among paid employees that one could argue that long hours are 'extinct'. The relatively high incidence of long working hours among the self-employed has often been explained by two factors. The first concerns the voluntary nature of long hours: as the self-employed tend to enjoy autonomy over when and the way in which work is undertaken, the 'disutility' associated with working hours can be relatively lower, thereby making long hours more acceptable to self-employed workers. The second is related to earnings instability among the self-employed: faced with large fluctuations in their earnings, they tend to work longer when they can, which tends to make their hours longer than those of paid employees. In a sense, long working hours can be seen by the self-employed as a type of 'self-insurance' (Parker *et al.* 2005). As a result, working hours are relatively unstable among the self-employed, sometimes swinging between short (even zero) and long hours. In comparison with employees, the distribution of working hours for the self-employed shows a more diversified (often bifurcated) pattern that tends to be concentrated at both ends of the distribution. These issues will be discussed in detail in Chapter 5 in relation to the informal economy.

In many other countries, however, such differences relating to employment status are very small, and in some cases paid employees are more likely than the self-employed to work long hours.[10] This is particularly the case in those countries which have a high incidence of long working hours (say, 30 per cent). Zimbabwe provides a striking example of this pattern where 40.6 per cent of paid employees were working more than 48 hours per week, while the proportion for the self-employed was relatively low at 29.2 per cent in 1999. This phenomenon appears to be related to the fact that in these countries many self-employed workers are forced to work shorter hours than they would like, due to the lack of available work (hence underemployment), and also, particularly for women in self-employment, because of temporal constraints resulting from a heavy burden of family responsibilities (see Chapter 4). The issue of underemployment will be discussed later in Section 3.7.

The Hours of Work Conventions (Nos 1 and 30) stipulate a 48-hour working week for industry and commerce and offices, respectively, and have been ratified by a number of countries. As we approach the centennial anniversary of Convention No. 1, it is interesting to see if the ratification of these standards is associated with a lower proportion of employees working more than this standard. As Figure 3.6 demonstrates, the ratification of these Conventions appears to have had an ambiguous impact in curbing excessive working hours. The proportion of paid employees who are working more than 48 hours (19.4 per cent) is equally high in countries that have ratified both Conventions as in those that have ratified neither.[11] Moreover, countries that have ratified only one of the two Conventions (e.g. Canada, France and Norway) have a lower incidence of 'excessive hours' than those that have ratified both. Further research is needed to explain this result, although some indicative discussions have been made (ILO 2005d; Lee and McCann 2007), and we explore the issue further in Chapter 7.

3.6.1 Global estimates

Finally, how many workers in the world are working more than 48 hours, the standard maximum stipulated in Conventions Nos. 1 and 30 and which appears to be essential for worker well-being? In making a global estimate, national incomes and the total volume of employment are taken into account; it turns out that our sample is fairly 'random' and also reasonably 'representative' (see Box 3.2). The result indicates that about one in five – 22.0 per cent, or 614.2 million workers – around the world are working more than 48 hours per week.

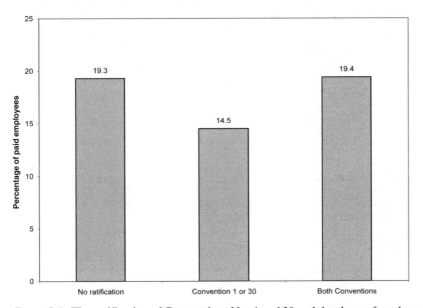

Figure 3.6   The ratification of Conventions Nos 1 and 30 and the share of workers who are working more than 48 hours per week (unweighted mean of national averages, based on latest figures available)

Source: ILO Database of International Labour Standards; see Box 3.1.

Box 3.2 Global estimates for workers working longer than 48 hours

A total of 54 countries were considered, after about ten countries were excluded from the sample for their questionable data quality or lack of comparability. The simple mean average of the national estimates is 20.1 per cent, and when weighted by total employment, it increases to 23.3 per cent.

As the effects of population size and incomes may affect the proportion of workers working more than 48 hours, data on total employment and national incomes (GNI per capita) were collected from the ILO and World Bank databases. Data are available for 125 countries. One major obstacle was that data on the distribution of working hours were not available for certain large countries such as China and India. To ensure the reliability and validity of the global estimates, data were collected separately for these two countries. The Indian estimate (20.6 per cent) came from the Report on Factory Act 2000 (http://labourbureau.nic.in/FA2K%20Main%20Page.htm), while the Chinese figure used (21.8 per cent) refers to the average proportion of workers working 48 hours or more in three major cities (Zeng *et al.* 2005).

A logistic regression was carried out (a country included in the sample = 1; otherwise, 0), which concluded that employment volume and national incomes do not have a significant influence and that the sample can therefore be considered 'random'. The result did not change even when China and India were included in the sample. The global estimate was made on the 'prediction' of the proportion of workers working 48 hours or more based on the averages over the sample weighted by total employment and national income levels.

Estimation summary

	More than 48 hours (%)
Sample (54 countries)	
• Sample average	23.3
• Predicted (OLS regression on total employment and national incomes per capita (GNI))	22.0
Full (125 countries)	
• Predicted on GNI	21.8
• Prediction interval for weighted average of GNI, including China and India	22.0 (18.5–25.4)
• Prediction interval for weighted average of GNI, without China and India	22.1 (18.5–25.8)

3.7 Short hours and underemployment

Along with workers working long hours, there are those who are working rather short hours. In industrialized countries, short hours have been considered as a viable option for those who have difficulties in combining full-time work with other commitments, notably to the family (Anxo 2004; Fagan 2004). However, short hours are often not well received by these workers due to the disadvantages associated with part-time work (e.g. wages, promotion and training), and not surprisingly there are a considerable number of part-time workers who would like to have a full-time job (Lee 2004). By contrast, short hours in developing countries are understood to be predominantly problematic, because it is commonly believed that most of these workers belong to the category of 'time-related underemployment', which is also known as 'invisible underemployment'. This section examines these two related issues: short hours (or part-time employment) and time-related underemployment.

3.7.1 Short hours

Table 3.5 presents the share of workers working short hours, using the threshold of 35 hours whenever data are available. First, it is striking that the proportion of short hours is high in many countries. In some countries such as Albania and Georgia, more than 40 per cent of workers (32 per cent of paid employees and 55 per cent of the self-employed) were working less than 35 hours. As mentioned earlier, short hours are also common in high-income countries where they are often recommended as a way of reconciling work and family life. By contrast, it is believed that the high incidence of short hours in developing countries is often the result of a slack labour market and poor economic performance. If this is the case, it is plausible that with the growth of the economy the incidence of short hours would decrease, as the labour market becomes more likely to able to offer full-time jobs. This is probably why the relationship between the incidence of short hours and national income per capita (GNI) shows a U-shaped curve (see Figure 3.7).

Second, in developing countries with a high incidence of short hours, this incidence tends to be concentrated on self-employed women: men are less likely than women to work short hours, while paid employees are less likely than the self-employed to work short hours. In Guatemala, for instance, 61.8 per cent of self-employed women were working less than 35 hours in 2004, compared with 19.0 per cent of their male counterparts. This pattern is also found in other countries such as Honduras, Mauritius, Panama, Sri Lanka and Uruguay. This shows that in developing countries, short hours tend to be concentrated in informal jobs. One study demonstrates that in Chile more than half of all part-time workers (54 per cent) did not have any written contracts and about half of them had permanent contracts. Not surprisingly the overwhelming majority (63 per cent) of part-timers did not contribute to

Table 3.5 The proportion of workers with shorter hours

Country	Year	Paid employee (%)			Self-employed (%)			Age	Hours cutoff
		Both	Female	Male	Both	Female	Male		
Albania	2001	32.0	32.4	31.7	54.8	58.9	52.4	15+	<35
Armenia	2004	23.2	35.1	12.5	40.4	52.2	32.7	25+	<35
Australia	2004	25.0	43.6	9.5	31.5	56.4	18.9	25+	<35
Azerbaijan	2003	12.9	20.0	8.1	22.9	29.3	18.0	25+	<30
Bolivia	2000	22.3	36.4	16.2	32.2	36.2	28.3	15+	<35
Bulgaria	2004	2.5	3.4	1.6	12.6	16.3	10.6	15+	<35
Canada	2004	19.0	30.3	8.2	26.9	45.4	17.4	25+	<35
Croatia	2004	5.8	7.2	4.6	34.1	18.3	13.7	15+	<35
Cyprus	2004	6.6	10.6	3.0	20.3	41.9	11.5	25+	<35
Czech Republic	2004	5.1	8.3	2.2	7.0	15.6	3.6	25+	<35
Estonia	2003	8.4	12.1	4.6	12.3	9.9	4.2	15+	<35
Ethiopia	2004	10.2	12.4	8.9	33.6	42.3	26.0	10+	<35
Finland	2004	13.7	19.0	8.3	20.6	26.6	17.7	25+	<35
France	2004	20.1	33.9	7.4	10.9	23.5	4.9	25+	<35
Georgia	2004	34.0	46.0	22.0	47.0	51.8	42.5	25+	<36
Guatemala	2004	17.7	32.0	11.2	35.8	61.8	19.0	25-60	<35
Honduras	2001	12.2	13.2	11.6	25.8	52.7	16.7	10+	<35
Hungary	2004	5.3	7.8	2.9	5.2	9.1	3.3	25+	<35
Indonesia	2003	16.8	25.9	12.8	25.5	36.1	21.0	15+	<35
Ireland	2004	23.1	41.5	6.6	9.1	28.7	5.2	25+	<35
Israel	2004	22.4	35.3	10.6	23.7	41.0	16.6	25+	<35
Japan	2004	23.7	40.0	12.3	25.3	41.4	14.1	15+	<35
Korea, Republic of	2004	8.8	14.3	5.3	14.0	17.3	11.7	25+	<35
Lithuania	2004	15.2	19.7	10.5	41.8	46.3	38.4	25+	<35
Luxembourg	2004	18.0	40.9	2.0	13.7	28.7	5.7	15+	<35
Macedonia, FYR	2003	3.1	3.5	2.9	17.3	21.1	15.0	15+	<35

Country	Year							Age	
Madagascar	2001	21.9	31.1	16.7	22.2	26.4	17.7	15+	<35
Malta	2004	16.9	34.8	8.0	13.3	0.0	10.8	15+	<36
Mauritius	2004	24.0	35.6	18.0	40.0	59.2	33.5	25+	<35
Mexico	2004	13.5	26.2	6.7	26.4	48.2	13.7	25+	<35
Moldova, Republic of	2004	6.1	9.0	2.9	12.3	15.2	9.2	25+	<35
Netherlands	2004	40.5	73.3	13.6	35.8	70.3	17.6	15+	<35
New Zealand	2004	25.2	41.5	9.1	31.5	56.1	20.2	25+	<35
Norway	2004	27.9	43.3	13.3	21.1	37.2	16.1	16+	<35
Pakistan	2003	9.5	30.1	6.2	9.3	45.9	6.5	10+	<35
Panama	2004	12.5	14.2	11.3	45.8	64.2	36.5	15+	<35
Peru	2004	16.9	NA	NA	27.5	NA	NA	25+	<35
Poland	2004	10.1	15.0	5.9	23.4	30.5	18.6	15+	<30
Portugal	2004	6.9	11.4	2.9	30.2	41.8	21.8	15+	<35
Romania	2004	1.9	2.5	1.5	22.6	27.8	18.2	15+	<36
Russian Federation	2004	4.1	6.0	2.3	33.0	40.1	27.1	25+	<30
Slovakia	2004	3.7	5.5	2.1	4.0	9.8	2.0	15+	<35
Slovenia	2004	5.3	5.3	3.5	21.5	21.2	14.5	25+	<40
Spain	2004	11.5	23.1	3.5	9.4	19.9	4.6	25+	<35
Sri Lanka	2003	32.9	36.2	31.4	43.5	58.7	36.7	25+	<35
Switzerland	2004	33.1	58.0	12.8	38.2	61.4	21.1	25+	<35
Tanzania, United Republic of	2000	6.5	NA	NA	38.0	NA	NA	10+	<40
Thailand	2000	6.5	6.2	6.6	12.2	13.5	11.1	15+	<35
United Kingdom	2003	16.2	34.8	2.7	14.4	34.7	7.2	25+	<35
United States	2004	23.4	31.3	16.5	33.6	47.2	25.7	16+	<35
Uruguay	2004	24.7	38.3	12.7	36.8	47.3	30.6	25+	<35
Zimbabwe	1999	4.7	6.8	3.8	37.1	39.0	33.6	15+	<35

Source: see Box 3.1.

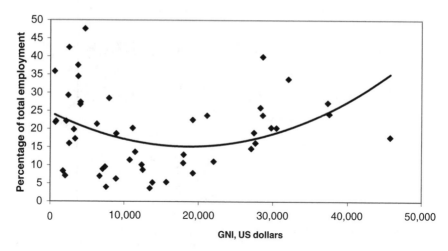

Figure 3.7 Incidence of short hours by national income

Sources: see Box 3.1 and Table 3.5; World Bank Database.

the insurance and pension systems in that country (Leiva 2000; see also Saboia 2002 for Brazil).

This reflects the fact that many informal jobs in these countries are no more than a short-term coping strategy for survival or underemployment. However, it should also be noted that the considerable gender gaps in Table 3.5 suggest that work–family constraints appear to play a role in determining the incidence of short hours, a point which will be discussed in detail in Chapter 4. If other factors such as geographical (e.g. rural or urban) and age factors (high incidence of short hours among young and old workers) are considered as well, a fairly broad range of factors actually affect working time decisions concerning short hours. While due to the paucity of data it is not possible to know the extent to which these various constraints can affect working time decisions (cf. Blackden and Wodon, eds, 2006), some evidence is useful. In Indonesia, for example, the 1995 population survey data show that about 58 per cent of workers working less than 35 hours per week reported that they did not need to work, and 26 per cent (mostly women) stated that they were working short hours due to their housekeeping responsibilities (Dhanani 2004). (Other minority responses included school (6 per cent) and 'lost hope' (2 per cent).) Thus the question is the extent to which part-time work is voluntary.

3.7.2 Time-related underemployment

According to the 1998 resolution of the International Conference of Labour Statisticians, 'time-related underemployment exists when the hours of work of an employed person are insufficient in relation to an alternative employment situation in which the person is willing and available to engage' (paragraph 7). In other words, workers who experience time-related under-employment are working short hours 'involuntarily'. Therefore, this indicator, along with unemployment rates, can provide useful information regarding how effective the labour market is in providing full employment

Table 3.6 Time-related underemployment (2001, percentage of total employment)

Country	Total	Men	Women	Hours cutoff
Armenia	16.0	NA	NA	39
Australia	7.2	5.1	9.9	35
Austria*	1.1	0.5	1.9	30
Belgium	2.8	1.0	5.4	30
Canada	4.7	2.9	6.7	30
Colombia**	19.4	NA	NA	32
Costa Rica	10.1	9.8	10.7	47
Czech Republic	0.6	0.2	1.2	30
Denmark	1.6	0.7	2.6	30
Ecuador	7.0	5.5	9.4	40
Finland	3.4	1.5	5.5	30
France	2.5	1.1	4.3	30
Germany*	1.7	0.7	3.1	30
Greece	1.4	0.8	2.6	30
Guatemala**	15.5	3.0	4.3	40
Hong Kong, China**	3.3	NA	NA	35
Hungary	0.4	0.3	0.6	30
Iceland	1.1	0.3	2.0	30
Ireland	1.8	1.2	2.6	30
Italy	2.1	0.9	4.3	30
Japan	1.8	0.8	3.3	35
Luxembourg	0.7	0.2	1.5	30
Netherlands	0.9	0.6	1.3	30
New Zealand	6.0	3.7	8.8	30
Nicaragua	15.4	12.9	18.3	40
Norway	0.9	0.8	1.1	30
Pakistan*	2.8	2.5	5.0	35
Panama	7.3	7.2	7.6	40
Paraguay	8.3	5.4	12.9	30
Peru**	20.1	NA	NA	35
Philippines	8.3	NA	NA	40
Poland	1.8	1.4	2.3	39
Portugal	1.5	0.3	2.9	30
Slovakia	0.5	0.1	0.9	30
Spain	1.5	0.5	3.2	30
Switzerland	0.8	0.5	1.1	30
Thailand*	4.0	4.0	4.0	40
United Kingdom*	1.9	1.3	2.5	30
United States	0.7	0.5	1.0	30

Source: ILO (2005a).

Note
* 2000 figure; ** 2002 figure.

to those who would like to have it. For example, relatively low unemployment rates in many developing countries are often simply due to the fact that unemployment is not a viable option for many workers and, therefore, they take any available jobs even though they may be for short hours and low pay.

Despite its importance for understanding the situation regarding working time in both industrialized and developing countries, data are limited for developing countries. When data are available, comparability is problematic, as national definitions of time-related underemployment vary considerably among countries (see further ILO 2005a). With this caveat in mind, the available data indicate that the proportion of time-related underemployment is much higher in developing countries than in industrialized countries. For example, as Table 3.6 shows, the figures in Armenia (16.0 per cent), Colombia (19.4 per cent), Nicaragua (15.4 per cent) and Peru (20.1 per cent) are considerably higher than in other countries. Most industrialized countries have much lower levels of underemployment, typically below 5.0 per cent, with the exceptions of Australia (7.2 per cent) and New Zealand (6.0 per cent). However, even the high figures reported in Table 3.6 for developing countries appear to be underestimated ones. For instance, other sources indicate that time-related underemployment in the Philippines is much higher, at 17.0 per cent of total employment, and other countries with higher proportions of underemployment, such as Cambodia, Indonesia and Viet Nam, are not included in this table (see Asian Development Bank 2005: table 2.3).

Given that workers experiencing time-related underemployment would like to work more, it is important to know the extent to which this preference is realized. While there is a growing body of studies about transition from involuntary part-time work to full-time work in industrialized countries (see for example O'Reilly and Bothfeld 2002), little is known about developing countries. An interesting study on Trinidad and Tobago found that about 40 per cent of workers in 'visible underemployment' had taken full-time jobs in three months, while many others remained in the same situation (25.5 per cent) or had withdrawn from the labour market (20.3 per cent) (Görg and Strobl 2003).

3.8 Distribution of working hours: bifurcation and double challenges

So far we have looked at different segments of working-hour distributions. As a way of wrapping up our discussions, it would be useful to briefly examine the overall distributional patterns in working hours, in relation to the different working time regimes discussed in Section 3.4. Types E and F in Figure 3.3 are particularly relevant here.

First, the distribution patterns of working hours in many countries are skewed to the right, which means that the standard hours have lost their relevance as a standard. Probably the best example of this situation is found in the Republic of Korea where longer hours affect more workers (see Figure 3.8). As we have seen in our discussions on the effective regulation index (ERI), this is fairly common. Table 3.3 shows that observance rates do not exceed 70 per cent in the majority of developing and transition countries around the world, including Armenia, Bolivia, Croatia, Ethiopia, Georgia, Guatemala, Honduras, Pakistan, Peru, Sri Lanka, the United Republic of Tanzania, Thailand and Zimbabwe. While we have seen that observance rates are only loosely related to income levels, the Korean case can be seen as an interesting outlier where enforcement remains poor despite remarkable economic growth and, paradoxically, the reduction of actual working hours has been primarily attempted through the reduction of statutory hours, most recently to a 40-hour working week (see Lee 2003).

As discussed earlier, the working time challenge that most developing and transition countries are facing comes not only from long hours and low observance but also from the massive presence of short hours, often associated with time-related underemployment. For this reason, the overall working hours distribution pattern in these countries is close to a uniform distribution. Several country examples are provided in Figure 3.9. In all of the countries in Figure 3.9, workers are basically split into two major groups and only a minority of workers are working somewhere around the standard hours, say between 40 and 48 hours per week. The most striking example in this regard is Bolivia, where working hours are strongly bifurcated between very short and very long hours. The bifurcation of working hours is particularly strong in the informal economy (see Chapter 5).

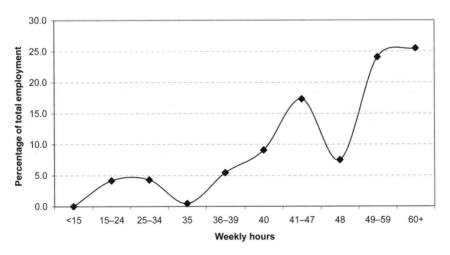

Figure 3.8 The distribution of working hours in the Republic of Korea (2004, percentage of total employment)

Source: see Box 3.1.

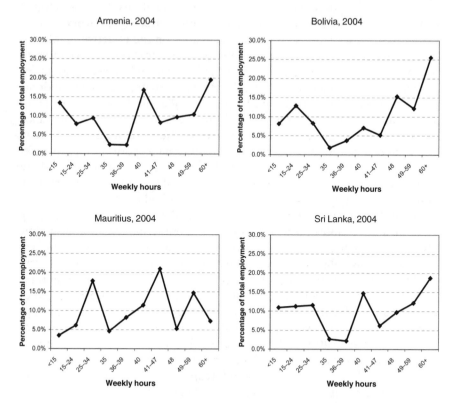

Figure 3.9 Working-hour bifurcation in selected countries: double challenges

Source: see Box 3.1.

3.9 Conclusions

In this chapter, we have reviewed actual working hours from various angles. First, from a historical perspective, we have observed that developments in working hours are rather uneven, depending on the degree of social intervention as well as economic development. Of course, the forms that social intervention can take are varied, ranging from legislation to financial support for a specific working-hour pattern that is perceived as socially desirable.

Second, when the focus is placed upon the manufacturing sector, average weekly working hours have been relatively stable for the last ten years in many countries. There is no sign that developing countries are 'catching up' with industrialized ones, and gaps between countries remain substantial. However, average figures mask the differences in the distribution of working hours across countries. In developing countries, the incidence of both long hours and short hours is high, and whenever this is the case, average figures could potentially be misleading.

Third, the aspect of long working hours has been examined based on the universal threshold of the 48-hour working week and the relative concept of observance, the latter of which can be defined in relation to the existing statutory normal hours. The 48-hour working week was introduced almost a century ago, but our analysis indicates that while the incidence of long hours (i.e. the proportion of workers working more than 48 hours per week) tends to have decreased in many countries over the last ten years, long hours are still widespread. Our estimation indicates that roughly one out of five workers (or 22 per cent) are working longer than 48 hours per week.

Fourth, observance rates tend to be low in many countries. In fact there is no reason to believe that 'stricter' standards (i.e. shorter statutory normal hours) can lower the observance rate, as the evidence shows that many developing countries have low observance rates despite their 'less-stringent' regulations. The ERI developed in this chapter, which attempts to capture both the *de jure* and *de facto* aspects of working-hour regulation, shows that the relationship between statutory hours, economic development and observance is rather complicated, such that any generalization would be difficult to make (cf. World Bank 2004).

Finally, on the other side of the working time challenge lies short hours, which are particularly widespread among women and the self-employed. A considerable proportion of these short-hours workers are likely to be underemployed and would like to work more, and they are also more likely to fall into the trap of poverty. Combined with long working hours, many developing and transition countries are faced with the bifurcation of working hours between short and long hours, or put in a different way, between income poverty and time poverty.

Thus, we have focused on macro-level developments, especially on variations across countries. As hinted at earlier, the developments in working hours that are identified in this chapter often play out differently for different groups of workers, depending on demographic characteristics (such as gender and age), industries (e.g. manufacturing versus service sectors), and probably more importantly for many developing countries, the formal versus the informal economy. These issues will be subjects of Chapters 4 and 5.

4 Gender, age and working time

4.1 Introduction

In Chapter 3, we looked at some of the macro-level trends that are shaping working time around the world, both in terms of hours of work and the ways in which those working hours are being organized. For individual workers, there has been, broadly viewed, a move away from workers working the 'normal' or 'standard' working hours laid down in laws and collective agreements, and towards diversity in the number of hours that are actually being worked. This diversification includes both long hours of work – with more than one-fifth of the workforce working even excessive hours of over 48 a week – and also hours that are shorter than the norm, which may represent time-related underemployment.

In Chapters 4 and 5, we turn our attention to some of the concerns that are simmering just beneath the surface of these broad, macro-level trends in working time around the world. First, there is the question of the diversification of the global workforce, and how the specific circumstances of certain groups of workers affect their hours of work. Perhaps the most dramatic evidence of this diversity concerns women workers: in the last few decades, women have gone from a relatively marginal role in non-agricultural employment to a much more significant one in most parts of the world, even nearing parity with men in a few countries such as China in terms of their labour force participation (ILO 2005a). Nonetheless, the ways in which women participate in paid work are in many cases substantially different from men's participation in the workforce, and this has profound implications for their working hours – for example, women's much higher rates of short (or part-time) hours (see e.g. Saboia 2002; Messenger, ed., 2004; OECD 2004) and also their higher rates of participation in the informal economy (ILO 2002a).

Similarly, the ageing of the global workforce is raising questions about the appropriate level of labour force participation of older workers; these questions relate to both their working hours and the adequacy of social protection systems for the elderly (where such systems exist). These and other factors can also interact with each other in any of a myriad number of ways: just as one example, the increased labour force participation of women combined with increased migration can mean a lack of the traditional extended family support for providing child- and elder care to family members, thus increasing the need for alternative means of support for such families.

In this chapter, we will consider the diversification in the global work-force and its accompanying effects on working time, with a particular focus on the two key factors mentioned above: *gender* and *age*. How and why do women's working hours and working time arrangements differ from those of men, and what are the implications of these differences for gender equality? How and why do working hours vary across age groups, and what are the implications of such variations? This chapter will review variations in working hours and in the organization of those hours (i.e. work schedules), with an emphasis on gender differences and differences by age group, thus offering some insights into the ways in which the increased participation of women in paid work and the ageing of the global workforce are impacting on working time around the world.

4.2 Differences in male and female labour market participation

Any discussion of working time and gender must begin by recognizing two essential points. The first point is that, in a little over two decades, women's participation in paid work has increased substantially in most of the world. There was a significant period of growth during the 1980s, but participation continued to increase marginally during the 1990s as well (see Table 4.1). For example, from 1993 to 2003, the total number of women in the global labour force increased by 20 per cent – from 1.0 to 1.2 billion workers – although their participation rate increased by only 0.4 per cent during the same period (ILO 2004: 2).[1] Nonetheless, the global labour force participation rate for women stood at a relatively low level (53.9 per cent) in 2003, compared with 79.4 per cent for men (ibid.).[2] The regions of the world with the highest levels of female labour force participation in 2003 were East Asia and sub-Saharan Africa, while the Middle East–North Africa and the South Asia regions recorded the lowest levels (ibid.: 5).

The second point is that, despite the increase in women's participation in paid work, women continue to bear the primary responsibility for *unpaid* work in households, including both domestic tasks (e.g. cooking, cleaning) and the provision of care to family members. With regard to care work, for instance, recent research based on time-use studies in the industrialized countries indicates that women continue to provide the vast majority of childcare in families (Ilahi 2001; European Commission and Eurostat 2003). And although comprehensive data on time use are unavailable in most developing countries, where such data are available the results can truly be eye-opening. For example, in Brazil, a nationwide survey of women in 2001 by the Fundação Perseu Abramo (the Perseu Abramo Foundation) found

Table 4.1 Changes in global labour market indicators by gender (1993–2003)

	Female		Male		Total	
	1993	*2003*	*1993*	*2003*	*1993*	*2003*
Global labour force						
participation (millions)	1006.0	1208.0	1507.0	1769.0	2513.0	2978.0
Employment (millions)	948.0	1130.0	1425.0	1661.0	2373.0	2792.0
Unemployment (millions)	58.2	77.8	82.3	108.1	140.5	185.9
Global labour force						
participation rate (%)	53.5	53.9	80.5	79.4	67.0	66.6

Source: *Global Employment Trends Model 2003* (ILO 2004, Table 1.1, p. 2 and Table 2.1, p. 5).

that in 96 per cent of all Brazilian households women were the ones who had the primary responsibility for handling domestic tasks, and 57 per cent of the women with partners (married or not) who were interviewed reported that their partner had not performed *any* housework in the previous week (Sorj 2004: 25). The difference in the average weekly hours that the women devoted to household tasks compared with their partners was astonishing: the women reported spending an average of 48 hours per week on domestic tasks, while their male partners spent only 5.6 hours on such tasks – thus, the difference in household work is the equivalent of a full paid working week (44 hours) in that country (ibid.). Even if the comparison is narrowed down only to those in paid work, similar findings are reported; for example, the results of a time-use survey conducted in the Republic of Korea in 1999 showed that women workers spent an average of nearly two and a half hours per day on household tasks and family care, compared with only 25 minutes for male workers (Yoon 2001: 92).

4.2.1 Temporal constraints on availability

These two factors, taken together, lead to the inescapable conclusion that, while women are increasingly being found in paid work, their temporal availability for such work is going to be significantly constrained by the time that they need to devote to their household/domestic responsibilities. That is, given the weight of these responsibilities, one would expect to find that women will of necessity be somewhat limited in the number of hours that they can spend on paid work activities and also in the times of the day/week when they are available for paid work. A number of other recent studies provide a substantial body of evidence indicating that the presence of children in a household – particularly young, pre-school children – substantially reduces women's paid labour supply, either in terms of their labour force participation, their working hours, or both (see, for example, Fagan and Burchell 2002; Anxo 2004; Anxo and Boulin, eds, 2005).

Hungary (Galasi 2002) provides an excellent illustration of the phenomenon of temporal constraints on women's participation in paid work. Based on a gender analysis, this study finds that both marriage and the presence of children in the household increase men's paid working hours and reduce women's paid working hours.[3] The presence of children alone results in working hours that are between 13 and 19 per cent longer for men than for women (Galasi 2002: 62), and the more children in the family the greater the effect of this factor on hours worked. Thus, the findings of this study suggest that women of any given age would be willing to work longer hours in paid employment *if not for their family obligations*.[4] The Hungary country report concludes that:

> Our analysis suggests that in the 1990s observed gender differences in weekly hours of work at least partially reflect a long-lasting gender inequality problem resulting from a gender division of labour where paid work is primarily considered as men's duty, and most of the unpaid (household) work is generally considered the responsibility of women.
>
> (Galasi 2002: 95)

Given this important temporal constraint, it is not surprising that the ways in which women participate in paid work are often substantially different from men's participation in the labour force, and that these differences, in turn, have some profound implications for their working time. First, according to ILO LABORSTA data on working hours in the non-agricultural sectors, the average actual hours of work of employed men exceed those of employed women in almost every country for which data are available. The sole exception to this pattern is the Philippines, where the average hours of women slightly exceeded those of men (see Box 4.1).

Women's temporal constraints on their working hours are widely reported. For example, in Malaysia it was estimated that the percentage of women who stopped work due to childcare reasons was 23 per cent (Nagaraj 2004: 46). The Malaysia study goes on to conclude that marriage and family remain constraints to female labour force participation. Likewise, the Peru report emphasizes the temporal constraints on the scope and degree of women's labour market participation, including their working hours: 'women's participation in the labour market [due to] their family responsibilities occurs mainly in those areas that allow them to share their time between caring for small children and work, which are basically independent activities' (Aparicio Valdez 2001: 17).

4.2.2 Patterns of work

The second difference in male and female participation is illustrated by the data on the distribution of working hours presented in Tables 4.2 and 4.3 (using data from the 2005 special survey of ILO member States on the

***Box 4.1* Role reversal: longer hours of paid work for women in the Philippines**

Given the temporal constraints that family responsibilities typically impose on women's participation in paid employment, the average actual hours of work of employed men exceed those of employed women in almost every country for which data were available for this report. The sole exception to this pattern is the case of the Philippines. In the Philippines, women in paid employment averaged 41.3 hours of work per week in 2002, compared with 40.4 hours a week for employed men. Interestingly, employed women were between two and three times more likely than men to work exceptionally long hours of over 64 hours per week.

It appears that these longer average working hours for employed women in the Philippines are being driven by long hours of work in the service sector. Average weekly hours in this sector are quite long, particularly in certain of its subsectors, such as the wholesale and retail trade (48.8 hours a week) and hotels and restaurants (48.6 hours per week). In fact, almost half of all those workers in the country who are working more than 40 hours per week are in the service sector, which has grown substantially in the last decade.

All of this raises an important question: given the long hours of paid work of many Filipino women, how are they able to balance work and family?

Source: ILO LABORSTA (2002 data).

distribution of working hours). The tables show two dominant patterns: one pattern for men, and a second, very different, one for women. For men, we see a pattern of long working hours (49 hours a week or more). Although this pattern varies substantially across countries and regions – for example it is markedly lower for wage employees in Europe – it leads to the same gender pattern within nearly all the countries that responded to the survey: namely, the proportion of men working long hours is greater than the comparable proportion of women. The only exceptions to this pattern are Zimbabwe and Ethiopia.

For women, on the other hand, Tables 4.2 and 4.3 reveal a pattern that is essentially the reverse of that for men: high proportions of women working part-time hours – defined here as less than 35 hours a week[5] – and from a gender perspective, proportions of part-time working that are dramatically higher for women than for men. Only one country, Thailand, had a higher proportion of males than females working part-time in wage employment, and even in that country the proportions were essentially the same. In fact, two-fifths of all countries responding to the special survey reported that 30 per cent or more of women in wage employment were working part-time; as will be discussed in Chapter 5 on working time in the informal economy, the proportions of women working part-time in self-employment are even higher in most of these countries. Although many of those countries which show high proportions of women working part-time hours are industrialized countries, this phenomenon is by no means limited to them, and in fact, this group is quite diverse, as was discussed in Chapter 3.

On the other hand, there were relatively few countries which reported that less than 10 per cent of women in wage employment were working part-time hours, and they were very heavily concentrated in the transition countries of Eastern Europe, including Bulgaria, Croatia, the Czech Republic, Hungary, the Former Yugoslav Republic of Macedonia, Romania, the Russian Federation, Slovakia and Slovenia (and of course, the proportions of men working part-time in these countries is even less). As the experience of the Czech Republic suggests, this very limited use of part-time *wage* employment arises from the fact that it appears to be in the interests of neither workers nor employers in those countries (Berkovsky *et al.* 2002). From the perspective of workers, their lack of interest is primarily due to the fact that the wages available in part-time positions are typically lower than the average wage, and total earnings are (by definition) considerably less; from the perspective of employers, the costs of part-time workers are similar to those of full-timers (e.g. social contributions, which are often calculated on a per employee basis) while the benefits (in terms of the number of hours that workers are available to work) are fewer (ibid.; Vaughan-Whitehead, ed., 2005).

By contrast, the only countries with substantial proportions (over one-fifth) of men working part-time in wage employment were Albania (31.7 per cent), Georgia (22.0 per cent), and Sri Lanka (31.4 per cent). Likewise, all of the country reports on working time and work organization that included data on the distribution of working hours confirm that there are greater proportions of men than women working long hours (49 or more per week), and greater proportions of women than men working short hours.

4.3 Work schedules and family responsibilities

Temporal constraints due to women's family responsibilities have important implications not only for the number of hours of paid work that they are able to perform, but also on the timing of that work as well. In the industrialized countries, for example, some firms structure work schedules specifically to appeal to working mothers, such as part-time daytime schedules from Monday to Friday that allow mothers to work when their children are attending school (Purcell *et al.* 1999; Fagan 2004; Messenger, ed. 2004). Although such schedules may have their own problems, in many developing countries the possibility of balancing work and family through such 'family-friendly' work schedules is simply non-existent, at least not for workers in wage jobs in the formal economy. As a result, workers with family responsibilities – predominantly women – may be forced by family constraints into

Table 4.2 Proportion of workers working long hours, by gender (2004–5[a], percentage of workers)

	Both		Female		Male		Hours cutoff
	Total employment	Paid employees	Total employment	Paid employees	Total employment	Paid employees	
Industrialized countries							
Australia	20.41	17.7	9.2	7.8	29.1	26.1	50+
Cyprus	14.60	6.3	6.0	3.3	21.2	9.0	49+
Finland	9.65	4.5	5.3	2.4	13.7	6.6	49+
France	14.68	8.6	7.9	4.9	20.4	11.9	49+
Ireland	11.60	5.5	3.0	1.8	18.4	8.9	49+
Israel	25.45	23.2	11.0	10.1	37.7	35.3	50+
Japan	17.71	17.0	8.3	7.2	25.1	24.7	49+
Korea, Republic of	49.53	45.7	42.6	36.4	54.0	51.6	49+
Luxembourg	4.23	0.9	2.4	0.4	5.5	1.2	49+
Malta	9.36	5.3	2.5	0.0	12.4	7.2	49+
Netherlands	6.95	1.4	1.7	0.3	11.0	2.2	49+
New Zealand	23.55	16.4	10.8	7.8	34.0	24.9	49+
Norway	5.25	3.3	1.8	1.2	8.4	5.4	49+
Portugal	10.63	5.2	7.1	2.8	13.6	7.4	49+
Spain	12.09	6.0	6.4	3.0	15.7	8.0	49+
Switzerland	19.23	16.6	7.8	6.4	28.4	25.0	49+
United Kingdom	25.74	24.9	13.5	13.1	34.5	33.5	49+
United States	18.08	17.3	10.8	10.2	24.3	23.5	49+
Transition countries							
Albania	7.70	6.0	5.0	3.7	9.3	7.4	49+
Armenia	29.93	24.2	17.1	12.3	40.1	34.9	49+
Azerbaijan	10.60	8.8	5.3	3.5	14.4	12.5	51+
Bulgaria	6.48	4.1	5.0	3.4	7.8	4.7	49+
Croatia	11.91	9.9	4.6	0.0	16.3	12.3	49+
Czech Republic	17.65	9.3	7.2	3.9	25.6	14.1	48.5+
Estonia	9.79	7.4	6.0	4.5	13.5	10.3	49+
Georgia	12.00	13.9	8.2	7.7	15.7	18.8	51+

Hungary	7.31	5.1	3.3	2.3	11.0	7.9	49+
Lithuania	4.55	3.2	3.1	2.1	5.9	4.4	49+
Macedonia, FYR	18.73	7.1	14.8	4.6	21.4	8.8	49+
Moldova, Republic of	4.85	3.9	3.5	2.8	6.4	5.1	48+
Poland	19.29	14.1	11.1	7.5	25.8	19.8	50+
Romania	18.19	16.6	14.7	14.3	21.2	18.6	46+
Russian Federation	3.15	2.5	1.8	1.4	4.5	3.6	51+
Slovakia	9.23	5.3	4.1	2.9	13.4	7.4	50+
Asia							
Indonesia	51.15	53.0	42.0	44.7	55.1	56.6	45+
Macao, China	39.07		35.4		42.4		50+
Pakistan	44.39	39.6	14.4	22.1	50.9	42.5	49+
Sri Lanka	26.65	25.3	17.2	17.6	30.8	28.7	49+
Thailand	46.74	34.7	42.3	31.2	50.1	37.3	50+
Africa							
Ethiopia	41.21	43.2	37.3	43.2	44.2	43.1	49+
Madagascar	16.67	22.6	14.9	16.0	18.3	26.4	49+
Mauritius	22.06	20.6	16.4	16.0	24.8	23.0	49+
Zimbabwe	29.20	40.6	24.2	42.5	33.7	39.9	49+
Americas							
Bolivia	37.69	37.9	33.6	20.4	40.9	45.4	49+
Guatemala	28.45	30.2	23.0	23.1	31.4	33.5	49+
Honduras	32.28	36.0	32.4	35.5	32.2	36.3	49+
Mexico	26.21	24.2	16.2	12.2	31.8	30.8	49+
Panama	17.27	14.6	13.0	12.1	19.9	16.3	49+
Uruguay	22.11	18.3	13.8	9.8	28.6	25.9	49+

Source: see Box 3.1.

Note
a The latest figures available; see Table 3.4 and Statistical annex.

Table 4.3 Proportion of workers working short hours, by gender (2004–5[a], percentage of workers)

Country	Paid employees			Self-employed			Hours cutoff
	Both	*Female*	*Male*	*Both*	*Female*	*Male*	
Industrialized countries							
Australia	25.0	43.6	9.5	31.5	56.4	18.9	<35
Canada	19.0	30.3	8.2	26.9	45.4	17.4	<35
Cyprus	6.6	10.6	3.0	20.3	41.9	11.5	<35
Finland	13.7	19.0	8.3	20.6	26.6	17.7	<35
France	20.1	33.9	7.4	10.9	23.5	4.9	<35
Ireland	23.1	41.5	6.6	9.1	28.7	5.2	<35
Israel	22.4	35.3	10.6	23.7	41.0	16.6	<35
Japan	23.7	40.0	12.3	25.3	41.4	14.1	<35
Korea, Republic of	8.8	14.3	5.3	14.0	17.3	11.7	<35
Luxembourg	18.0	40.9	2.0	13.7	28.7	5.7	<35
Malta	16.9	34.8	8.0	13.3	0.0	10.8	<36
Netherlands	40.5	73.3	13.6	35.8	70.3	17.6	<35
New Zealand	25.2	41.5	9.1	31.5	56.1	20.2	<35
Norway	27.9	43.3	13.3	21.1	37.2	16.1	<35
Portugal	6.9	11.4	2.9	30.2	41.8	21.8	<35
Spain	11.5	23.1	3.5	9.4	19.9	4.6	<35
Switzerland	33.1	58.0	12.8	38.2	61.4	21.1	<35
United Kingdom	16.2	34.8	2.7	14.4	34.7	7.2	<35
United States	23.4	31.3	16.5	33.6	47.2	25.7	<35
Transition countries							
Albania	32.0	32.4	31.7	54.8	58.9	52.4	<35
Armenia	23.2	35.1	12.5	40.4	52.2	32.7	<35
Azerbaijan	12.9	20.0	8.1	22.9	29.3	18.0	<30
Bulgaria	2.5	3.4	1.6	12.6	16.3	10.6	<35
Croatia	5.8	7.2	4.6	34.1	18.3	13.7	<35
Czech Republic	5.1	8.3	2.2	7.0	15.6	3.6	<35
Estonia	8.4	12.1	4.6	12.3	9.9	4.2	<35
Georgia	34.0	46.0	22.0	47.0	51.8	42.5	<36
Hungary	5.3	7.8	2.9	5.2	9.1	3.3	<35
Lithuania	15.2	19.7	10.5	41.8	46.3	38.4	<35
Macedonia, FYR	3.1	3.5	2.9	17.3	21.1	15.0	<35
Poland	10.1	15.0	5.9	23.4	30.5	18.6	<30
Romania	1.9	2.5	1.5	22.6	27.8	18.2	<36
Russian Federation	4.1	6.0	2.3	33.0	40.1	27.1	<30
Slovakia	3.7	5.5	2.1	4.0	9.8	2.0	<35
Slovenia	5.3	5.3	3.5	21.5	21.2	14.5	<40
Asia							
Indonesia	16.8	25.9	12.8	25.5	36.1	21.0	<35
Pakistan	9.5	30.1	6.2	9.3	45.9	6.5	<35
Sri Lanka	32.9	36.2	31.4	43.5	58.7	36.7	<35
Thailand	6.5	6.2	6.6	12.2	13.5	11.1	<35
Africa							
Ethiopia	10.2	12.4	8.9	33.6	42.3	26.0	<35
Madagascar	21.9	31.1	16.7	22.2	26.4	17.7	<35
Mauritius	24.0	35.6	18.0	40.0	59.2	33.5	<35
Zimbabwe	4.7	6.8	3.8	37.1	39.0	33.6	<35

Table 4.3 Continued

Country	Paid employees			Self-employed			Hours cutoff
	Both	Female	Male	Both	Female	Male	
Americas							
Bolivia	22.3	36.4	16.2	32.2	36.2	28.3	<35
Guatemala	17.7	32.0	11.2	35.8	61.8	19.0	<35
Honduras	12.2	13.2	11.6	25.8	52.7	16.7	<35
Mexico	13.5	26.2	6.7	26.4	48.2	13.7	<35
Panama	12.5	14.2	11.3	45.8	64.2	36.5	<35
Uruguay	24.7	38.3	12.7	36.8	47.3	30.6	<35

Source: see Box 3.1.

Note
a The latest figures available; see Table 3.5 and Statistical annex.

taking jobs that offer them the possibility of caring for their children while they are working, such as the case of plantation workers in Kenya, although this may then create other difficulties (see Box 4.2 below).

Box 4.2 Plantation work and family responsibilities in Kenya

Workers in the plantation and agricultural sector in Kenya, most of whom are women, normally work for an average of 46 hours per week. The typical work schedule runs from Monday to Saturday, with eight-hour days during the week plus six hours on Saturday. As workers in this sector are typically paid on a piece-rate basis, working hours may be extended if the worker is unable to finish their piece-work targets during the scheduled time.

'Balancing work and family' is *quite literally* what is happening in Kenya's plantation and agricultural sector. Typically, mothers carry their infants and young children balanced on their backs while they progress with their work on the plantations. Though this behaviour is officially prohibited, it is in fact quite routine. When their babies are hungry, for example, working mothers stop to breastfeed them and then continue on with their work.

While this situation is obviously physically arduous for the mothers, it has both advantages and disadvantages. On the one hand, the women are able to care for their children while they work. On the other hand, though, children may be exposed to pesticides and other toxic chemicals that are used on the plantations. In addition, older children may also be forced to work if their mothers need help in completing the established piece-work targets on time.

Source: Mwatha Karega 2002.

As was discussed earlier in this chapter, women's need to fit their work schedules around their family responsibilities may encourage them to enter self-employment, which (almost by definition) offers them more flexible working hours and/or the ability to work for pay in their own homes (this will be further discussed in Chapter 5). Of course, this type of flexibility may come at a very high price, given that many types of self-employment in developing and transition countries are in the informal economy – with the low earnings and the lack of social protection that this implies (see e.g. ILO 2004). In a similar manner, fitting paid work around their family responsibilities may also encourage women to attempt to balance work and family via working at times when their spouses or partners are at home, such as at nights or on weekends.

4.4 Working time flexibility

The availability of policies and programmes designed to support workers with family responsibilities can help to substantially increase the extent of women's participation in paid employment – including their working hours. In addition to affordable, high-quality childcare, 'family-friendly' working time policies, such as flexible daily starting and finishing times (flexi-time) and paid time off work to deal with family problems, can help workers to more effectively manage their work and family responsibilities.[6] The importance of such measures is illustrated by findings from a series of ILO surveys on work and family conducted during 2002 in a total of seven countries – Australia, Brazil, Hungary, Malaysia, Mauritius, the Philippines and the Russian Federation. These work and family surveys gathered information on the family responsibilities of employees and the extent to which enterprises in those countries have established policies to help employees balance work and family.

4.4.1 Policies and programmes

Based on the hypothesis proposed above regarding the crucial importance of both the duration and the organization of working time for successfully balancing work and family life, an attempt has been made to estimate the extent to which three types of employee-oriented working time flexibility are available to workers: (1) flexibility regarding the daily work schedule; (2) flexibility regarding the use of paid annual leave (holidays); and (3) flexibility regarding the use of other paid leave (e.g. sick leave) for family needs (see Table 4.4, Panel A). The main results relating to working time and work–family balance are presented in Table 4.4, and only workers with a child are considered (Mauritius is excluded from the analysis due to comparability problems).

Panel A of Table 4.4 shows that the gender gaps in working hours are substantial, as discussed earlier, again with the notable exception of the

Philippines. The biggest gap is found in Australia where part-time work is widely exercised – predominantly by women. Interestingly, however, women workers' relatively short hours do not necessarily mean that they have a relatively lower incidence of reported feelings of overwork. In fact, with the exception of Australia, there is very little difference between men and women in the incidence of their reported feelings of overwork. In Hungary, for example, the average female worker was working five and a half hours less than her male counterpart, but the extent of reported feelings of overwork was slightly higher for women workers. This may be due both to the spillover effects of gender inequality in the division of housework on feelings of overwork, as well as to women's well-known preferences for shorter working hours (see e.g. Fagan and Burchell 2002; Fagan 2004). In the case of Australia, however, it appears that the working hours difference between genders (16.3 hours) is large enough to 'compensate' for the unequal gender division of housework and thus generate a lower incidence of feelings of overwork among women workers (a value of 0.77 for women versus 1.05 for men).

When it comes to working time flexibility, variations across countries are substantial, but gender gaps are rather small and do not show any systematic pattern. In comparison to Australia, where shorter hours are combined with greater flexibility for women workers, such a combination does not exist on a notable scale, although the chance of securing such flexibility is higher overall for women workers. It is also interesting that workers' flexibility over their working time is not necessarily low in developing countries, as is demonstrated by the Malaysian figures. Of course, such flexibility may not be 'systematized' or 'institutionalized', but may instead be available only on an *informal basis* through individual negotiations with managers at the workplace. Nonetheless, this could still be an invaluable method of helping women workers in addressing urgent and important family matters, especially considering that short hours (part-time work) is not a viable option for them due to the low wages of the vast majority of workers in most developing countries.

4.4.2 Workers' attitudes towards flexibility

Next, we turn to the question of how working time is associated with workers' feelings about work–family balance. The correlations matrix provided in Panel B in Table 4.4 provides some useful insights regarding this question.[7] First, when it comes to women workers with a child, as expected, workers' feelings regarding the difficulty of managing work–family balance are positively associated with their working hours and their reported feelings of overwork (these two items are positively correlated with each other) and negatively correlated with all three types of employee-oriented working time flexibility. In other words, longer hours are related to higher levels of concern about managing work and family, and employee-oriented working

Table 4.4 Working time and work–family balance in selected countries: coefficients matrix (2002)

		I Length of working time: Weekly hours in the main job	II Flexibility over daily schedule: Could start work late or leave early if needed without losing pay (yes = 1, no = 0)	III Flexibility over holidays: Can usually take holidays at times that suit family (yes = 1, no = 0)	IV Flexibility over the use of paid leave: Could take paid leave (sick leave or other) to handle urgent family matters (yes = 1, no = 0)	V Overwork: Feeling of overwork (never = 0, sometimes = 1, often = 2)	VI Work–family balance: Feeling about managing work and family (mostly easy = 0, sometimes easy and sometimes difficult = 1, mostly hard = 2)

Panel A: *Mean values (workers with a child)*

Country	Gender						
Australia	M	45.8	0.46	0.55	0.58	1.05	0.69
	F	29.3	0.74	0.74	0.52	0.77	0.63
Brazil	M	44.4	0.73	0.36	0.34	1.01	0.76
	F	39.5	0.72	0.37	0.39	0.94	1.03
Hungary	M	45.6	0.34	0.55	0.68	1.18	1.02
	F	40.1	0.31	0.49	0.7	1.23	0.94
Malaysia	M	49.1	0.48	0.76	0.8	0.7	0.47
	F	44.6	0.51	0.77	0.79	0.74	0.45
Philippines	M	45.4	0.43	0.33	0.43	1.14	0.52
	F	45.6	0.54	0.47	0.5	1.02	0.58
Russian	M	42.6	0.34	0.26	0.2	1.26	0.89
Federation	F	39.0	0.33	0.37	0.37	1.23	1.03

Panel B: *Correlations matrix (Spearman's) for workers with a child*

Men: total employment

	I	II	III	IV	V	VI
I	1					
II	0.107*	1				
III	0.017	0.175*	1			
IV	0.035	0	0.266**	1		
V	0.033	-0.058	-0.185**	-0.104*	1	
VI	-0.025	-0.163	-0.163**	-0.05	0.311**	1

Women: total employment

	I	II	III	IV	V	VI
I	1					
II	-0.066	1				
III	-0.036	0.173**	1			
IV	0.153**	-0.051	0.114**	1		
V	0.145**	-0.169**	-0.129**	-0.022	1	
VI	0.100**	-0.136**	-0.235**	-0.092*	0.360**	1

Women: paid employees

	I	II	III	IV	V	VI
I	1					
II	-0.087*	1				
III	-0.021	0.182**	1			
IV	0.137**	-0.52	0.072	1		
V	0.179**	-0.175**	-0.134**	0.008	1	
VI	0.088*	-0.114**	-0.230**	-0.087*	0.412**	1

Source: ILO surveys on work and family, 2002, unpublished data.

* Result is statistically significant at the 0.05 level of significance.
** Result is statistically significant at the 0.01 level of significance.

Notes

(1) Mauritius is excluded due to incomparability. (2) Total sample size is 1,570 (137 for Brazil, 312 for Malaysia, 163 for the Philippines, 470 for Hungary, 266 for the Russian Federation, 222 for Australia). (3) 'Flexibility over the use of paid leave' was derived from the question: 'If you suddenly had to take time off from work to attend to an urgent family matter how could you do that?' When respondents reported that they could use sick leave and/or other paid leave, the value of 1 was assigned. (4) Results for male employees are not reported separately because those results are essentially the same as those for all employed men (total employment). For further details regarding the survey, please contact travail@ilo.org.

time flexibility is related to lower levels of concern about work–family balance. The correlations are particularly strong for feelings of overwork (0.360) and flexibility over the use of paid annual holidays (–0.235). When the focus is narrowed down from all workers to paid employees, the overall results remain unchanged.

Second, the relationship between employee-oriented working time flexibility and concerns about managing work and family is much weaker for male workers with family responsibilities. For men, difficulty in managing work and family is positively associated with reported feelings of overwork and negatively associated with flexibility over the use of paid annual holidays. The latter result might imply that, for men, organizing annual holidays (vacation) to meet the wishes of their families is a crucial dimension of work–family balance (hence, the capability to take holidays when their families want to do so is highly appreciated), while the lack of other significant results would imply that other family matters are taken care of by their wives/partners.

Finally, with regard to the relationship between the duration and the organization of working time, it has been observed that in many industrialized countries, flexible arrangements such as *informal* flexi-time are often traded off for longer working hours, in what might be viewed as a kind of 'fringe benefit' associated with long working hours, particularly for higher-level or more qualified employees such as managerial and professional staff (see e.g. Golden 2001; Kelly and Kalev 2006; Lee and McCann 2006). Such an observation can be applied to flexibility over daily working hours for surveyed workers in the countries shown in Table 4.4, *but only among men*. For men, longer working hours are indeed positively associated with a greater degree of access to informal flexi-time. For women, however, longer working hours are actually associated with *reduced access to informal flexi-time*, although the actual effect is relatively small (–0.087). Nonetheless, this means that those women workers who work longer hours effectively have a 'double disadvantage', in that they are also less likely to be able to access informal flexi-time to help them balance work and family. In contrast, there is a clear correlation – and, thus, an implied tradeoff – between longer hours and increased flexibility over the use of other types of paid leave (e.g. sick leave) to handle urgent family matters, *but only for women*. These two findings, taken together, imply that men working long hours are more likely to vary their daily working hours in response to family demands, while women working such long hours are more likely to take leave days, perhaps because the family matters requiring their attention are more time-consuming in nature.

4.5 Working time and age: variable hours of work over the life course

Age, like gender, represents a crucially important dynamic that shapes the socioeconomic circumstances in a country in many different ways, including both participation in the paid labour force and working hours. The age structure of the population in any country will, to a substantial degree, determine the proportion of the total population which is economically active at any given time. This occurs simply because, generally speaking, the youngest and oldest members of society are less likely to participate in the labour market than prime-age individuals. Younger individuals, on the one hand, are likely to be participating in formal schooling until sometime during their teenage years, while older individuals, on the other hand, are likely to have exited the labour force by sometime during their sixties (or even earlier, for example in a number of EU Member States such as Luxembourg). The result is the familiar three-part division of the life course: initial formal education,[8] market work (perhaps combined with some continuing formal education and/or on-the-job training) and, finally, retirement.

Of course, the timing of both the end of formal education and the beginning of retirement may vary considerably, both across individuals and more broadly. For example, the timing of retirement – with its implied withdrawal from paid work – is dependent in part upon the extent to which public and/or private pension systems providing an adequate retirement income exist in a given country. Obviously, a variety of circumstances affects the participation of individuals in the labour market. In a similar manner, the particular circumstances of different age groups of workers, combined with the regulation of working time, can affect their working hours as well. Although the three-part division of activity – and in consequence, of time – over the life course has recently been called into question by some authors in an industrialized country context,[9] in the vast majority of countries around the world this tripartite division remains largely intact.

4.5.1 Patterns of hours over the life course

The tripartite division of working time over the life course is clearly revealed in Figure 4.1, which presents data on hours of work by age group from selected country reports on working time and work organization.[10] Across five of the seven countries in this figure, we can see a similar, distinct pattern: somewhat shorter average weekly hours for younger workers under the age of 25 years, with weekly hours rising to a plateau during prime age – which here encompasses the age categories between 25 and 54 years. As workers age, their average weekly working hours begin to decline – as we see in the 55–64 category of older workers – and their working hours continue to decline as they pass the typical retirement age of 65 years or older, which is illustrated by the final age category. The dominant pattern of working hours by age group in this figure is perhaps best illustrated by the case of Brazil, which clearly shows average weekly hours of work rising from 37.4 per week in the youngest age group to a peak of 42.1 in the 25–39 age group, and then gradually falling off until it reaches a low of 32.5 hours a week in the oldest age group (65 years and older). In some regions of the world, however, the available evidence suggests that the *average* hours of older workers do not differ substantially from those of other age groups. This situation appears to be the case in many EU Member States, where the working hours of those older workers aged 55–64 years who remain in the labour force are similar, on average, to those of other age groups, although their working hours have become increasingly diverse (Ghosheh *et al.* 2006).[11]

In Figure 4.1, the patterns of working hours by age group in China and the Republic of Korea are notable outliers. The results for China that are presented in this figure – which were derived from an enterprise survey in three major cities (Beijing, Guangzhou and Changsha) – clearly show a pattern in which younger workers work longer hours than workers in the other age groups. This pattern is confirmed by the presence of a negative correlation between age and working hours in China (Zeng *et al.* 2005: 13).[12] In the Republic of Korea, on the other hand, working hours are quite long among all age groups – but even longer among both younger and older workers. These variations in working hours by age can be explained both by differences in the industries in which different age groups work and by

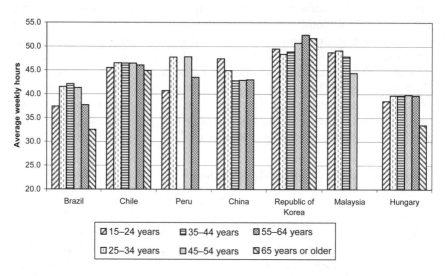

Figure 4.1 Average weekly hours of work by age group (percentage, 2000)

Notes

Brazil: figures are for 1999. Age categories are as follows: 15–19 years; 20–24 years; 25–39 years; 40–59 years; 60–64 years and 65 years or more.

Peru: the first age category is 14–24 years.

China: figures are for 2004 (enterprise survey). Age categories are as follows: less than 25 years; 26–35 years; 36–45 years; 46–55 years and 56 years or more.

The Republic of Korea: the last two age categories are 55–59 years and 60 years or older.

Malaysia: age categories are as follows: 20–24 years; 25–29 years; 30–49 years and 50–64 years.

Hungary: age categories are as follows: 15–19 years; 20–29 years; 30–39 years; 40–49 years; 50–54/59 years and 55/61–74 years.

Source: ILO country study reports on working time and work organization, Brazil, Chile, Peru, China, the Republic of Korea, Malaysia, Hungary.

differences in their contractual status (i.e. whether the workers have permanent or temporary contracts): younger and older workers are more likely to find a job in industries with longer working hours and on temporary contracts, which are more vulnerable to overtime and long working hours (Yoon 2001).

4.5.2 Part-time work

Another important variation in working hours over the life course concerns the pattern of part-time working for workers in different age groups. As has been observed in the industrialized countries, there has been an increasing diversification in working hours for older workers, and, in particular, a higher incidence of short hours (Ghosheh *et al.* 2006). In fact, it is older, younger and women workers who provide the primary sources of part-time workers in these countries.

Figure 4.2 provides an indication, via data from six of the 15 country studies commissioned for this book, of the incidence of short working hours by age group. As the figure shows, the highest proportions of short hours by age group are indeed found at the two ends of the age distribution – among both younger workers and especially older workers.[13] The share of part-timers among the 65 and older age group is particularly striking in the cases of Brazil, Chile, Mexico and Hungary.

The Russian country study (Chetvernina *et al.* 2004: 73) also reports a similar pattern after recent, dramatic increases in the proportion of both older and younger workers working part-time hours; these doubled and tripled, respectively, in a period of only two years.[14] By contrast, Peru really tells two different stories: for men, it is primarily younger and older workers who work part-time, while for women, the share of part-timers remains fairly high over the entire life course (between one-third and two-fifths of all workers).[15] These results are in line with earlier studies on the working hours of older workers (e.g. Jolivet and Lee 2004), which find a higher proportion of part-timers among older workers than other age groups.

Thus, as we have seen, the average working hours of both younger workers and retirement-age workers are typically somewhat lower than those of prime-age workers, and the proportion of part-timers is higher – this is particularly true in the case of retirement-age workers. An important exception, however, is prime-age women workers with family responsibilities, whose temporal availability for paid work is constrained by the time devoted to domestic and caring tasks, as discussed previously. Men's working hours over the life course tend to be more linear than women's (Echeverría 2002; see also Galasi 2002). In Chile, for example, men's working hours remain reasonably stable for prime-age workers from the age of 25 until they reach the normal retirement age in that country (i.e. 65 years old), leading to an inverse U-shaped distribution. Women's hours of work, on the other hand, vary far more over their lives; the pattern of women's working

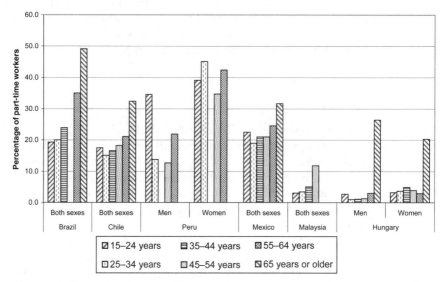

Figure 4.2 Share of workers working short hours by age group (percentage, 2000)

Notes

Brazil: figures are for 1999; part-time = less than 30 hours per week. Age categories are as follows: 20–24 years; 25–39 years; 40–59 years; 60–64 years and 65 years or more. This age category represents only 0.68 per cent of all workers.

Chile: figures are for 1998. For this table, part-time is defined as less than 40 hours per week; normal hours in Chile were 48 hours per week in 2000.

Peru: figures are for the first quarter, 2000; part-time = less than 35 hours per week. Age categories are as follows: 14–24 years; 25–44 years; 45–54 years and 55 years or more.

Mexico: part-time = less than 35 hours per week.

Malaysia: part-time = less than 30 hours per week. Age categories are as follows: 20–24 years; 25–29 years; 30–49 years and 50–64 years.

Hungary: part-time = less than 30 hours per week. Age categories used are 15–19 years; 20–29 years; 30–39 years; 40–49 years; 50–54/59 years and 55/61–74 years.

Source: ILO country study reports on working time and work organization, Brazil, Chile, Hungary, Peru, Mexico, Malaysia.

hours by age cohort typically shows an M-shaped distribution due to the decrease in working hours that occurs during women's typical childbearing and child-rearing years (which is the 'point' in the 'M'). For example, the gap between women and men in their hours of paid work in Chile is indeed the largest during women's typical childbearing and child-rearing years. In this case, this time period corresponds to the age categories of 25–34 years, when the reported gender gap is 6.1 hours, and 35–44 years, when the reported gender gap is 6.8 hours. So, it appears that the effects of age on the dynamics of working hours also interact with those of another important factor – gender – resulting in an even larger gender gap between the ages of 25 and 44 years than at other stages of the life course, due to the importance of children as a determinant of women's paid working hours.

Finally in any discussion of age, it has to be acknowledged that the ageing of the global workforce also has important implications for the adequacy of social protection systems for the elderly. From the perspective of working time, it appears that older workers tend to work more when pension systems are unable to provide a 'decent' retirement income or in countries where such systems are simply non-existent. To illustrate this situation, we consider the case of long working hours among retirement-age workers in Mexico (see Box 4.3 below).

Box 4.3 Long hours among retirement-age workers in Mexico

Even with the major proportion of older workers aged over 55 working on a part-time basis, there are nonetheless also substantial numbers of older workers *in the same countries* who are working long and even excessive hours (over 48 hours per week). The case of Mexico provides a good illustration of this phenomenon. In Mexico, the average age of the working population is on the rise, and many workers over 60 years of age are not only continuing to work but even working long hours. In fact, this study (Esponda 2001) found that over half of all workers over 65 years of age were working 40 hours a week or more, and 23 per cent of these workers were working excessively long hours – more than 48 hours a week.

The analysis suggests that the long working hours among retirement-age workers are a reflection of the inadequacy of the available social protection systems in that country. The fact that weekly hours among these workers were even higher in a time of economic crisis (e.g. 1995) offers further evidence of their dependence on wage earnings. The Mexico country report concludes that:

> several groups within the population (60 years of age and older) that theoretically should be enjoying a decent pension ... nonetheless not only remain active but are also working more than 48 hours per week, offering clear evidence of the failure of the current social security system. (p. vii)

> Source: Esponda 2001.

4.6 Conclusions

This chapter has reviewed a few of the significant changes in the dynamics of the global workforce, in order to understand their implications for working time in countries around the world. Regarding the dynamics of working time for different groups of workers, the chapter considered two key demographic factors that have important implications for working hours and patterns – gender and age.

We can now see that both gender and age carry important implications for working time. First, gender is clearly a crucial factor differentiating working hours among workers. In particular, even though women are increasingly engaged in the paid workforce, their temporal availability for paid work appears to be significantly constrained by the time that they need to devote to their household/domestic responsibilities. These temporal constraints manifest themselves in a dramatic imbalance between the sexes in average working hours. For men, there is a pattern of long hours working (49 hours per week or more) in many countries, although the proportion of employees affected varies quite substantially across countries. For women, we see a working time pattern that is essentially the reverse of that of men: high proportions of female employees who are working part-time hours that are, moreover, dramatically higher than the comparable proportions of male employees working part-time hours. The end result is that there is a clear 'gender gap' in working hours in all regions of the world.

The availability of policies and programmes designed to support workers with family responsibilities can help to substantially increase the extent of women's participation in paid employment – including their working hours. In addition to affordable, high-quality childcare, 'family-friendly' working time policies, such as flexible daily starting and finishing times (flexi-time) and paid time off work to deal with family problems, can help workers to better manage their work and family responsibilities. Workers' flexibility over their working time is not necessarily lower in developing countries, but such flexibility may be available only on an *informal basis* through individual negotiations with managers at the workplace. According to results from a work–family survey, for men there tends to be a tradeoff between longer hours and flexible daily hours (informal flexi-time), while for women the tradeoff is between longer hours and flexibility in using paid leave, such as sick leave, for family reasons.

Age, on the other hand, appears to be considerably less powerful but nonetheless important as a factor in shaping working hours. The variability in working hours by age group is actually quite modest; in particular there are considerable proportions of older workers aged 55–64 years who are continuing to work hours that are not much different from those of prime-age workers, although the distribution of their working hours is more diverse. It is only for the oldest age group – those workers 65 years or older – that we see a substantial reduction in their working hours, primarily in the form of a higher incidence of short-hours or part-time working.

To sum up, we have seen that demographic factors such as gender and age have to varying degrees been influencing working time, but such influence has gained particular importance in certain economic sectors. The service sector, in which job creation has been particularly intensive through attracting disadvantaged groups of workers identifiable in terms of their gender and age, deserves special attention. Another important area on which to focus is the informal economy, where the majority of economic activities are now undertaken in many developing countries. In the next chapter, Chapter 5, we turn our attention to working time in these two vitally important economic sectors.

5 Tertiarization, informalization and working time

5.1 Introduction

This chapter will consider how various aspects of the structure of national economies are affecting working time, drawing extensively on the 15 ILO-commissioned country studies. While there are a number of structural economic changes that could be investigated, it is necessary to choose a few specific developments on which to focus the present analysis. Two such developments would appear to have particularly important implications for working time. The first aspect we shall examine is the 'tertiarization' of national economies – that is, the dramatic expansion in size and importance of the service sector in many countries, in terms of its contribution to both economic output and total employment. The hours of work and the ways in which working time is organized in service industries such as the retail trade is often very different from working time patterns in traditional industries such as manufacturing, mining and construction (Messenger, ed., 2004). In fact, as we will see, the service sector is exercising an important influence on working time patterns around the world. This chapter will review working hours and work schedules that are commonly deployed in the services sectors of the economies in developing and transition countries, as well as how these working time patterns vary by subsectors within services.

The second structural aspect that will be considered is the continuing and even increasing importance of the informal economy – particularly in many developing countries, but also in the transition economies and some industrialized countries as well (ILO 2002a). The lack of a legal and regulatory framework to structure working time in the informal economy, and differences between various types of informal economy workers (e.g. the self-employed compared with domestic workers), has meant that much of what transpires in informal employment, including working hours, is often a 'black box'. What do we know about working hours in the informal economy, and how do these patterns vary by country and across different regions of the world? This chapter will assemble the available evidence to address these questions, with a focus on the largest group of informal workers: the self-employed.

5.2 The rise of the service sector across the world

One of the most dramatic changes in the structure of the world's economy over the last 30 years has been the profound 'tertiarization' in the nature of economic activity – that is, the substantial increase in the size of the service sector, particularly in terms of employment. Recent studies analysing the sectoral composition of employment in industrialized countries (e.g. OECD 2000) have shown that there has been a substantial increase in the service sector's share of total employment in those countries. For example, in developed economies such as Canada, Denmark, France, the Netherlands, the United Kingdom and the United States, nearly three-quarters of all jobs are in services (ibid.: 85).

What is less well understood, however, is that this broad trend towards an increasing share of employment in services also applies in a wide array of developing countries. A broad range of countries from all over the world witnessed an increase in the size of the service sector between 1980 and 2000. As is shown in Table 5.1, this includes countries as diverse as Bulgaria, Brazil, Egypt, Hungary, Malaysia, Mexico, Namibia and the Philippines. While not all countries have followed this trend – Chile, for example – nonetheless it is clear that the service sector represents nearly half of total employment in many developing countries. Many of the services industries are also major sources of female employment, such as education, health services, the retail trade, and hotels and restaurants (OECD 2000).

Although the growth of service sector jobs as a share of total employment is a significant trend, this trend takes on even greater importance because of its implications for future growth in employment. In an analysis of employment growth in industrialized countries over the period 1986–98, the OECD concluded that:

> Virtually all net employment growth is due to increased service employment. Indeed, job losses in agriculture and industry partially offset job gains in services in one-half of the countries. This simple analysis suggests that policy makers probably should look to services as the dominant source of further employment gains.
>
> (OECD 2000: 109)

An ILO study (ILO 2005b) makes a similar point regarding the employment implications for the service sector in some developing countries. In analysing the sectoral composition of employment in Asian countries, this report notes that (using a 4 percentage point threshold) there has been a significant increase in the share of services employment in China, the Republic of Korea, Malaysia, the Philippines, Singapore and Thailand (as well as in Japan) – an increase which coincided with substantial declines in agricultural employment in five of these countries. This report therefore concludes that, 'In this sense, the process of economic development in these countries is

Table 5.1 Share of total employment in the service sector in selected countries (%)

	1980	1990	2000
Industrialized countries			
Canada	66.1	71.3	74.1
France	55.4	67.6	73.9
Japan	54	58.2	63.1
Switzerland	55	63.6	69.1
United States	65.9	70.9	74.5
Transition countries			
Bulgaria	32.9	37.3	45.5
Czech Republic	39.1	42.2	54.8
Hungary	NA	53.7[a]	58.7
Romania	26.3	27.4	31
Asia			
China	11.7	9.5	12.9
Malaysia	38.7	46.5	49.5
Pakistan	26.8	28.9	33.5
Philippines	32.8	39.7	46.5
Africa			
Egypt	35.7	40.1	49.1
Kenya	55.4	60.5	61.9[b]
Namibia	37.2	29	56
Americas			
Brazil	46.1[c]	54.5	59.2[c]
Chile	65.4[d]	55.5	62.2
Colombia	64.6	67.7	73.3
Ecuador	62[e]	66.3	67.6
Jamaica	NA	54[f]	60[f]
Mexico	24.1	39.6	55.2

Source: ILO, *Key Indicators of the Labour Market*, third edition, 2003a.

Notes
a For Hungary, the 1990 figure in fact corresponds to 1992.
b For Kenya, the 2000 figure in fact corresponds to 1999.
c For Brazil, the 1980 and 2000 figures correspond to 1981 and 2001, respectively.
d For Chile, the 1980 figure in fact corresponds to 1982.
e For Ecuador, the 1980 figure in fact corresponds to 1988.
f For Jamaica, the 1990 and 2000 figures correspond to 1991 and 1998, respectively.

characterized not by industrialization as such with regards to employment, but rather by shifting shares of employment from agriculture to services' (ILO 2005b: 26).

In addition to its clear implications for employment growth, the service sector is also exercising an important influence on working time patterns. In the industrialized countries, it is clear that the service sector has been the driving force for the diversification of working hours observed in those countries (see Messenger, ed., 2004). The incidence of part-time work, for example, is much greater in services than in the manufacturing sector in industrialized countries (OECD 2001), leading to an increase in the diversification of hours in those industries in which part-time work is commonplace. However, in addition, hours of work in services are often longer than those in manufacturing. A quick comparison of working hours in manufacturing versus services in ten countries from across the world, which is presented in Table 5.2, indicates that this pattern holds for most of these countries. Of the countries presented, only one country (France) has shorter hours of work in manufacturing than all of the service sectors; similarly, only in one country (Thailand) are the hours of work the longest in manufacturing. In the other eight countries shown in Table 5.2, the average hours of work in manufacturing fall somewhere in the middle of the range: generally lower than the average hours in certain service subsectors such as transport, storage and communications, but also generally higher than the average hours in other service subsectors, most notably education.[1]

5.3 Working hours in the service sector

With this background, we now turn our attention to the question of actual working hours in the service sector. We will begin by providing an overview of working hours in the different service subsectors in a broad array of countries around the world, and then turn to a more in-depth analysis of actual hours of work in specific subsectors, based largely on information from our country study reports.

Average hours of work in various subsectors that comprise the service sector are presented in Table 5.3 for a range of different countries, using the categories of economic activity established under revision 3 of the International Standard Industrial Classification (ISIC).[2] From figures presented in this table, several general points become apparent.

The first point to note is that (as expected) working hours across all the subsectors of the service sector are substantially shorter in the industrialized countries than in either the transition countries or in the developing countries in any region of the world. There are obviously some exceptions, however, such as the case of Greece, where actual hours of work, particularly in certain service subsectors (e.g. wholesale and retail trade etc., hotels and restaurants), are much higher than those in the other industrialized countries shown here. This situation undoubtedly reflects the relatively small proportion of part-time workers in Greece (9.9 per cent for men, 16.5 per cent for women in the service sector) compared with the share of part-timers in most other industrialized countries (for example, in the old EU-15, it is 16.6 per cent for men and 29.4 per cent for women (Eurostat 2005)).

Looking at the various service subsectors, the table highlights that average weekly hours of work are particularly long in certain industries – notably, wholesale and retail trade, etc., hotels and restaurants, and transport, storage and communications. Likewise, average weekly hours are relatively short in a few subsectors – particularly in education – but also in category L, which consists of public sector employees in a range of governmental functions

Table 5.2 Average weekly working hours in manufacturing versus services in selected countries (2002)[a]

	Manufacturing (F)	Wholesale and retail trade, repair of motor vehicles, motorcycles and personal and household goods (G)	Hotels and restaurants (H)	Transport, storage and communication (I)	Financial intermediation (J)	Real estate, renting and business activities (K)	Public administration and defence, compulsory social security (L)	Education (M)	Health and social work (N)	Community, social and personal service activities (O)
Australia (2002, EMP)[b]	38.5	32.2	31.7	39.2	36.3	36.2	34.7	32.6	30.2	31.1
Brazil (2002, TE)[b]	43.2	44.8	48.8	48.7	40.1	43.5	41.4	35.4	41.6	38.5
Costa Rica (2003, EMP)	49	49	48	52	46	49	47	39	46	43
France (2002, EMP)[c]	35.31	38.05	41.04	37.92	38.26	38.85	37.83	36.5		
Japan (2003, TE)[d]	43.1	42.1	40.6	47.9	42.8	38.6	43	37.2	38.1	40.6
Lithuania (2002, EMP)	38.6	39.5	41.2	41.3	39.1	38	39.8	32.6	37.7	37.2
Mexico (2001, EMP)	45.1	45.4	47	51.2	42.4	45.8	45.3	31.2	40	41.6
Slovenia (2002, EMP)	36	37	37.8	38.1	35.3	36.4	34.7	33.8	36.2	34.4
Thailand (2001, EMP)	59.3	45	48.8	50	52.9	50.7	NA	42	53.4	39
Turkey (2002, TE)	51.9	57.9	63.5	52.8	45	50.6	44.7	36.8	44.3	51.7

Source: ILO Labour Statistics Database, hours of work by economic activity, classification ISIC-Revision 3 (labour force survey data only).

Notes

a Where LABORSTA data for 2002 are unavailable, comparable data for the most proximate alternative year are used.

b EMP = data presented are for employees only; TE = data presented are for total employment.

c For France, some of the tabulation categories have been combined.

d For Japan, repair of motor vehicles, motorcycles, and personal and household goods are included under Category O instead of Category G.

Table 5.3 Average weekly working hours in services (by subsector, 2002)[a]

	Wholesale and retail trade, repair of motor vehicles, motorcycles and personal and household goods (G)	Hotels and restaurants (H)	Transport, storage and communication (I)	Financial intermediation (J)	Real estate, renting and business activities (K)	Public administration and defence, compulsory social security (L)	Education (M)	Health and social work (N)	Community, social and personal service activities (O)	Private households with employed persons (P)
Industrialized countries										
Australia (2002, EMP)[b]	32.2	31.7	39.2	36.3	36.2	34.7	32.6	30.2	31.1	18.2
France (2002, EMP)	38.1	41.0	37.9	38.3	38.9	37.8	36.5			
Greece (2002, TE)	45.0	48.0	45.0	39.0	42.0	38.0	26.0	39.0	41.0	38.0
Italy (2002, TE)	41.4	42.4	39.6	37.6	38.3	35.1	27.1	35.5	37.7	31.2
Japan (2003, TE)[c]	42.1	40.6	47.9	42.8	38.6	43.0	37.2	38.1	40.6	
New Zealand (2002, EMP)	33.2	30.1	37.7	35.1	34.5	35.6	28.6	29.0	32.3	16.5
Spain (2002, TE)	37.4	40.4	37.7	35.4	34.3	32.9	25.7	32.9	34.6	26.5
Switzerland (2002, EMP)	35.5	32.8	37.9	39.7	35.7	37.3	31.9	31.4	31.2	17.2
Transition countries										
Croatia (2002, EMP)	41.8	44.7	43.1	40.5	41.0	40.6	39.0	40.8	40.1	
Georgia (1999, EMP)	44.5	47.7	43.2	40.6	37.8	43.2	26.2	35.6	36.8	36.1
Latvia (2002, TE)	43.0	42.3	43.0	38.5	39.6	39.8	32.7	39.9	37.5	30.3
Lithuania (2002, EMP)	39.5	41.2	41.3	39.1	38.0	39.8	32.6	37.7	37.2	33.7
Poland (2002, EMP)	40.9	40.2	42.1	39.7	39.7	40.1	30.0	38.9	38.1	
Slovenia (2002, EMP)	37.0	37.8	38.1	35.3	36.4	34.7	33.8	36.2	34.4	26.6
Asia										
Israel (2002, TE)	40.6	37.4	41.1	38.7	38.9	39.6	25.6	32.0	33.2	30.4
Macau, China (2002, TE)	52.9	55.5	47.0	43.9	54.3	39.1	41.4	43.4	54.0	55.2
Philippines (2002, TE)	48.8	48.6	47.6	41.4	45.7	39.7	36.3	40.5	36.1	54.0

Table 5.3 Continued

	Wholesale and retail trade, repair of motor vehicles, motorcycles and personal and household goods (G)	Hotels and restaurants (H)	Transport, storage and communication (I)	Financial intermediation (J)	Real estate, renting and business activities (K)	Public administration and defence, compulsory social security (L)	Education (M)	Health and social work (N)	Community, social and personal service activities (O)	Private households with employed persons (P)
Thailand (2001, EMP)	45.0	48.8	50.0	52.9	50.7		42.0	53.4	39.0	49.0
Turkey (2002, TE)	57.9	63.5	52.8	45.0	50.6	44.7	36.8	44.3	51.7	43.2
Viet Nam (1999, TE)	50.2	50.6	50.7	47.2	46.7	45.4	44.6	46.3	46.8	49.1
Africa										
Botswana (1995, EMP)	52.2	54.7	50.7	40.6	51.5	37.3	34.7	38.5	39.1	51.0
Gambia (1998, EMP)d	44.7	48.1	41.7	39.7					46.8	
Americas										
Argentina (2002, TE)	47.1	44.7	51.4	44.2	41.1	36.7	25.5	35.9	33.5	27.4
Brazil (2001, TE)	44.8	48.8	48.7	40.1	43.5	41.4	35.4	41.6	38.5	40.1
Colombia (2002, EMP)e	44.9		50.6	42.3	42.2				38.2	
Costa Rica (2003, EMP)	49.0	48.0	52.0	46.0	49.0	47.0	39.0	46.0	43.0	36.0
Mexico (2001, EMP)	45.4	47.0	51.2	42.4	45.8	45.3	31.2	40.0	41.6	37.7
Panama (2002, TE)	46.7	46.0	44.8	43.5		42.6	38.2	41.5	42.3	41.4
Uruguay (2002, EMP)	44.8	44.8	47.3	40.2	44.8	43.5	29.5	36.9	38.2	31.3

Source: ILO Labour Statistics Database, hours of work by economic activity, classification ISIC-Revision 3 (labour force survey data only).

Notes

a Where LABORSTA data for 2002 are unavailable, comparable data for the most proximate alternative year are used.
b EMP = data presented are for employees only; TE = data presented are for total employment.
c For Japan, repair of motor vehicles, motorcycles, and personal and household goods are included under Category O instead of Category G.
d For Gambia, survey results were influenced by a low response rate.
e For Colombia, France and Uruguay, some of the tabulation categories have been combined.

(public administration, defence, social security programmes). The working hours in other subsectors, such as real estate, renting and business activities, vary dramatically by country, which range from a low of 34.3 hours per week in Spain to a high of 54.3 hours per week in Macau, China. Interestingly, there also appears to be a dramatic cross-country variation – from a low of 16.5 hours a week in New Zealand to 55.2 hours a week in Macau, China – in the weekly hours of individuals in category P (private households with employed persons), the service subsector category that includes domestic workers.

With these broad comparisons in mind, we now turn to some evidence from the sectoral analysis of working time presented in the country study reports. Beginning with the Americas, the transport, storage and communications subsector appears to have the longest average weekly hours in many of the countries studied. In Chile, for example, weekly hours in that subsector average 53.7 per week – the longest for any industry in the country – roughly equal to the weekly hours worked in mining and quarrying (53.6 per week), a sector that has traditionally recorded very long hours in that country (Echeverría 2002: 53). In Brazil, it is once again the transport, storage and communications subsector that shows the longest working week among all the major industry groupings, with a working week of 48.4 hours (Saboia 2002: 13). Similarly, in Jamaica 28 per cent of all workers in this industry worked more than 49 hours per week – by far, the highest percentage of any major industry group in that country (Taylor 2004: 54). For the Asian countries studied, Malaysia also shows very long hours in transport, storage and communications; in fact, the average working week remained quite high – 51.8 hours, with 42.6 per cent of all workers in that industry working over 50 hours per week (Nagaraj 2004: 35). China, however, is a different story: based on household surveys conducted in three major cities in that country (Beijing, Guangzhou and Changsha), weekly hours of work in this subsector averaged only 41.3 hours per week (Zeng *et al.* 2005: 11). Likewise, the hours of work in this industry appear more modest in the case of some transition economies, such as in the Czech Republic (41.1 hours per week) and in Hungary (43.2 hours per week) (Berkovsky *et al.* 2002: 105; Galasi 2002: 122).

Long hours of work in the wholesale and retail trade subsector were also consistently reported across those countries studied. For example, in Mexico there are a higher proportion of workers working over 48 hours per week in this industry than in any other, 36.2 per cent of all workers (Esponda 2002: 17). Moreover, it should be noted that the share of women working such long hours in the Mexican wholesale and retail trade is even higher: 51.4 per cent (ibid.). Likewise, in Chile, the *average* hours of work in this industry exceed 48 hours a week, and women work longer hours in this industry than in any others except for hotels and restaurants – 46.7 hours per week on average (Echeverría 2002: 53). In Peru, the average working week for workers in the wholesale and retail trade was 49 hours per week in 2000; only domestic workers showed a longer average working week (Aparicio Valdez 2001: Appendices). In Asia as well, we see longer than average hours of work in the wholesale and retail trade. In China, the combined category of wholesale and retail trade with restaurants and hotels shows an average working week of 46.5 hours[3] (Zeng *et al.* 2005: 11). And in Malaysia, the wholesale and retail trade shows the highest percentage of workers working over 50 hours a week in any industry – 44.8 per cent in 2000 (Nagaraj 2004: Appendices). All of these figures appear quite stunning when compared with the situation in most of the industrialized world, where the retail industry has come to be dominated by part-time workers in many countries (see, for example, Messenger, ed., 2004).

Box 5.1   Excessive hours of work in the security industry: a global phenomenon

The legal hours of work in the security industry are among the highest of any industry in the world. This is due to the fact that security workers are considered to be engaged in what is termed 'intermittent work', involving only physical presence at the workplace, which is often subject to laxer hours limits (see Chapter 6 for a discussion on this issue). Data on the *actual* hours of work in the security industry can be hard to come by, however, as there is no standard industry category (ISIC) that corresponds precisely to this industry.

One of the country studies commissioned for this report sheds some light on this global phenomenon. This study indicates that, in Jamaica, workers in the security industry are working an average of 12 hours per day for six days a week – for an astounding total of 72 hours per week (Taylor 2004: 75). These excessive hours appear to be due, in large part, to working double shifts totalling 24 hours at least twice a week (ibid.). However, the situation in Jamaica is hardly unique. In South Africa, for example, security industry employees commonly worked 60 or even 72 hours a week until 2000 (South Africa Department of Labour 2000: 75). In that year, though, a sectoral determination agreement was established to reduce the working hours of all security industry employees in that country down to the 45-hour standard working week within a three-year period, although the ultimate impact on their actual hours remains to be seen (Lundall 2002).

Average weekly hours of work are also quite long in hotels and restaurants in many of the countries studied (where these are delineated separately; see Note 2). In Hungary, for example, usual weekly hours were the highest of any subsector in that country, averaging 45.2 hours per week (Galasi 2002: 122). Average weekly hours in hotels and restaurants were also quite high in

Chile, at 49.8 hours per week, and the working hours of women are longer than in any other industry in the country – 48.4 hours per week (Echeverría 2002: 56).

At the other extreme, the shortest average working hours across the countries studied were most typically found in the education subsector – where education is delineated separately – or, where this is not the case, in the broad category of community, social and personal services, which includes education, public administration and defence, health and social services, as well as an array of recreational and personal services.[4] For example, the average working week in the education subsector was only 37.7 hours in the Czech Republic and 38.5 hours in Hungary (Berkovsky *et al.* 2002: 107; Galasi 2002: 122). Similarly, the average hours of work in social services and public administration were only 34.7 and 39.4 hours, respectively, in those countries in 1999, and the working hours in social and other community services in Chile were only 42 hours per week – dramatically less than the national average of 47.9 hours per week in 2000 (Echeverría 2002: 55).

From a slightly different perspective, it is also interesting to consider which of the service subsectors have higher or lower rates of part-time working. Once again, limitations on the available data impact on the analysis; in this case, it is necessary to use the broader categories of economic activity established under revision 2 of the International Standard Industrial Classification (ISIC). These data, showing the proportion of workers working part-time hours (either less than 30 or less than 35 depending on the country) in seven countries from different parts of the world, are presented in Table 5.4.

The most striking result that emerges from this table is the relatively high proportions of workers in the community, social and personal services subsector who are working part-time in many of these countries – particularly Brazil (60.1 per cent), the Russian Federation (46.2 per cent), Jamaica (38 per cent),[5] Mexico (31.1 per cent) and Hungary (18.3 per cent). This may help to explain why the average working hours in this subsector are relatively short, as discussed above. In a similar vein, it is also very noticeable how small the proportions of individuals working part-time are in the transport, storage and communications subsector – the highest share of part-timers in that subsector is only around 10 per cent (in Jamaica and Mexico). Once again, this is in line with the findings discussed above, which indicated that this subsector appears to have the longest hours of any of the service subsectors. Nonetheless, even in subsectors with fairly long overall hours of work – notably, the wholesale and retail trade and hotels and restaurants (which are combined under ISIC-Revision 2) – there are still some countries with significant proportions of part-timers in those subsectors, that is Mexico, Brazil and South Africa. As all of these countries have a fairly high level of development, there is reason to believe that they may be demonstrating a movement towards a reliance on part-time work in these subsectors that is observed in many industrialized countries; this is particularly evident

Table 5.4   Proportion of workers working part-time hours in service subsectors (percentage, 2000)

	Total economy	Wholesale and retailing, restaurants and hotels (6)	Transport, storage and communi- cations (7)	Financing, insurance, real estate and business services (8)	Community, social and personal services (9)
Brazil (<30 h)	26.1	24.9	9.6	16.3	60.1
Hungary (<30 h)	3.2	4.5	0.9[a]	4.8	18.3
Jamaica (<35 h)	11	8	10	20	38
Malaysia (<30 h)	5.3	3.8	2.1	1.7	6.4
Mexico (<35 h)	22	24.1	9.9	19.9	31.1
Russian Federation (<30 h)	9.7	N/A	5.9	N/A	46.2
South Africa (<30 h)	7.8	19.42	5.34	3.08	7.6[b]

Sources: ILO country study reports on working time and work organization; South Africa Department of Labour 2000.

Notes
a Only transport and storage.
b Only government sector plus laundries and dry cleaning services.

in the retailing industry, in which short-hours staff are often deployed to cover peak periods.

5.4 Work schedules in the service sector

Of course, hours of work are only half of the picture; the timing of when these working hours occur – that is the arrangement of working time or *work schedules* – is equally important. Some important aspects of work schedules include the extent to which companies use shift work, including night work; weekend work; and various types of 'flexible' working time arrangements, which may include the averaging of working time over extended periods (i.e. more than one week), flexi-time schemes that allow workers to vary the starting and ending times of their working day, and similar approaches.[6]

5.4.1 Shift work

Unfortunately, reliable comparative information on work schedules around the world is essentially non-existent. Nonetheless, the information available from the 15 country studies provides some useful insights into work schedules in the service sector in those countries. First, we can see that shift work is a traditional method of organizing working time that allows companies to extend their operating hours beyond the working time of any individual workers. The use of various types of shift patterns, including night shifts, is quite common across all regions of the world. In Asia, shift work is widely employed in China, the Republic of Korea and Malaysia. The same situation also holds for the Americas, as well as for the formal economy in the African countries studied – Mauritius, Senegal and Tunisia[7] (Richards 2005; Ndiaye 2004; Alouane *et al.* 2003). The transition economies, however, appear to be (at least in part) an exception to this general rule on shift patterns. This is particularly the case in the Russian Federation, where 57.6 per cent of all enterprises still operated with no shift system in 2002 – i.e. they had only one group of workers who were all working the same hours – primarily, it would appear, due to 'the limited market for their products' (Chetvernina *et al.* 2004: 91).

Box 5.2 Extended opening hours in the retail trade: the case of Malaysia

Retailing is one of the fastest-growing sectors in Malaysia, with large increases in both retail space and occupancy over the last decade. With high levels of demand and changing consumer preferences, opening hours of retail outlets have gradually expanded over time. For example, Giant, one of the largest supermarket chains in the country, used to be open from 8:30 am until early in the evening six days a week; it had shorter hours on Sundays and was closed on holidays. Now this company's stores are open from 8:30 am to 10 pm seven days a week (and until midnight on Saturday), 365 days a year.

Some stores have gone even further: one supermarket, a relatively new chain to Malaysia, TESCO, decided to begin 24-hour operations in March 2004. However, after complaints that supermarket/hypermarket operations were hurting small businesses, the Malaysian Ministry of Domestic Trade and Consumer Affairs stepped in with an order prohibiting 24-hour operations for such supermarket chains. This government order also established standardized opening hours for all supermarkets and hypermarkets: 10 am to 10 pm on Monday to Friday and 10 am until midnight or 1 am at weekends and public holidays.

Source: Nagaraj 2004: 57–58.

There are, however, some interesting cross-country differences regarding shift work. In China, for example, 36.1 per cent of employees undertake shift work, but they are highly concentrated in the manufacturing sector; in the service sector, only the wholesale and retail trade/hotels and restaurants subsector (ISIC-Revision 2) demonstrates an extensive use (19.3 per cent) of shift working (Zeng *et al.* 2005: 4). The Republic of Korea, with a similar overall proportion of shift work, nonetheless shows much higher proportions of shift workers in the service sector: 30.2 per cent in the wholesale and retail trade/hotels and restaurants subsector; 48.3 per cent in the community, social and personal services subsector; and 64.9 per cent in transportation, storage and communications (Yoon 2001: 48). The use of shift systems is slightly less common in Chile: 23 per cent of companies use shift systems and around one-quarter of all employees are engaged in shift work; within the service sector, two-shift systems are most prevalent with the exception of financial services, in which three-shift continuous operations predominate (Echeverría 2002: 83). By contrast, in Jamaica shift work is the dominant working time arrangement in nearly every major industry group, with two service sub-sectors – transport, storage and communications and the wholesale and retail trade/hotels and restaurants subsector (ISIC-Revision 2) registering excep-tionally high proportions of shiftworkers, 93 and 75 per cent, respec-tively (Taylor 2004: 76). Similarly, an enterprise survey conducted for the Senegal country study found that the vast majority of enterprises surveyed, 89 per cent, employed shift systems (Ndiaye 2005: 48). By way of comparison, only 14 per cent of all employees in the United Kingdom are regular shift workers, although it is again the transport, storage and communications subsector in which shift work is most common – around one-quarter of all employees in that subsector regularly work shifts (IDS 2005). And in the EU-25, 17.7 per cent of all employees are working on shifts, although a substantially higher proportion of employees in the transition economies of the new EU Member States[8] are working shifts (28.4 per cent) than in the old EU-15 (15.8 per cent); overall, there is a similar proportion of shift workers (16.6 per cent) in the service sector as in the EU as a whole (Eurostat 2005).

5.4.2 Night work

Night work is often an integral part of shift work systems, whether fixed or rotating ones, particularly in three-shift continuous operations and its vari-ants, but increasingly in some two-shift operations as well, given enterprises' increasing deployment of 12-hour shifts. In Chile, for example, 61 per cent of those companies that have a shift system also make use of night work; this suggests (given the overall percentages of shift work and shift workers mentioned above) that around 15 per cent of all employees perform night work in that country (Echeverría 2002: 83). Interestingly, the available figures for night working in many of the other countries studied were quite similar: 17.5 per cent of employees in China do night work at least once a month; 24 per cent work do the same in the Czech Republic; and 20 per cent of employees in Senegal work nights at least once per week (Zeng *et al.* 2005: 4; Berkovsky 2002: 50; Ndiaye 2005: 49). By contrast, less than 10 per cent of all employees in Brazil (9.0 per cent) and Hungary (9.5 per cent) are engaged in regular night working (Saboia 2002: 47; Galasi 2002: 166).

Box 5.3 The increasing fragmentation of working time: the case of split shifts in Peru

Recent research in several industrialized countries, such as France and the United Kingdom (e.g. Gadrey *et al.* 2006; Rubery *et al.* 2006), has shown a tendency towards an increasing 'fragmentation' in working time. That is, enterprises are attempting to tailor working hours more and more closely to fluctuations in market demands, particularly in the service sector industries such as retailing and hotels and restaurants.

Although the available information is insufficient to confirm this tendency in developing and transition countries, there is nonetheless some evidence of such a trend in our country studies. Peru provides a good illustration of this phenomenon. In Peru split shifts have become common in the education subsector, where cutbacks in public education funding have reduced classroom hours to around 600 per year, the shortest school year in Latin America. Students attend school for only four or five hours per day – either in the morning or the afternoon – and so teachers work in split shifts to accommodate this situation. This is an approach that is now spreading to other services, such as financial services, telecommunications, fast food restaurants, hotels, retail stores and casinos. In many cases, such 'fragmented' shift systems are employed in combination with job rotation to minimize the hours of individual workers, particularly younger workers. It appears that this trend has also been facilitated by legislation establishing a minimum threshold of one-half of the normal working day in order to qualify for basic employment benefits and conditions (e.g. the minimum wage).

Source: Aparicio Valdez 2001: 43–44.

5.4.3 Weekend work

Turning now to weekend working, there appears to be – similar to the situation in many industrialized countries, such as Canada (see e.g. Zeytinoglu and Cooke 2006) – a greater likelihood for individuals to work weekends in the wholesale and retail trade/hotels and restaurants subsector (ISIC-Revision 2) in most of the 15 countries studied. In China, for example, the overall figure for weekend working was 22.5 per cent of workers, but the corresponding figure was 36.4 per cent of workers in trade/hotels and restaurants (Zeng *et al.* 2005: 5–6). A similar phenomenon is also observed in Hungary, where 47 per cent of workers in hotels and restaurants reported working regularly on Saturdays and 39 per cent of them reported regular Sunday work; these figures are *triple* the overall proportion of workers who are working regularly on Saturdays and Sundays – only 16.9 and 11.6 per cent, respectively (Galasi 2002: 166). And in Jamaica, where reported levels of weekend work are generally much higher than in the other countries studied, the combined category of trade/hotels and restaurants is once again among the top subsectors for weekend working, with 70 per cent of enterprises in this category reporting that they operate on Saturdays and Sundays, along with 80 per cent of the firms in transport, storage and communications, and 75 per cent of firms in the tourism industry[9] (Taylor 2004: 80–81).

5.4.4 Other flexible working time arrangements

In addition to the more traditional approaches of shift work, night work and weekend work, other types of 'flexible' working time arrangements similar to those observed in the industrialized countries – albeit with country-specific adaptations – appear to be emerging in many developing and transition countries. Although no reliable figures exist on the specific incidence of such arrangements (which are difficult to quantify even in many of the industrialized countries), one of the most commonly observed 'flexible' working time arrangements are 'hours averaging' or 'modulation' schemes (sometimes also referred to as 'annualized' hours schemes if they allow averaging over an entire year), which allow for variations in hours of work over multiple-week periods. Typically, hours averaging schemes set an *average* number of hours to be worked per week (e.g. 40 hours) over a specified period of time, called the 'reference period', which may vary from several weeks up to as long as an entire year in some cases. This approach allows firms to increase hours of work during periods in which the volume of work is high, which can then be offset by reduced hours of work at other times when the company's workload is less. Of course, to the extent that 'unsocial hours' working at night and at weekends (and overtime work as well) is already widely deployed, the incentive for firms to introduce these types of flexible working time arrangements would be diminished.

Nonetheless, while these sorts of arrangements do not appear to be widespread across the developing and transition countries, hours averaging schemes are becoming increasingly important in some countries, such as Brazil, China, the Czech Republic and Hungary. For example, the 'modulation of the working week' is 'one of the proposals for making the working week more flexible that has rallied [the] most support in recent years in Brazil' (Saboia 2002: 51). This type of scheme has received considerable support from both Brazilian industry and trade unions, perhaps because the modulation of working hours to tailor working time more closely to market demands is usually combined with a reduction in the length of the average working week – a practice similar to that in countries such as Germany. Such schemes seem to be more common in manufacturing than in services, however. In China, hours averaging is known as 'comprehensive working time', and this arrangement appears to be widespread in major urban centres – 12.2 per cent of workers were working under this scheme (Zeng *et al.* 2005: 7). These issues will be taken up again in Chapters 6 and 7.

5.5 The 'informalization' of national economies

Another important change in the structure of the global economy over the last several decades – particularly, though not exclusively, in developing countries – has been the further 'informalization' of many economic activities. Various alternative definitions of informal economic activity have been proposed, and many authors simply speak of the 'informal sector' or 'informal jobs', with the assumption that there is a broad, shared understanding of the phenomenon. However such informal activities are defined, there can be little doubt of their very real importance to the economic livelihoods – indeed the very survival – of hundreds of millions, if not billions, of workers around the world.

With regard to analysing informal economic activities, there has been a long-running debate regarding whether the appropriate unit of analysis should be enterprises or individual workers – or, at least, individual *jobs*. (For a comprehensive discussion of the history of this debate regarding the measurement of informal economic activities, see Hussmanns 2004). This difference in perspective has, in turn, led to disagreements regarding the appropriate use of terms such as 'informal sector', 'informal jobs', etc. However, the argument has continued to turn around the question of whether the focus should be on *employment in informal sector enterprises* or on *informal employment* regardless of whether the enterprises in question are considered to be informal or not. In the conclusions of the extensive discussion of the informal economy at the 90th Session of the International Labour Conference (ILC) in 2002, the ILO adopted the following definition of the *informal economy*:

> [A]ll economic activities by workers and economic units that are – in law or in practice – not covered or insufficiently covered by formal arrangements. Their activities are not included in the law, which means that they are operating outside the formal reach of the law; or they are not covered in practice, which means that, although they are operating within the formal reach of the law, the law is not applied or enforced; or the law discourages compliance because it is inappropriate, burdensome or imposes excessive costs.
>
> (ILO 2002c: 53)

The above definition can be considered a comprehensive one, in that it encompasses all informal employment regardless of the types of firms in which it occurs. In fact, this definition was based on a conceptual framework of the informal economy that combines the type of economic unit – i.e. formal sector enterprises, informal sector enterprises, and households – with the type of job as categorized based on employment status – i.e. own-account workers, employers, contributing family workers, employees and members of producers' cooperatives (ILO 2002a: 13). This conceptual framework was ultimately endorsed (with minor amendments) as an international statistical standard by the International Conference of Labour Statisticians (ICLS) in 2003 (ILO 2003b).

Using this conceptual framework, the ILO has developed estimates of the size of informal employment relative to all non-agricultural employment in a wide range of countries. These estimates, which are reproduced in Figure 5.1, help to quantify the important contribution of informal employment to overall employment across the developing world.

As can be seen from Figure 5.1, informal employment represents at least half of all non-agricultural employment in all regions of the developing world. This proportion would undoubtedly be even higher if agriculture had been included in the calculations. Another important observation is that informal employment generally represents a more important share of women's non-agricultural employment than men's – with the exception of North Africa and Asia (where men's and women's incidence of self-employ-ment is roughly equal). This is particularly the case in sub-Saharan Africa, where informal employment provides 84 per cent of all employment for women outside of agriculture.

Informal employment includes both self-employment in informal sector enterprises and wage employment (in both informal and formal sector enterprises) in which workers lack a secure contract, employment benefits or social protection (ILO 2002a). This includes a wide array of economic activities: domestic work in households, industrial outwork (homework), casual labour, and many different types of self-employment, both home-based and in public areas (e.g. street vendors).

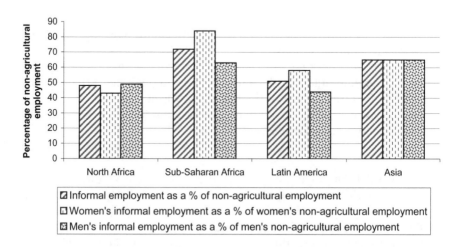

Figure 5.1 Informal employment in non-agricultural employment by gender (1994–2000)

Source: Reproduced from ILO (2002a), p. 19.

What is perhaps most striking about the composition of informal employ-ment, however, is just how much of it takes the form of *self-employment*. As shown in Figure 5.2, self-employment represents at least three-fifths of all informal employment in all regions of the developing world. In fact, self-employment accounts for well over one-third of total employment in the developing world (nearly half of total employment in Africa), compared with only around 12 per cent in the industrialized countries (ILO 2002a: 22). Only a handful of developing countries show a higher proportion of wage employment than self-employment in the informal economy – most notably South Africa, where, due to the legacy of apartheid (black-owned businesses were illegal under the apartheid regime), wage employment still predomi-nates (ibid.; Valodia 2001).

5.6 Working time in the informal economy: self-employment as a proxy measure

With this background, we now turn to the issue of working time in the informal economy. Unfortunately, there is no source of comparative data on working hours in the informal economy. However, given the fact that self-employment represents a dominant share of total informal employment in most developing countries (South Africa is an important exception), it is possible to use data on the working hours of the self-employed as a proxy

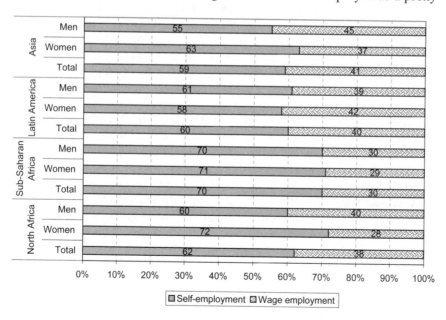

Figure 5.2 Wage employment and self-employment in non-agricultural informal employment by gender (percentage, 1994–2000)

Source: ILO (2002b), Table 2.2, p. 20.

measure for working hours in the informal economy as a whole. While it is important to keep in mind that some of these workers could be employers who own formal sector enterprises, the reality is that the vast majority of these individuals are going to be owners of their own private, unincorporated enterprises, which means that – by definition – they are considered to be in informal employment.[10]

There are two traditional theories that attempt to explain entry into self-employment in terms of a worker's economic utility. One theory – the 'career' or 'pull' theory – asserts that workers are pulled into self-employment due to their own particular knowledge and skills, as well as their need for qualitative benefits such as autonomy and flexibility (Knight 1933). The major competing theory – the 'default' or 'push' theory – holds that workers are pushed into self-employment when they lack decent opportunities in the wage and salary labour market (Schumpeter 1934); thus, this theory predicts that those workers who have the most limited options for wage employment (i.e. who can obtain only the lowest-paying positions or no job at all) and/or have particular barriers keeping them from obtaining wage positions would be the most likely to enter self-employment.

Although developed many years ago in a different economic context, one can easily imagine how these two theories can apply to the realities of self-employment in today's global economy. The 'pull' theory can reasonably describe the situation of those fortunate individuals – the managerial and professional elite, or as Reich (1992) calls them, 'symbolic analysts' – with high levels of education, well-developed, marketable skills and extensive experience that allow them to start their own businesses and earn more than they ever could in wage employment. In terms of working hours, with the 'pull' theory, one might reasonably expect to see most self-employed workers working very long hours in order to maximize the returns to their substantial human capital, a situation analogous to that of other so-called 'knowledge workers', whose working hours are typically quite long. This, in turn, implies that the distribution of working hours for these individuals would be highly concentrated in the longest hours categories. Of course, in addition to the expected financial compensation, there are also other factors that can affect individuals' motivations for entering self-employment; these factors include the non-pecuniary characteristics of the work, such as an individual's preference for greater control/autonomy regarding how the work is performed and their level of risk aversion (see, for example, Rees and Shah 1986). These other factors will, in turn, affect the degree to which the 'pull' of self-employment actually translates into long working hours in practice.

On the other hand, the 'push' theory seems to accurately capture the reality for the vast majority of self-employed workers in the developing world, for whom 'the informal sector has in fact become an employer of last resort for people who do not manage to find employment in the formal economy' (Torres 1998: 50). The 'push' theory would appear to have quite different implications for working hours from those of the 'pull' theory. If those workers who have the most limited options for wage employment and/ or have particular barriers preventing them from obtaining wage positions are being pushed into self-employment, then one might reasonably expect that these individuals would have no choice but to accept whatever work comes their way. In terms of working hours, this situation would suggest that the working hours of these self-employed workers would be highly variable – depending on their workload at any given time – which, in turn, would imply a diverse distribution of working hours, including variations *among* workers at a given time and perhaps also instability in hours across time for individual workers.[11]

More recently, several studies (most notably Carr 1996) have posited a new theory: that *gender is the key variable* for understanding why individuals enter self-employment. Carr asserts that women and men enter self-employment for fundamentally different reasons: while the traditional theories may be applicable to men, for many women – especially women with children – self-employment is a strategy that they employ to reconcile work and family. And, in fact, there is evidence that women entrepreneurs exhibit a different pattern of working hours than men. For example, Devine (1994) performed a detailed analysis of the work patterns of male and female self-employed workers in the United States, and found that self-employed women were more likely to work part-time hours than self-employed men; 40 per cent of all self-employed women worked part-time hours compared with just 15 per cent of self-employed men. Once again, although this theory emerges from research in an industrialized country context, the extensive recourse to self-employment by women in other regions of the world, particularly Africa and Latin America (see ILO 2002a) – and typically with far less support than that available to women in industrialized countries – suggests that the need to reconcile competing work and family demands may well be an issue affecting self-employed women's working hours in those regions as well. In terms of working hours, then, this theory would imply a clear split in working hours along gender lines; that is, there should be a much higher proportion of part-time hours among self-employed women than self-employed men.

With this background on the motivations for entering self-employment, we now turn to an analysis of the survey data on the distribution of working hours among the self-employed (which was explained in both Chapter 1 and in Chapter 3, Box 3.1). These data are displayed in Tables 5.5a, 5.5b and 5.5c.

5.6.1 Industrialized countries

Table 5.5a shows the working hours of self-employed workers in a subset of those industrialized countries that responded to the ILO special survey on the distribution of working hours. Self-employed workers without employees – typically called own-account workers or independent contractors – constitute a majority of the self-employed in most OECD countries, and it is precisely these individuals who report poorer working conditions and more

Table 5.5a Distribution of working hours for the self-employed by gender (percentage, industrialized countries)

Gender	Working hours	Canada 2004	France 2004	Ireland 2004	Japan 2004	Korea, Rep. of 2004	New Zealand 2004	Portugal 2004	Spain 2004	Switzer- land 2004	United Kingdom 2003	United States 2004
Both	<15	6.9	1.9	1.6	11.2	3.0	11.2	7.9	1.4	17.7	2.2	10.2
	15–24	9.0	4.3	3.5	24.2	5.6	9.7	12.0	3.9	11.0	5.5	15.5
	25–34	11.0	4.7	3.9		5.4	10.5	10.3	4.1	9.4	6.8	7.9
	35	4.9	3.7	1.4	6.8	0.5	3.3	2.1	1.4	2.5	1.2	5.8
	36–39	1.6	2.2	4.2		7.0	1.4	0.6	0.7	1.8	5.0	
	40	21.5	9.8	13.5	23.6	6.3	16.9	26.9	35.9	7.7	6.0	25.4
	41–47	7.6	10.6	4.1		11.0	9.7	9.0	11.3	12.6	21.9	6.6
	48	0.9	1.6	0.6		5.0	1.4	3.3	3.5	0.0	2.5	
	49–59	17.1	21.6	11.8	15.9	21.8	17.3	12.3	22.9	14.4	24.3	13.3
	60+	19.5	38.6	18.7	18.0	34.4	18.4	13.3	14.9	21.8	21.4	15.2
		100.0	99.0	63.3	99.7	100.0	99.8	97.7	100.0	98.9	96.8	99.9
Females	<15	13.4	3.9	6.2	17.2	3.3	22.5	11.7	3.1	31.7	5.7	16.2
	15–24	16.1	9.2	12.0	32.3	7.2	18.9	16.4	8.7	18.1	14.3	21.6
	25–34	15.9	10.4	10.5		6.8	14.7	13.8	8.1	11.6	14.7	9.4
	35	6.0	5.3	2.5	7.6	0.7	3.7	2.8	2.4	0.0	2.7	6.1
	36–39	1.6	3.0	6.8		8.5	2.0	0.9	1.2	0.0	7.9	
	40	17.5	12.5	15.3	18.7	6.3	12.3	20.9	36.1	6.3	5.9	20.6
	41–47	5.8	10.6	4.5		10.2	5.9	7.9	11.4	9.9	16.5	5.7
	48	0.7	2.0	0.0		4.0	1.3	2.8	3.4	0.0	2.3	
	49–59	12.3	16.4	7.4	11.6	18.8	9.9	9.6	14.5	7.1	14.4	10.2
	60+	10.7	24.9	7.6	12.1	34.2	8.9	10.8	11.0	10.4	12.3	10.2
		100.0	98.2	72.8	99.5	100.0	100.1	97.6	99.9	95.1	96.7	100.0

Males											
<15	3.5	0.9	0.7	6.9	2.8	6.1	5.2	0.7	7.5	0.9	6.8
15–24	5.4	2.0	1.8	18.1	4.5	5.5	8.8	1.6	5.8	2.4	11.9
25–34	8.5	2.0	2.6		4.4	8.6	7.8	2.3	7.8	3.9	7.0
35	4.3	3.0	1.1	6.1	0.4	3.1	1.6	0.9	2.5	0.7	5.7
36–39	1.5	1.8	3.7		5.9	1.0	0.4	0.4	0.0	4.0	
40	23.7	8.6	13.2		6.3	19.1	31.3	35.8	8.8	6.1	28.2
41–47	8.4	10.5	4.0	27.5	11.6	11.5	9.7	11.4	14.6	23.8	7.2
48	0.9	1.3	0.6		5.8	1.5	3.6	3.5	0.0	2.6	
49–59	19.6	24.0	12.7	19.1	23.9	20.6	14.2	26.7	19.8	27.8	15.1
60+	24.1	45.1	20.8	22.5	34.5	22.8	15.1	16.7	30.1	24.6	18.1
	99.9	99.2	61.2	100.2	100.1	99.8	97.7	100.0	96.9	96.8	100.0

Source: see Box 3.1 and Statistical annex.

Notes
Not all columns add up to 100 per cent due to reporting of 'unknown' working hours. Where 'unknown' hours are particularly high, these are noted below.
Ireland: 'unknown' hours figure for the self-employed is very high (36.7 per cent of total); this figure also includes individuals reporting variable hours.
Japan: different hours categories are used.
United Kingdom: figures presented in the table are for 2003.

Table 5.5b Distribution of working hours for the self-employed by gender (percentage, developing countries)

		Americas							Africa				Asia			
Gender	Working hours	Bolivia	Guate-mala	Hon-duras	Mexico	Panama	Peru	Uruguay	Ethiopia	Mada-gascar	Mauritius	Tanzania, United Rep. of	Indo-nesia	Pakistan	Sri Lanka	Thailand
		2000	2004	2001M	2004	2004	2004	2004	2004	2001	2004	2000	2003	2003	2003	2000F
Both	<15	9.8	12.5	8.9	7.6	20.1	11.0	13.5	7.3	2.2	11.2	27.7	2.6	1.6	14.4	3.3
	15–24	13.5	12.3	9.3	10.5	16.9	11.1	15.0	13.4	9.5	12.6	11.6	5.5	2.9	13.9	6.3
	25–34	9.0	11.0	7.6	8.2	8.8	8.8	10.3	12.9	10.4	18.5		9.9	5.6	15.1	2.5
	35	2.2	2.7	1.6	3.1	1.9	2.5	1.1	3.9	0.1	2.9	14.5			4.7	7.9
	36–39	4.1	4.5	5.1	7.4	2.1	3.4	1.8	4.2	20.2	6.4		29.6	12.9	2.1	
	40	4.3	6.1	7.8	4.4	9.5	2.3	16.3	6.2	0.1	4.0	23.6			10.9	
	41–47	5.4	11.5	30.9	13.7	5.8	6.4	4.1	8.2	11.8	14.0		37.2	19.1	5.1	23.2
	48	14.1	12.8	0.0	15.9	10.3	5.0	8.8	4.4	30.4	3.9				5.4	
	49–59	12.1	12.1	10.9	13.4	7.8	11.4	8.7	13.4	2.8	14.6	9.4	7.0	17.9	10.6	56.8
	60+	25.5	14.6	16.4	15.7	16.8	38.0	20.4	25.7	12.5	11.9	13.2	8.2	40.0	17.8	
		100.0	100.1	98.5	99.9	100.0	99.9	100.0	99.6	100.0	100.0	100.0	100.0	100.0	100.0	100.0
Females	<15	12.1	27.5	26.3	16.7	35.7		20.5	8.5	2.9	18.9		4.5	8.2	19.3	3.6
	15–24	14.7	21.2	15.9	19.2	19.5		17.1	18.2	11.8	22.5		9.9	14.8	19.9	7.1
	25–34	9.3	13.1	10.5	12.3	9.1		11.3	15.5	11.6	19.4		13.1	24.7	19.5	2.8
	35	2.7	2.7	0.9	4.5	2.8		1.3	4.1	0.1	3.1				5.7	9.6
	36–39	4.2	2.3	4.7	6.8	1.4		1.9	4.5	22.0	4.4		28.5	24.9	1.7	
	40	3.6	1.7	4.1	3.0	7.3		13.2	6.1	0.2	2.6				8.9	
	41–47	5.4	4.6	12.7	9.1	3.7		3.9	7.8	10.5	9.2		30.3	15.7	4.9	25.6
	48	10.9	4.1	0.0	6.4	4.4		6.7	2.7	26.1	2.2				3.5	
	49–59	12.2	7.6	5.2	9.6	4.8		6.8	10.6	2.7	8.4		5.5	6.0	6.5	51.3
	60+	24.8	15.3	17.9	12.3	11.3		17.2	21.5	12.1	9.3		8.2	5.7	10.1	
		99.9	100.1	98.2	99.9	100.0		99.9	99.5	100.0	100.0		100.0	100.0	100.0	100.0

Males													
<15	7.5	2.8	3.1	2.4	12.3	9.4	6.2	1.5	8.6	1.8	1.1	12.2	3.1
15–24	12.2	6.4	7.1	5.4	15.5	13.7	9.1	7.1	9.3	3.6	1.9	11.3	5.6
25–34	8.6	9.7	6.6	5.9	8.7	9.8	10.7	9.0	18.2	8.5	4.1	13.2	2.4
35	1.6	2.6	1.8	2.3	1.5	1.0	3.8	0.1	2.8			4.2	6.6
36–39	4.0	5.9	5.4	7.8	2.4	1.7	3.9	18.1	7.0	30.1	12.0	2.3	
40	5.0	8.9	9.0	5.2	10.6	18.1	6.3	0.1	4.5			11.7	
41–47	5.5	16.0	37.1	16.3	6.8	4.3	8.5	13.2	15.6	40.1	19.4	5.3	21.2
48	17.3	18.5	0.0	21.4	13.3	10.1	6.0	34.9	4.5			6.2	
49–59	12.1	15.0	12.8	15.6	9.3	9.7	15.8	2.9	16.7	7.7	18.8	12.5	61.1
60+	26.2	14.2	16.0	17.7	19.6	22.2	29.5	13.1	12.8	8.2	42.7	21.1	
	100.0	100.0	98.9	100.0	100.0	100.0	99.8	100.0	100.0	100.0	100.0	100.0	100.0

Source: see Box 3.1 and Statistical annex.

Note

The United Republic of Tanzania, Indonesia, Pakistan and Thailand: for these countries, different hours categories are used.

Table 5.5c Distribution of working hours for the self-employed by gender (percentage, transition countries)

Gender	Working hours	Albania	Armenia	Bulgaria	Croatia	Czech Republic	Estonia	Georgia	Hungary	Lithuania	Poland	Russian Federation	Slovakia
		2001	2004	2004	2004	2004	2003	2004	2004	2004	2004	2004	2004
Both	<15	7.5	13.3	1.1	10.0	1.0	2.3	18.5	0.9	1.9	11.7	16.5	0.6
	15–24	16.2	11.3	4.2	15.1	2.4	6.1	16.4	2.7	15.9	11.7	20.1	3.4
	25–34	31.1	15.8	7.3	9.1	3.5	4.0	13.0	1.6	24.0			
	35	3.6	4.1	1.3	0.0	1.3	1.3		0.1	4.9	12.2	38.3	3.6
	36–39	9.2	1.1	0.2	0.0	0.7	1.3	13.3	0.3	3.0			
	40	13.2	8.0	26.5	25.1	27.9	43.4		41.2	25.0	28.6	13.6	54.1
	41–47	6.6	5.0	3.0	10.9	5.6	5.5	10.2	2.8	11.7			
	48	4.1	3.8	9.1	0.0	0.6	1.3		10.0	2.5			
	49–59	5.1	15.0	11.1	10.9	28.4	20.3	6.1	8.2	7.7	14.9	10.2	37.9
	60+	3.4	22.6	6.2	13.6	27.9	14.4	2.7	8.7	2.0	17.2		
		100.0	100.0	70.0	94.7	99.3	99.9	80.2	76.5	98.6	96.3	98.7	99.6
Females	<15	8.8	16.7	1.8		1.8	0.0	22.5	1.3	2.6	15.3	19.6	1.3
	15–24	17.0	13.8	4.9		5.1	9.9	18.4	5.0	17.9	15.2	24.0	8.4
	25–34	33.1	21.7	9.6		8.6	0.0	12.0	2.8	25.8			
	35	3.7	4.4	1.3		2.5	0.0		0.1	5.8	15.0	36.5	6.0
	36–39	9.8	1.0	0.2		1.2	0.0	12.9	0.4	3.3			
	40	11.9	9.1	26.5		40.0	36.8		48.4	22.2	28.7	11.9	64.3
	41–47	7.2	5.2	2.9		5.4	0.0	8.4	3.2	11.4			
	48	3.0	3.4	9.3		1.0	0.0		0.8	1.6			
	49–59	3.4	12.6	10.2		19.9	18.7	4.8	5.6	5.8	11.6	6.8	19.4
	60+	2.1	12.1	5.4		13.5	11.7	1.8	5.4	2.1	9.9		
		100.0	100.0	72.1		99.0	77.1	80.8	73.0	98.5	95.7	98.8	99.4

Males										
<15	6.7	11.1	0.7	0.7	0.0	15.0	0.7	1.3	9.3	14.0	0.4
15–24	15.7	9.6	3.8	1.3	4.2	14.7	1.6	14.5	9.3	17.0	1.6
25–34	30.0	12.0	6.0	1.6	0.0	13.9	10.0	22.6			
35	3.5	3.9	1.3	0.8	0.0		0.2	4.2	10.3		
36–39	8.8	1.1	0.3	0.5	0.0	13.7	0.3	2.9		39.7	2.8
40	13.9	7.2	26.5	23.2	46.5	11.9	37.8	27.1			
41–47	6.4	5.0	3.0	5.6	0.0		2.6	12.0	28.5	15.0	50.5
48	4.8	4.0	9.0	0.5	0.0		1.1	3.2			
49–59	6.1	16.5	11.7	31.7	21.3	7.2	9.5	9.2	17.2	13.0	44.5
60+	4.1	29.5	6.7	33.5	16.0	3.5	10.3	2.0	22.2		
	100.0	99.9	69.0	99.4	88.0	79.9	74.1	99.0	96.8	98.7	99.8

Source: see Box 3.1 and Statistical annex.

Notes
Not all columns add up to 100 per cent due to reporting of 'unknown' working hours. Where 'unknown' hours are particularly high, these are noted below.
Albania: figures used in the table are for 2001.
Bulgaria: 'unknown' hours figure for the self-employed is very high (29.9 per cent of total).
Estonia: figures used in the table are for 2003.
Georgia: 20 per cent of self-employed workers report different working hours in different seasons.
Georgia, Poland and the Russian Federation: different hours categories are used.
Hungary: 'unknown' hours figure for the self-employed is very high (32.4 per cent of total).

insecure jobs, thus making them somewhat more analogous to self-employed workers in developing countries (ILO 2002a). Nonetheless, it must be noted that the situation of the self-employed in industrialized countries is often quite different from those in the rest of the world – they are more likely to have formal, incorporated businesses, employees, and in many countries (even with unincorporated businesses) to be required to participate in national social security, retirement and health insurance schemes (ibid.).

What we see in Table 5.5a is the classic pattern of working hours for the self-employed in the developed world – long hours are the rule. In line with the predictions of the 'pull' theory, self-employment in the industrialized countries attracts predominantly older individuals with relatively high levels of skills and/or formal qualifications, and the returns to education for such individuals appear to be higher in self-employment than in wage employment (see Messenger and Stettner 2000, for a review of the relevant literature). Thus, there is a strong financial incentive for these self-employed workers to work as many hours as possible. With only one exception (Portugal), every one of the countries presented in Table 5.5a shows at least 30 per cent of self-employed workers working an average of 49 hours a week or more. France presents a particularly dramatic case: in a country known for its 35-hour standard working week for employees, approximately 60 per cent of all self-employed workers in that country are working 49 hours a week or more, and nearly 40 per cent of them work 60 hours a week or more. Moreover, if we focus on self-employment by sex, we can see that men's self-employment in the industrialized countries is even more concentrated in the long-hours categories (49–59 hours per week and 60 hours a week or more) than self-employment in general. In all but two of the countries shown in Table 5.5a (Ireland and Portugal), more than 40 per cent of self-employed men are working 49 hours a week or more, and the proportions are considerably higher (50 per cent or more) in four of these countries (France, the Republic of Korea, Switzerland and the United Kingdom).

Women's self-employment, however, displays a pattern that, in terms of working hours, is quite different from men's in many industrialized countries. Overall, we can see from Table 5.5a that the working hours of self-employed women show a split between the long-hours (49 and over) and short-hours (under 35) categories, but with a higher incidence of short hours in most of these countries. While those women in long-hours self-employment are, like most men, probably attempting to maximize their incomes in line with the 'pull' theory, there is reason to believe that short-hours self-employment is a strategy being employed by women to attempt to balance their work and family responsibilities, as predicted by the gender theory of self-employment (see Carr 1996; Messenger and Stettner 2000). Switzerland is a case in point: in that country, over 60 per cent self-employed women are working less than 35 hours per week, and nearly half are actually working less than 25 hours per week. In the Swiss context – where incomes are generally high and the structure of the society assumes the presence of a parent at home during school periods – short-hours self-employment is a logical choice for women who wish to work for pay while handling their family duties. A similar phenomenon of short-hours self-employment among women is also observable for Canada, Japan, New Zealand and Portugal – all of which show around half of self-employed women working less than 35 hours a week – and, to a lesser extent, for the United Kingdom and even Ireland as well.[12]

5.6.2 Developing countries

Turning now to the developing countries, in Table 5.5b we see (as might be expected) a very diverse picture across countries, but nonetheless a very different picture in many of them. Some countries with relatively high levels of economic development, most notably Thailand, appear to follow the broad pattern seen in the industrialized countries: nearly 57 per cent of all self-employed workers in that country are working more than 50 hours per week, with very few self-employed workers (only around 12 per cent) working less than 35 hours a week. However, as Table 5.5b indicates, the more common pattern of working hours for the self-employed in developing countries is a *diverse and thus relatively flat distribution of working hours.* Moreover, if we look at the data more closely, we can also observe a split in working hours operating along gender lines: when we break down the hours distributions of the self-employed by sex, we see that it is largely (although not exclusively) women who are working shorter hours and predominantly men who are working longer hours.

The situation for many self-employed men in developing countries is what one might expect for any workers in these countries – high proportions of them are working long hours, given the very low earnings which are prevalent among the self-employed in much of the developing world (ILO 2002a). With only two exceptions (Indonesia and Madagascar), approximately 30 per cent or more of all self-employed men in every one of these countries are working long hours (49 hours a week or more) and the proportions are considerably higher – one-half or more of all self-employed men – in Ethiopia, Pakistan and Thailand.[13] In addition, if we compare the figures for self-employed workers working long hours in Table 5.5b with the proportions of long hours for wage employees in Table 3.4 (Chapter 3), we can see that higher proportions of the self-employed are working long hours than wage employees in almost all of these countries. Nonetheless, the proportions of self-employed men who are working short hours (less than 35 per week) is *also* greater than that of their wage-earning counterparts, suggesting that these men may also be more likely to be underemployed as well. The fact that self-employed men in many of these developing countries are more likely to have both long hours and short hours would appear to be in line with the 'push' theory's prediction of a diverse distribution of working hours among the self-employed who have limited employment options.

The situation for self-employed women in these developing countries, however, is much less diverse: with only one exception (Thailand), at least one-quarter of all self-employed women in every one of these countries is working less than 35 hours per week. Moreover, *the proportion of short-hours self-employment is considerably higher – approximately one-half or more of all self-employed women – in half of these countries*, specifically Guatemala, Honduras, Mexico, Panama, Uruguay, Mauritius, Pakistan and Sri Lanka. When women have to enter the paid labour market – often with little education and few if any marketable skills – they may end up getting 'pushed' into self-employment, perhaps, as some authors have suggested, to 'play the role of buffer in [a] period of economic difficulty' (see Lee and Wood 2005: 16). However, given the often profound temporal constraints associated with handling their domestic responsibilities (this point was extensively discussed in Chapter 4), the prevalence of short hours among self-employed women in developing countries seems more likely to be an indication that women may well be using self-employment as a means of obtaining flexibility in their working hours and possibly reduced hours as well (see Carr 1996; see also Maloney 2004).[14] This short-hours self-employment, in turn, may permit them to better reconcile their need for earnings from paid labour with their family responsibilities. For example, in Brazil, so-called 'irregular occupations', which can include self-employment as well as certain types of jobs in the formal economy,[15] offer women the opportunity to improve work–family reconciliation, albeit at the price of lower job quality:

> [I]rregular occupations ['unprotected employment without benefits provided by labour legislation'] offer women, especially wives, the possibility of working part-time. We would suggest that this is the main form of reconciliation between the conflicting demands of work and family. The weak public mechanisms to facilitate the integration of women lead female labour into lower quality occupations.
>
> (Sorj 2004: 47)

Overall, it appears that both the gender and 'push' theories of self-employment matter in explaining the working-hour patterns for women in the informal economy of the developing world, although the precise extent to which each theory affects their working hours is impossible to determine given the limited data available.

5.6.3 Transition countries

Finally, in the transition countries, Table 5.5c indicates a substantial proportion of short-hours self-employment – between one-third and one-half of all self-employed workers – in half of these countries. This pattern holds in the following transition countries: Albania, Armenia, Croatia, Georgia,

Box 5.4 Very long hours and low pay: the case of domestic workers

The self-employed are not the only workers in informal employment who often have to work very long hours. In fact, their hours are not typically as long as those of another group in the informal economy: domestic workers. Domestic workers are overwhelmingly female, and make up a large share of women's employment in many countries: for example, they account for 20 per cent of female employment in Latin America and the Caribbean (Chaney and Castro 1993, cited in Saboia 2002).

Domestic workers are in a rather unique situation because they work as employees of private households rather than of businesses: they are often treated as a special category under national labour laws with specific (less restrictive) rules on work hours and their personal relationships with host families are an essential component of their working conditions. Especially for domestic workers who live with their host families, this situation can make it difficult if not impossible to separate working time and personal time – a situation that can easily lead to excessively long hours of work. In Chile, for example, live-in domestic workers – virtually all of whom are women – averaged 59.3 hours per week (Echeverría 2002: 37).

A recent study of domestic workers in the Arab States (Esim and Smith 2004) sheds some new light on the working hours of domestic workers. Based on surveys of domestic migrant workers in Kuwait, the study found that (apart from part-time gardeners) hours of work are very long, *averaging* from 78 to 100 hours per week. For example, cooks worked an average of 88.4 hours per week, drivers 91 hours a week, security guards 99.7 hours per week and housemaids averaged 100 hours per week. A similar survey of household employers of these domestic workers found somewhat shorter but still long working hours: 66 hours a week for women and 60 per week for men, on average. In addition, overtime pay is typically not provided for these workers.

Source: Esim and Smith 2004: 51–52.

Lithuania and the Russian Federation. One major exception to this general pattern is the Czech Republic and, to a lesser extent, Estonia and Slovakia. These countries seem to be following the industrialized country pattern of self-employment, in which dominant proportions of self-employed workers – and particularly men – are working long hours (in line with the 'pull' theory).

The other major exceptions to the most prevalent pattern in the transition countries are Bulgaria and Hungary, both of which have high proportions of the self-employed whose reported working hours are 'unknown' (i.e. their working hours are not indicated at all).[16] This is an important issue in measuring working hours in the informal economy, as is illustrated by Figure 5.3 for the Republic of Moldova – a country which is not displayed in Table 5.5c due to the extraordinarily high proportion of self-employed workers (51.3 per cent) whose working hours are 'unknown' (not indicated). The case of the Republic of Moldova provides an illustrative example of the difference between usual working hours and actual working hours for informal economy workers; these differences arise from the fact that many of these workers say that they 'don't know' what their usual hours are. This result suggests that there may indeed be substantial variability in the working hours of a significant proportion of self-employed individuals.

Unlike the situation in both the developing countries and many of the industrialized countries, however, the pattern of short-hours self-employment in transition countries is *not* confined primarily to women. In fact, the figures for short-hours self-employment for men and women are of comparable magnitude in most of the countries presented in Table 5.5c (and particularly the Commonwealth of Independent States countries which responded to the ILO questionnaire); moreover, 30 per cent or more of all self-employed men are working less than 35 hours a week in the following countries: Albania, Armenia, Georgia, Lithuania and the Russian Federation.

The explanation for this puzzling phenomenon is not immediately apparent from the data presented in this table. However, one possible explanation appears to be the presence of 'extreme' age groups in the informal

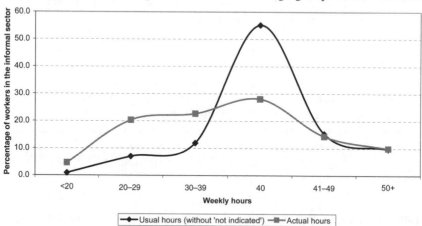

Figure 5.3 Usual versus actual working hours in the informal economy (the Republic of Moldova, 2003)

Note

The proportion of hours 'not indicated' in the informal economy was 45.7 per cent, compared with 15.3 per cent in the formal sector.

Source: ILO Bureau of Statistics 2004, Employment in the informal economy in the Republic of Moldova. Policy Integration Department Working Paper No. 41.

***Box 5.5* Work schedules in the informal economy: everything depends on the volume of work**

The working time country study report for Senegal includes an in-depth analysis of working hours and work schedules in the informal economy, based on interviews with informal economy workers. The study found that, on average, workers in informal employment work between eight and ten hours per day. However, there are some substantial differences in how these hours are organized in terms of work schedules. For example, commercial vendors and small-scale manufacturers (e.g. clothing, footwear, cosmetics, etc.) typically work from 9 am to 7:30 pm with a lunch break of 30–60 minutes between 2 and 5 pm. Auto mechanics work between 9 am and 6 pm with an hour for lunch between 2 and 3 pm. And fishermen may work either days (from 8 or 9 am to 5 pm), nights (from 7 pm to 5 or 6 am), or for extended periods at sea of 10 to 15 days, followed by a similar number of rest days. Some informal economy workers work much longer hours, however: taxi drivers, for example, regularly work 14–18 hours a day, from as early as 5 am until as late as midnight.

Another interesting point from the study concerns paid holidays and paid annual leave in the informal economy – or, rather, the lack of them. When asked about paid holidays and leave, informal workers often just smiled at the ridiculousness of the question. They said that time off means no income, which is something that they typically cannot afford, although many of them did indicate that they normally observe a few major religious holidays.

Perhaps the most important finding that emerges from the Senegal study, however, is that – according to the workers themselves – everything depends on the volume of work. For example, commercial vendors and mechanics in Senegal may extend their hours until 9 pm if the available work justifies it. They will also work on the traditional weekly rest day (i.e. Sunday) if an increase in work activities requires it, or, in the case of the vendors, during holiday periods when the volume of their customers typically increases substantially. In addition, women – particularly those working as commercial vendors – spoke of specific problems linked to being female and/or married, including having to return home at midday to prepare lunch or do housework; some preferred to divorce rather than attempt to continue to balance these competing demands. This finding is in line with other studies that consider working hours in the informal economy, such as Tipple (2006), who concludes, 'For production HBEs (home-based enterprises) ... the intensity of work is dependent on the volume of orders' (p. 175).

Source: Ndiaye 2004: 57–60.

economy in these countries. For instance, in the Russian Federation, the informal economy, particularly self-employment, includes substantial proportions of both youth aged 15–19 and older workers aged 60–72 years (Chetvernina *et al.* 2004). We have already seen (in Chapter 4) that these age groups tend to have shorter hours than prime-age groups, and the former do indeed have very short hours, between 22–23 and 24–25 hours, respectively (ibid.: 67). Moreover, the incentives for shorter hours in these age groups are particularly strong; while self-employment for these individuals is their primary employment, the income derived from their self-employment activities is, in fact, only a secondary source of income for them. In fact, these workers are also receiving income transfers in the form of either schooling assistance or old age/retirement/disability pensions, respectively; this situation is thus somewhat analogous to that of women with family responsibilities, in that there are temporal constraints on the number of hours that these individuals are available for paid work. In addition, it should be noted that those working short hours also include a substantial proportion of farm workers, who are more likely to have been 'pushed' into self-employment by a lack of employment alternatives in rural areas, and thus to be underemployed (ibid.).

5.7 Conclusions

This chapter has reviewed a few of the significant changes in the structure of the global economy, in order to understand their implications for working time. Regarding structural economic changes and their effects on working time, the chapter examined, first, work hours and work schedules in the expanding service sector (tertiarization) and, second, the situation regarding working time in the informal economy.

Working time in the service sector varies substantially across its component subsectors. In general, it is clear that average hours of work are particularly long in certain subsectors, most notably the wholesale and retail trade, hotels and restaurants, and transport, storage and communications. The security industry, with the longest legal hours of any industry, also has extraordinarily long actual hours of work as well. Likewise, both the governmental sector (i.e. public administration and defence, and compulsory social security) and particularly the education sector have relatively short hours. Finally, work schedules in the service sector indicate that, while shift work is quite common across all regions of the world, the proportion of workers working in shifts varies dramatically across countries and across industries.

This chapter also examined working time in the informal economy. Given that self-employment represents at least three-fifths of informal employment in developing countries, this chapter used data on the working hours of the self-employed as a proxy for working hours in the informal economy as a whole. The results of this analysis indicate that the self-employed in industrialized countries generally work very long hours, although substantial proportions of self-employed women in some of these countries work short hours, most likely as a strategy for balancing work and family.[17]

In contrast, the more common pattern of working hours for the self-employed in developing countries is a diversification of working hours, with a relatively flat distribution of hours that includes substantial proportions of workers working long hours (49 hours per week or more) and short hours (less than 35 hours per week). Gender appears to be a key variable affecting the working hours of the self-employed in developing countries, too. In general, self-employed men in developing countries were working long hours, although the proportions of self-employed men working short hours are *also* greater than those for their wage-earning counterparts, suggesting that this latter group of men is likely to be underemployed. By contrast, for self-employed women in developing countries, short hours are the rule; this suggests that many women are using self-employment as a means of obtaining reduced hours, in order to earn some money while simultaneously handling their family responsibilities.

Finally, the pattern of self-employment in transition countries appears somewhat different from that found in either the industrialized or developing countries. Although there are considerable variations, the most common pattern in these countries is high proportions of short-hours self-employment – which are comparably high for *both men and women*. It appears that the primary explanation for this phenomenon is that self-employment is concentrated among 'extreme' age groups – youth less than 20 and older workers over 60 – both of whom use short-hours self-employment as a secondary source of income to supplement social income transfers.

Having reviewed all of these trends and developments in the structure and dynamics of working hours in terms of regulation, actual practice and variations by different groups of workers and economic sectors, we need now to examine what policy issues have been discussed and debated in different countries. It is to these policy developments that we now turn in Chapter 6.

6 Working time issues in developing countries

6.1 Introduction

The opening chapters of this book reviewed the legal standards that limit working hours and the hours actually worked in countries across the world, highlighting the situation in developing countries. The subsequent chapters added detail to this broad picture by considering two of the forces shaping working hours in developing countries, tertiarization and informalization, and examining working time developments through the lenses of gender and age. This chapter adds to the preceding analysis by looking at the response to working time developments found in the social and economic policies of developing countries. In doing so, it attempts to highlight the broad themes of these policies and to explore the forces that underlie them and influence the likelihood of their success.

This chapter draws primarily on the series of country studies prepared for this book, and focuses on policy directions in the countries they cover. A review of additional literature has also been carried out on these and other countries, and is drawn on particularly where regional trends are reviewed. To complement these sources and provide more detail on legal measures, the chapter also includes information from the ILO's Database of Working Time Laws (see Chapter 2). Even relying on this range of sources, however, a definitive picture of trends in working time policy is not yet possible. Instead, this chapter attempts to identify and highlight any particularly interesting approaches and experiences, and to explore any striking similarities or differences among countries from different regions. It aims to offer some of the detail on national working time policies in countries beyond the industrialized world that is so often missing from debates on the impact of globalization on working hours.

To this end, Section 6.2 builds on the opening chapters by examining two factors that can undermine measures to prevent long hours: the need to work long hours in developing countries to compensate for low wages, and the reliance on overtime in preference to other methods of advancing productivity. It then turns to the more recent policy theme that accompanies the long-standing preoccupation with reducing hours, the quest for flexibility in working hours (Section 6.3); and considers the sometimes fraught relationship between working time arrangements, the harmonization of paid work and family life and gender inequality (Section 6.4). Section 6.5 questions whether working time policies strongly influence workplace practice, reviewing the factors that can weaken their impact, and includes a discussion of the plight of workers in the informal economy.

6.2 Reducing working hours

In outlining the global trends in legal hours limits, Chapter 2 highlighted a broad and persistent adherence to the initial goal of working time policy, the reduction of working hours. The following chapter, however, highlighted the extent of long hours, estimating that more than one in five workers across the world work for more than 48 hours a week. This section builds on these chapters by exploring two of the factors that fuel long hours and which therefore need to be addressed if initiatives to reduce working hours are to be successful: the influence of wages on working hours and the recourse to long hours to compensate for low hourly productivity.

6.2.1 Time or money: working time and wages

The need to give careful attention to the relationship between working time and wages has long been recognized as one of the guiding principles for the reduction of working hours.[1] The experience of developing and transition countries confirms this need, which is particularly acute in this context. Across these countries, for example, overtime payments often constitute a regular and substantial element of wage packages and are relied on to ensure a decent standard of living, as is clear in a number of the countries examined in depth in this volume, including China, the Czech Republic, the Republic of Korea and Mexico (Zeng *et al.* 2005; Berkovsky *et al.* 2002; Yoon 2001; Esponda 2001). Under these circumstances, resistance to initiatives towards reducing overtime work can be expected, and this is the case in many countries.

In Hungary, for example, many workers appear to be dissatisfied with the new stricter rules on overtime discussed in Chapter 2, and it is suggested that any trade union effort to enforce the new limits on both overtime and standby work would be likely to encounter resistance, given the widespread dependence on the associated wage supplements (Galasi 2002). This experience is reinforced by case studies from across the new EU Member States that demonstrate worker opposition to reductions in overtime due to its substantial contribution to their incomes (Vaughan-Whitehead, ed., 2005). Similarly, in Senegal, unions have strongly opposed proposals to compensate overtime with time-off rather than wage premiums (Ndiaye 2005).

In order to understand the complexity of the working hours and wage relationship, however, it is important to note that the pecuniary advantages of working long hours are often insubstantial when compared with normal hours. Mexico provides an illustrative example. Table 6.1 shows the average wage earnings of different groups of workers by their number of working hours. It also demonstrates how benefit entitlements vary depending on the number of working hours. Standard paid employees (wage earners working between 35–48 hours) earned less than employers but more than any other group of workers, with the sole exception of male pieceworkers who worked more than 48 hours. Focusing on variations within each group of workers, longer hours improve earnings considerably, except for wage earners, both male and female.[2] However, the earnings advantage associated with long hours must be compared with the substantial penalties involved with respect to benefit entitlements. As Table 6.1 shows, the likelihood of receiving various benefits, including bonuses and paid holidays, is considerably higher among those with standard working hours than among groups that work short and long hours. For instance, about 66.6 per cent of male standard-hours workers were entitled to paid holidays. However, the ratio is much

Table 6.1 Working hours, earnings and benefits (Mexico, 2000)

	Men			Women		
	<35 hours	*35–48 hours*	*>48 hours*	*<35 hours*	*35–48 hours*	*>48 hours*
Composition (%)	12.7	59.4	27.9	30.7	55.0	14.3
Monthly income						
Employers	3333	4300	4500	3612	4228	3500
Self-employed	1290	1667	2150	688	1290	1505
Wage earners	1806	2193	2150	1800	2021	1720
Pieceworkers	1290	2150	2580	516	1290	1505
Monthly income (wage earners = 100.0)						
Employers	152.0	196.1	205.2	178.7	209.2	173.2
Self-employed	58.8	76.0	98.0	34.0	63.8	74.5
Wage earners	82.4	100.0	98.0	89.1	100.0	85.1
Pieceworkers	58.8	98.0	117.6	25.5	63.8	74.5
Benefits (%)						
Bonus	10.1	65.6	24.3	21.2	68.2	10.6
Paid vacations	10.4	66.6	23.0	21.2	68.9	9.9
Profit sharing	5.4	72.2	22.4	8.8	78.9	12.3
IMSS[a]	7.1	67.6	25.3	13.3	74.4	12.3
ISSSTE[b]	27.5	58.7	13.8	44.0	52.2	3.8
Retirement saving system	9.8	67.4	22.8	20.5	70.0	9.5
Housing credit	10.7	68.2	21.2	21.6	70.4	8.0
Private health insurance	9.0	56.5	34.5	21.3	61.5	17.2

Source: Restructured from Esponda (2001).

Notes
a Instituto Mexicano del Seguro Social.
b Instituto de Seguridad y Servicios Sociales de Los Trabajadores del Estado.

lower for short-hours workers, at 10.4 per cent and for long-hour workers at 23.0 per cent. A similarly wide gap is also shown for female workers.

At the same time, and as hinted at earlier, low hourly pay can induce workers to work longer, and again there is some evidence of this phenomenon in countries across the world. A study in the Philippines, for example, has shown that low hourly pay and long working hours are significantly correlated, even concluding that 'long hours of work are a reasonably good indicator of low-hourly pay for time-rated wage and salary workers' (Mehran 2005). And in Viet Nam, where long hours are also widespread, overtime wages have also been found to form a significant proportion of wages, around 14 per cent of total wage income (ILO 2003c: table 15).

6.2.2 Working time, productivity and work organization

Working time policies have long been recognized as having a role in improving productivity. Indeed, this was a strand of the debate during the deliberations on the first international standard in 1919 (Murray 2001). More recently, it has formed a goal of measures to reduce hours in western Europe, perhaps most visibly in Germany (see further Bosch and Lehndorff 2001). In developing countries in particular, the relationship between working time and productivity is weak and increases in output are often fuelled by overtime work. In Mexico, for example, the productivity increases of recent years appear to have been caused primarily by long workdays rather than a more efficient use of working time (Esponda 2001). And with respect to Chile, Echeverría suggests that unproductive or very low performance 'face time' constitutes a significant element of long workdays and is the result of deficient work organization (Echeverría 2002).

When integrated with broader initiatives on skill development, the role that working time reductions can play in advancing productivity by, in part, encouraging changes in work organization, is often missing from the debate, even in industrialized countries. In developing countries, it appears to be particularly hard for this vision of hours reductions and the relationship between hours and productivity to take hold, especially in the absence of national measures to encourage it. In China, for example, Frenkel and Kuruvilla (2002) have reported an emphasis on numerical and wage flexibility that is infrequently accompanied by moves towards functional flexibility. And Vaughan-Whitehead has noted, with respect to Central and Eastern European countries, that private firms operating in very competitive environments too often fail to take measures to improve the quality of employment or make investments in the skills of their workforces, with the inevitable negative long-term consequences for productivity (Vaughan-Whitehead 2005).

Working time policies in some developing and transition countries, however, have recognized this aspect of working hours reductions, and initiatives have been taken towards rewarding higher productivity rather than long hours. In Malaysia in particular, increasing productivity appears to be widely viewed as essential to competitiveness. The tripartite National Labour Advisory Council has produced guidelines on introducing productivity-linked wages, a technique that appears to be slowly gaining acceptance (Nagaraj 2004). There is also a strong emphasis on functional flexibility, including through a human resource fund to which firms are required to contribute and from which they receive refunds on their investments in training (Frenkel and Kuruvilla 2002). In Senegal, too, the conclusion of a *Charte Nationale sur Le Dialogue Sociale* in 2002 was partly aimed at promoting productivity by strengthening social dialogue at the enterprise-level (Ndiaye 2005).

6.3 Working time flexibility

In industrialized countries, the emergence of flexibility in working hours as a tool for employers to adjust labour inputs or, more recently, a method for workers to better balance their jobs with other elements of their lives, has been well documented (see, for example, Golden and Figart 2000; Messenger, ed., 2004). The facilitation of working time flexibility and its impact on workers now widely accompanies the traditional themes in debates on working time policy and informs concrete measures. Chapter 5 has reviewed the extent of various forms of working time flexibility, focusing on the service sector. This section adds to that analysis by reviewing policies that promote the flexibilization of working time in developing countries and the broader issues that underlie them.

As discussed in Chapter 5, information on national- and firm-level policies on working time flexibility and the extent to which techniques for working time flexibility are used in practice is very limited. As a consequence, we draw here primarily on the national studies that were carried out for this report and the information on legal measures contained in the ILO's Database of Working Time Laws. The lack of research on this element of the trends in working time renders this section inevitably impressionistic, and it is premature to draw any firm conclusions about global or regional trends. However, by exploring developments in the limited number of countries on which this information is available, we offer a more in-depth picture than is usually available on policy directions regarding working time flexibility.

It is clear that in developing and transition economies, interest in working time flexibility, its benefits and risks, and the most effective ways to realize it, has emerged more recently than in industrialized countries. This interest is not uniform, and in some countries an awareness of the forms of working time flexibility and their implications is not widespread. In the Russian Federation, for example, flexibility in working hours does not yet appear to be the subject of surveys or academic discussions and is seldom on the agenda of policy debates (Chetvernina *et al.* 2004). The primary interest in flexible working time arrangements is on the part of managers; and even among them, it appears to be confined to large companies. And in China, although discussions about flexible employment patterns and working time have been taking place since the statutory hours limit was lowered to 40 hours in 1995, they appear to be largely limited to government and academic circles, and the issue is seldom raised by unions and employers (Zeng *et al.* 2005).

In a number of transition and developing countries, however, working time flexibility has taken centre stage in debates on employment and social policy. This is perhaps most prominent among the new Member States of the European Union,[3] which include two of the countries discussed in depth throughout this book, the Czech Republic and Hungary. Their entry into the EU entailed an obligation on these countries to coordinate their employment and social policies with those of the other Member States. As a consequence, all of the new members developed and periodically review national policies as part of the EU-wide employment policy coordination process, the European Employment Strategy (EES), and have taken steps to implement the EU-level legislation, including the Working Time Directive[4] and the Part-time Work Directive[5] (Tang and Cousins 2005). The promotion of flexibility is not, however, confined to the EU. In Jamaica, for example, it has been on the agenda since the mid-1990s. All the major social partner organizations have issued policy statements on the subject, and in 2001 the government issued a set of proposals in a *Green Paper on Proposals for the Introduction of Flexible Work Arrangements* (Taylor 2004).

Where interest in working time flexibility arises, the techniques that are being promoted and deployed mirror those that have been prominent in western countries over the last two decades: permitting weekly hours limits to be averaged over longer periods; allowing work to be performed more extensively during 'unsocial' hours, including during weekly rest periods; promoting and regulating part-time work and other 'non-standard' working time arrangements; and allowing workers access to arrangements that allow them to better reconcile their work and family lives. These techniques are examined in turn in the remainder of this section, which ends with a discussion of the extent to which these kinds of techniques are actually available.

6.3.1 Hours averaging

As mentioned in Chapter 5, among the primary techniques directed towards flexibility in working hours is to average weekly hours limits over a defined period, allowing work to be performed beyond this limit without resort to overtime pay in individual weeks of the reference period. Legal provisions that permit hours averaging are prominent in the laws of industrialized countries. Indeed, certain weekly limits are in themselves averages, including the 40-hour limit in the Dutch working time legislation, which is expressed as an average over a 13-week period. In other jurisdictions, hours averaging is of more restricted application, and often is permitted only through collective agreements.

This technique for facilitating flexibility in working time appears to be increasingly influential in legal instruments in a number of transition and developing countries. It is particularly prominent in Central and Eastern Europe, partly due to the influence of the EU Working Time Directive, which is well known for the range of deviations it permits from its 48-hour limit on total weekly hours. In Hungary, for example, the social partners can agree to introduce hours averaging, and it appears that the number of collective agreements containing an annual reference period have significantly increased in recent years (Vaughan-Whitehead, ed., 2005). Beyond the EU, the Russian legislation allows hours averaging where the conditions of production make it impossible to observe the weekly hours limit (Chetvernina *et al.* 2004).

Hours averaging is also permitted and has been deployed in other regions. In Brazil, it was introduced during the 1990s in the wake of trade deregulation, underpinned by a desire to cut costs to respond to foreign competition (Saboia 2002). And a recent change to Senegalese labour law permits hours averaging to be agreed by the social partners, although this development has encountered resistance from the trade unions, who favour overtime hours (Ndiaye 2005). Among Asian countries, in China, hours averaging is permitted in certain industries (including transportation, postal and telecommunications services, aviation and fisheries), although the legislation does not contain any guidance on the length of the reference period (Zeng *et al.* 2005). And in the Republic of Korea, two types of flexible working hours systems are permitted, the bi-weekly and monthly systems, which permit the weekly limit to be averaged over a two-week and a monthly period, respectively (Yoon 2001).

Where hours averaging is permitted, the concern arises that workers should be protected from being required to work very long hours during certain parts of a reference period. It also has the potential to result in work schedules that are subject to substantial or unpredictable variations and thereby conflict with a worker's family life or preferences on time allocation. Certain of the legislation in developing countries attempts to prevent these kinds of work schedules. Some specify procedural requirements for the adoption of hours averaging schemes. A number of laws, for example, require consultation with workers' representatives or a reference to the labour inspectorate. In the Republic of Korea, the use of the flexible working hours systems must be preceded by an agreement between employer and workers' representatives; and the Dominican Republic's weekly limit can be averaged only with the authorization of the relevant government authority. In contrast, in Singapore, individual employees and workers can agree that the 44-hour limit will be averaged over a two-week period.

Another central protective technique to avert long hours is to specify an absolute limit on the hours than can be worked in individual weeks of a reference period. Again, these kinds of protections are available in legal measures in some developing countries. The averaging of the 44-hour limit in Singapore, for example, is not permitted to generate working weeks of longer than 48 hours. And in the Republic of Korea, the bi-weekly system is subject to an absolute maximum of 48 hours and the monthly system to a 56-hour maximum.

6.3.2 Flexibilization and weekly rest periods

An area in which the social impact of the flexibilization of working time has been particularly prominent, and given rise to sometimes heated public debates, is where it infringes on weekly rest periods by permitting more extensive forms of work to be performed on these days. As we saw in Chapter 2, the designation of one or two days as a weekly rest period available in principle to all workers, which was discussed in that chapter as a method of limiting working hours, has also traditionally been aimed at preserving periods of time that are reserved for the entire community (Supiot 2001). As was noted, the weekly rest day is perhaps the most deeply rooted of the traditional working time protections, and almost all countries specify a minimum period of weekly rest. The vast majority of these require that it coincide with the customary rest day, whether this is a Friday or a Sunday.

In countries in which approaches towards the weekly rest period have been altered in recent years, two directions have been taken, towards either providing for a longer period of weekly rest or liberalizing the prohibition of work on rest days. In some regimes that have a working week of six days, the developments around weekly rest are in the direction of extending it to two days. In Malaysia, the adoption of a five-day working week is one of the priorities of the main trade union body, the Trades Union Congress (Nagaraj 2004). Although legislative change has not been forthcoming, some developments have taken place at firm-level, and a number of organizations that had previously operated a five-and-a-half or six-day working week have granted their staff alternate Saturdays as rest days. Most notably, civil servants are now entitled to two Saturdays off per month and the postal services and banks and finance companies have also adopted this arrangement. And in the Republic of Korea, where workers are entitled to a half-day on a Saturday, a bi-weekly/Saturday-off system has been incorporated in the legislation, which permits firms to average the weekly limit over a two-week period with both Saturday and Sunday designated as rest days (Yoon 2001).

The second approach being taken towards the weekly rest period is to liberalize rest-day work, albeit usually within a generally applicable limit. Work during the weekly rest day has always been permitted under national laws, in certain sectors or by certain categories of workers; for example, for urgent work, in the emergency services, in the public interest, or in tourism. The current direction, however, is towards extending the categories for which rest-day work is permitted. This is the case, for example, in a number of Central and Eastern European countries, and Sunday work appears to be rapidly expanding in this region, notably in the retail sector (Vaughan-Whitehead, ed., 2005). In Chile too, the introduction of work schedules in certain sectors that include Sunday as a compulsory workday, except on two Sundays of each month, attracted most of the attention in the debate around recent legislative reforms. Among the countries covered by this report, the most extreme example of a divergence from the traditional approach to weekly rest is found in Jamaica, where the 2001 *Green Paper on Proposals for the Introduction of Flexible Work Arrangements* included a proposal to treat all seven days as normal working days (Taylor 2004).

Where the question of altering laws that designate Sunday as a rest day has arisen, the debate has included contributions from religious groups. Amendments to the Labour Code in Hungary, for example, were highly controversial, and involved not only mass demonstrations by unions but also the intervention of the Catholic Church, which issued a statement declaring that Sundays and public holidays should be preserved as non-working days (Galasi 2002). In Chile too, representatives of the Catholic Church pointed to the negative effects of long workdays and Sunday work on families, and called for Sunday to be reserved as a day of rest (Echeverría 2002). And in Jamaica, a number of Christian denominations have been involved in the debate on Sunday work, including in consultative forums. They have voiced their support for flexible hours in principle, but opposed initiatives to treat Sundays, and Saturdays in the case of the Seventh Day Adventist Church, as a part of the working week (Taylor 2004).

6.3.3 Part-time work and other 'non-standard' working time arrangements

Part-time work is among the most prominent measures to be promoted and used in industrialized countries as a form of flexibility in working hours (see, for example, Fagan and O'Reilly, eds, 1998). As we saw in Chapter 1, in developing countries many individuals work short hours, of below 35 hours per week; however, as seen in Chapter 5, these workers tend to be concentrated in the informal economy. Jobs in the formal economy that have been consciously designed to involve regular part-time hours are much rarer. In the new EU Member States, for example, part-time work is limited, mainly involuntary, and taken up primarily by the retired, the disabled, young entrants to the labour market, and the unemployed, who receive social security payments but are in need of additional income (Vaughan-Whitehead, ed., 2005). The limited presence of part-time work in developing countries can be attributed primarily to its impact on workers' incomes, in that the relatively lower wages earned for working shorter hours are not adequate to support workers and their families (Tang and Cousins 2005; Vaughan-Whitehead 2005).

In some countries, however, the promotion of part-time work has become a central theme of employment and social policies. The role it has taken in a number of European countries, of encouraging under-represented groups, and, in particular, women, to enter the labour market is also present in some developing countries, including Malaysia and Chile, as will be discussed below in the context of the impact of working time arrangements on gender equality. The complementary approach of mandating equal treatment for part-time workers, however, appears to be much less pronounced in other regions, although it is beginning to be addressed in some countries. The policy suggestions on flexible work issued by the Jamaican government in 2001, for example, call for an increase in part-time jobs that are attached to benefits such as life and health insurance, sick leave and annual leave (Taylor 2004).

Night work and shift work do not appear to be central to the current policy debates around working time in developing countries. They do, however, form part of flexibility policies in certain countries. One example is Hungary, where recent amendments to the Labour Code, tailored towards promoting working time flexibility, entailed a reduction in the statutory wage supplement required for night work (Galasi 2002). There are also signs, in some countries, of a degree of reluctance to work in shifts and at night, including for work–family reasons. Case studies conducted in the new EU Member States, for example, have found workers opposing overtime reductions not only because of the loss of income, but also because of the tendency for overtime to be replaced with shift work, including night shifts (Vaughan-Whitehead, ed., 2005).

Flexi-time schemes, which permit workers a degree of control over their hours provided they work certain specified 'core' hours each day, and the more sophisticated time-banking schemes, are also beginning to garner interest in developing countries, at least at the policy level (see Chapter 4 for the impact of those types of flexibility on family life). In some countries, for example, labour laws have been amended to facilitate and regulate flexi-time work. In the Russian Federation, the law permits these schemes where there is agreement with the employer; the normal schedule is not possible or effective; and where they would ensure a more effective use of time and improve efficiency. The Russian legislation also specifically permits the use of flexi-time by women with children and includes an equal treatment provision, which entitles workers on flexi-time schemes to the same conditions for the rating and remuneration of work, benefits and other employment rights as other workers. In the Republic of Korea, too, flexi-time is promoted by the Labour Standards Act, in which it is termed a 'discretionary time system'. Employers are required to agree with workers' representatives on the contents of the schemes, including the length of the accounting period and the core and flexible hours. In Jamaica, the public sector regulations were recently amended to introduce flexi-time for civil servants (Taylor 2004). And in Senegal, recent 'flexibility' amendments to the Labour Code included the introduction of a variant of flexi-time known as 'individualized hours' (Ndiaye 2005).

Flexi-time schemes do not appear to be widely used in practice in transition and developing countries, although there are signs of their presence in some. The national study on Brazil describes agreements that experiment with hours-banking, including a pioneering agreement between Scandia do Brasil Ltd and the Sao Bernardo do Camp Metalworkers Union, concluded in May 1996 (Saboia 2002). Moreover, research conducted for the study in Jamaica demonstrates an interest in flexi-time schemes among individual workers. More than 80 per cent of employees in the small-scale survey expressed an interest in schemes that would permit them to vary the start and end of their working days (Taylor 2004).

The other forms of flexible working time arrangements that have gained prominence in industrialized countries do not appear to be as well developed in developing and transition countries or to play a major role in policy debates or legal reforms. An exception is the interest in compressed working weeks that has emerged in the Czech Republic, where some trade unions have called for the introduction of four-day working weeks comprised of nine- or ten-hour days (Berkovsky *et al.* 2002). And in Hungary, amendments to the Labour Code in 2001 permitted employers to require on-call work, while stipulating a number of limitations on it, including that workers have a right to one week's notice of when they will be required to work and that such work be subject to daily and weekly hours limits (Galasi 2002).

6.3.4 Worker-oriented flexibility

The policy goals most frequently called on in developing countries to justify hours averaging and other flexibility measures are those well rehearsed in the OECD countries, of advancing productivity and competitiveness and promoting employment. And again, as in industrialized countries, the primary support for moves towards working time flexibility has come from employers, and the main forms of flexibility involved have been the types that they tend to favour. In both the Republic of Korea and Senegal, for example, it was employers who initiated demands for the kinds of flexibility ultimately embodied in the legislation (Yoon 2001; Ndiaye 2005). The response of workers' organizations to the changes being proposed has often been hostile or lukewarm. In the Republic of Korea, the introduction of hours averaging schemes was opposed by the trade unions, who feared they would be open to abuse and could have negative health and safety impacts (Yoon 2001). In the Russian Federation, the federal trade unions have been negative about working time flexibility, primarily due to concerns about its impact on wages (Chetvernina *et al.* 2004). However, the approach of the Russian unions appears to be slowly changing, and their more recent demands are towards a firm regulation of flexible working hours coupled with an extended role for collective bargaining.

Although the primary stress is on the employer-side benefits of working time flexibility, the vision of flexibility as a benefit to both workers and employers is present in a limited number of developing countries. Again, this vision appears to be most widespread in Central and Eastern Europe, mainly due to the influence of the EU. In the Czech Republic, the National Action Plans submitted as part of the EES support flexible forms of employment and working time arrangements as balancing the needs of employers and workers (Berkovsky *et al.* 2002). This goal has also formed part of government policy in Senegal, where the ability of workers to adapt their work schedules to their personal lives was included among the policy goals of recent legislative reforms (Ndiaye 2005).

Individual choice over working time arrangements is also reflected in legislative measures in some countries. A right to refuse to work overtime is available to pregnant workers in a number of laws. Consent to perform overtime is required in the Russian Federation from mothers of children younger than three. Other groups subject to limitations on overtime work include disabled workers, whose consent is required in Lithuania; and students, who have the same protection in Bulgaria. In the Russian Federation, overtime is permitted only with the consent of both individual workers and their representatives. And in Jamaica, the government's 2001 proposals on working time, the *Green Paper on Proposals for the Introduction of Flexible Work Arrangements*, includes a proposal that overtime be made voluntary, as a way of 'protecting employees from this loss of power over their daily schedules' (Taylor 2004). Similar 'individual choice' rights can apply to work on weekly rest days. In a number of countries, for example, pregnant workers have to give consent in order to work on the rest day. These entitlements also extend to mothers for a specified period after childbirth in Latvia. And in Lithuania, consent to rest day work is required from workers who are raising a child of younger than 14 years or a disabled child of up to 16 years.

6.3.5 The extent of flexible working time arrangements

Despite these initiatives in policy documents and legislation to facilitate and promote working time flexibility, the extent to which these measures are deployed in practice appears to be limited. Berkovsky *et al.* point out, for example, that although Czech policy documents refer to flexibility, the issue has not garnered widespread attention and there have been no significant discussions between the social partners and the government, nor any legal changes (Berkovsky *et al.* 2002). In Jamaica too, despite intermittently vigorous policy discussions, legal change has not so far been forthcoming (Taylor 2004). And in Malaysia, interviews with employer and worker representatives found them to agree that working time arrangements are not significantly changing (Nagaraj 2004).

A central factor in the limited use of these forms of working time flexibility in developing and transition countries would appear to be the widespread availability of a range of alternative options, in particular overtime and informal work. In Central and Eastern Europe, for example, flexibility has often been found to be achieved by either creating informal jobs or working long hours (Chetvernina *et al.* 2004; Tang and Cousins 2005; Vaughan-Whitehead, ed., 2005). And in the Republic of Korea, although flexible arrangements are increasingly used, employers can also resort to various types of non-standard work and make frequent and extensive recourse to overtime, although the impact of the recent reduction in the statutory weekly hours has yet to be felt (Yoon 2001).

With regard to hours averaging, the extent to which this technique is actually being used is difficult to track, given the current state of the research. However, a number of the national reports prepared for this study suggest that it is not widespread. The Czech Republic's annualized hours scheme appears to be confined mainly to the agricultural and construction sectors (Berkovsky *et al.* 2002). And in the Republic of Korea, the deployment of hours averaging provisions has been lower than was initially hoped: only 13.4 per cent of enterprises have adopted the bi-weekly scheme and just 1.9 per cent use the monthly system (Yoon 2001). Moreover, as discussed in the previous section, part-time work is not extensive in the formal economy, mainly due to low wages.

Partly too, the adherence to traditional ways of organizing working time may result from low levels of awareness and knowledge of the various forms of flexibility that exist. In a number of countries, there seems to be a widespread lack of awareness and even confusion about the nature of flexible working time and the kinds of schedules it entails. Interviews conducted with Malaysian employers' organizations and unions, for example, have indicated considerable differences in their understanding of the term 'flexible work' (Nagaraj 2004). And this may also be true of individual workers. In Jamaica, for example, just over half the workers interviewed for this report confessed that they had no knowledge of flexible working time arrangements (Taylor 2004).

6.4 Work–family and gender equality

An aspect of working time arrangements that has come to be recognized in the working time policies of industrialized countries during the latter part of the last century is that they influence the ease with which workers can balance their jobs and family lives, and thus can be crafted to allow workers to better realize this balance (see, for example, Fagan 2004). The need to assist developing country workers to care for their children and other family members is equally compelling. Indeed, it is becoming ever more urgent in light of the trend, outlined in Chapter 4, towards increasing numbers of women entering the paid labour market. Moreover, in the countries that are at the centre of the HIV/AIDS pandemic, care giving for the ill and dying is a responsibility taken on by many workers, many of whom combine their paid work with caring not only for their immediate family, but also sick members of their extended family, friends, and the orphaned children of relatives (Heymann 2005).

The absence of work–family policies, in combination with a strict gender-based domestic division of labour, prevents women from participating in the formal economy, channelling them into unpaid work in the household and/ or into the informal economy. In the Republic of Korea, for example, long working hours are associated with low female participation rates, squeezing women out of the labour market into full-time caregiving (Lee 2003). Similarly, the rapid drop in women's employment rates in some Central and Eastern European countries has been attributed in part to the removal of work–family supports from many workplaces during the transition period (Vaughan-Whitehead 2005). In contrast, in Slovenia, where a high level of accessible childcare provision survived the communist era, only 12 per cent of mothers are full-time caregivers (Tang and Cousins 2005).

These kinds of concerns are only beginning to be addressed in developing countries. In some, interest is been shown in the kinds of measures available in industrialized countries, including initiatives that allow working time arrangements to play a role in facilitating work–family balance, by allowing workers to give birth to children and then return to work, breastfeed, care for their children in the early months of their lives and beyond, and care for other family members. Measures that have been tied to work–family reconciliation in industrialized countries, such as flexi-time schemes, breastfeeding breaks and family emergency leave, appear not to be widespread. For example, despite the critical role of breastfeeding in preventing disease in infants, in a set of small-scale surveys in 180 countries, Heymann found that many women are unable to breastfeed for extended periods, in part due to a lack of flexibility in their working hours (Heymann 2005).

The role ascribed to part-time work in a number of European countries, of facilitating women's entry into the labour market by allowing them to combine paid and care work, is a more prominent policy measure being pursued in some developing countries. In Malaysia, for example, concerns have been raised that the labour supply may function as a constraint on growth (Nagaraj 2004). Traditionally, labour shortages in Malaysia have been addressed by importing overseas labour. In recent years, however, attempts have been made to identify ways of increasing women's labour force participation, in an attempt to recruit the substantial proportion of women currently outside of the labour force. The government's recent five-year plan, the *Eighth Malaysian Plan*, confirms its commitment to increasing the participation of women, although there have so far been no legislative developments on part-time work. In Hungary too, part-time work has been promoted by the government for the same reason (Galasi 2002); and a similar policy approach is being pursued in Chile, to increase the employment of both women and young people (Echeverría 2002).

These kinds of policies may be having an impact in some sectors. In Central and Eastern Europe, for example, although flexibility in working hours is limited, there are signs that women are working fewer hours, and managing to more successfully combine work and family, in the public sector and in certain activities in the tertiary sector (Vaughan-Whitehead 2005). In many developing countries, however, as was discussed in the previous section, part-time work is not widely available and is unrealistic, since it would substantially reduce household incomes. A further concern that threads through policies in employment that address part-time work is that there is often an association between part-time jobs, lower wages and benefits, and other poor terms and conditions of employment. In developing countries, empirical evidence of the association of part-time work with lower hourly wages, access to fringe benefits and social insurance, and employment protection is not widely available (Lee and Wood 2007). However, there is some evidence that the same pattern is present in developing countries. In the Republic of Korea, for example, part-timers are disadvantaged with respect to promotion and career development, and their wages appear to be less than half of the hourly wages of full-time workers (Lee 2003). However, ensuring high-quality part-time work, such as by mandating a right for part-timers to be treated comparably with full-time workers, does not appear to be widely contemplated in developing countries. One exception is Jamaica, where, as mentioned in Section 6.3.3, the government has called for part-time jobs to be created that extend benefits to the workers involved (Taylor 2004).

6.5 Policy and practice: enforcement, exclusion and the informal economy

As Chapter 3 has highlighted, one of the primary questions about working time policies in developing and transition countries is the extent to which they influence workplace practices. This is a particularly resonant issue where these policies are implemented in the form of legal rights for individual workers. In exploring this relationship, Chapter 3 drew on the notion of an 'observance rate' to assess the influence of the weekly hours limits contained in working time legislation. It found that a significant proportion of employees in many countries work beyond the applicable weekly hours limits, in some cases exceeding 40 per cent of the workforce (see also Lee and McCann 2007).

This research suggests that a major challenge for the effectiveness of working time policies is to find ways to ensure that legal measures are observed in practice. Moreover, this is a problem that can be assumed to be of broader import than the standards on weekly hours, and it appears from the national studies carried out for this report that it is relevant to other legal measures. Legislated rights to additional payments for overtime work, for example, appear to be frequently ignored. Unpaid overtime is widespread in Hungary, the Czech Republic and also in the Russian Federation, where as many as one-third or one-half of workers do not receive overtime compensation (Galasi 2002; Berkovsky *et al.* 2002; Chetvernina *et al.* 2004). In China too, the enterprise and employee surveys carried out for this report found that overtime premiums were not being paid to around half of employees who worked overtime on weekdays and almost one-third of those who worked overtime on holidays (Zeng *et al.* 2005). Moreover, a number of enterprises were found to offer alternative forms of compensation, not envisaged in the legislation, such as shift exchanges, changes in shift rotation and other 'home-made' rewards. In contrast, however, the surveys conducted in Senegal suggest that overtime premiums are usually paid (Ndiaye 2004).

Provisions that require overtime work to be voluntary also appear to be widely breached in some countries. In Chile, for example, where overtime should be worked only with the agreement of the employee, it appears that around 10 per cent of companies require it without prior agreement (Echeverría 2002). In the Republic of Korea, too, there is some evidence of employers exerting considerable pressure on their employees to work beyond normal hours (Yoon 2001). And the rules prohibiting work on weekly rest days and holidays appear to be widely flouted in Jamaica, as are those prohibiting women working extended workdays or at night (Taylor 2004). The degree of observance appears to vary, however, depending on the size of firms and the presence of unions. In the Czech Republic, for example, deviations from the law appear to be particularly likely in small private enterprises without a union presence and in Hungary, in small- and medium-sized firms and larger non-unionized establishments (Berkovsky *et al.* 2002; Galasi 2002).

The primary reasons for the deviance from these and other working time standards in individual countries are difficult to determine and substantial research remains to be done. However, it is clear that a range of factors can play a role. These include the strength of the enforcement of the law, the degree of awareness of the legal rights, the deviations from the principal norms that are permitted by the legal measures, and the extent and treatment of informal sector work. The national studies drawn on for this book offer a starting point on some of this kind of detail. Weak enforcement, for example, is recognized as contributing towards the disregard for statutory standards in both the Russian Federation and the Republic of Korea, and the limited capacity of the labour inspectorate has been highlighted in Senegal (Chetvernina *et al.* 2004; Yoon 2001; Ndiaye 2005).

A lack of legal literacy and complex legal texts may also be a factor. In Hungary, the Labour Code is claimed to be widely incomprehensible to the general public; and the experience in China suggests that the implementation of the overtime rules is hindered by a poor understanding of the law on the part of employers (Galasi 2002; Zeng *et al.* 2005). Further, non-observance of working time laws may also be partly attributable to the broader culture towards compliance with labour legislation. Disregard for the law in the Russian Federation, for example, which appears to have taken root during the period of transition from the Soviet model, is at a level that has been characterized as 'legal nihilism' (Chetvernina 2004). In the Republic of Korea, a recent survey found that a substantial proportion of workers believe they should undertake overtime if required, whether or not overtime payments are made; and among white-collar and professional workers in particular, long hours are highly valued as an indication of commitment to their employers (see Lee 2003).

Another significant issue for the effectiveness of all employment rights, including those related to working time, is the scope of the relevant legislation, and, in particular, the extent to which certain groups of workers are excluded from its coverage or consigned to lower levels of protection. With regard to exclusions embodied in working time legislation, the technique of exempting managers from hours limits, familiar from industrialized countries, is also common in legislation in other regions. More prevalent in the laws of transition and developing countries, however, is the treatment of workers engaged in 'intermittent work', characterized as involving substantial periods of inactivity or requiring no more than the worker's presence at the workplace. These workers are often subject to laxer hours limits (see further McCann 2006). And security guards and domestic workers are singled out to work longer hours in a number of countries, not only through intermittent work exceptions but also by way of specific exclusions. It is therefore significant that they are often found to work very long hours, a point highlighted in Chapter 5. In contrast, in Chile progress has been made towards addressing the exclusion of intermittent work, which was not previously subject to the statutory hours limits and is now covered by it, with some exceptions (Echeverría 2002).

In contrast to the exceptions specified in the legislation, disguised employment represents an attempt to entirely evade the statutory regime by designating workers as independent service-providers, rather than employees. This technique seems to be widely used in transition and developing countries, where there is evidence that workers are often hired under civil or commercial contracts, despite working in accordance with the legal definitions of employment (Vaughan-Whitehead 2005). These workers can remain in the same job while shifting between contracts or conclude an additional commercial contract to carry out a different activity from that performed under the contract of employment. Although small-firm exceptions seem to be more prominent in other areas of labour law, a prominent exception is the Korean legislation, which exempts firms of fewer than five workers from hours limits (Lee and Wood 2007).

Finally, workers in the informal economy who are not genuinely self-employed will be covered by the labour law regimes of most countries. They are, however, unlikely to see their rights enforced by government agencies or the courts. Yet, as we saw in Chapter 5, the informal economies of many developing countries account for a vast number of workers, and their hours can be very long. The challenge for working time policy, then, is to improve the conditions of these workers, including their working hours, either through ensuring the fulfilment of their legal rights, through formalization, or techniques that incorporate both. Despite advances in measures to extend social protection to informal sector workers, however, there appears to be little evidence so far of initiatives specifically directed towards improving working hours (Fenwick *et al.* 2006). However, a number of suggestions as to how this can be done are beginning to be debated in the labour law literature, and these are considered in the following chapter.

6.6 Conclusions

Chapter 2 revealed that, over the last decade, developing and transition countries have tended either to persevere with existing legal standards that limit normal weekly working hours or to take steps to reduce them. Chapter 3, however, confirmed that, despite these measures, the working hours of many individuals remain worryingly high. The present chapter explored two of the reasons for long hours in developing countries, highlighting, first, that they are often necessary for workers to earn a decent wage and, second, that they can function as a substitute for other techniques aimed at advancing productivity.

The chapter then turned to a more recent objective of working time policy, that of ensuring flexibility in working hours, which it revealed to be prominent in a number of countries, although often more in rhetoric than reality. It appears that, in many countries, these 'formal' forms of flexibility are not highly influential on workplace practices due to the availability of backdoor methods, such as a reliance on overtime or informal employment. Moreover, employee-oriented forms of flexibility are not as prominent as those traditionally favoured by employers. Part-time work is being promoted in some countries, including as a work–family measure, but remains relatively rare, given the low wage levels in developing countries. Moreover, data on working conditions in part-time jobs are underdeveloped, as are measures to ensure their quality.

Finally, the factors that contribute towards the divergence between legal measures on working time and actual working time arrangements were reviewed, an issue that will be returned to in the next chapter.

7 Summary and implications for policy

The preceding chapters of this book have reviewed working time around the world from a variety of perspectives: from regulatory frameworks and national policies on working time to trends in actual working hours, and from the consequences of tertiarization and informalization on working hours to the specific experiences of different groups of workers, such as those workers with family responsibilities. This final chapter will begin by summarizing the main findings. It will then turn to a discussion of the implications of those findings for working time policies in developing and transition countries, based on the 'decent working time' policy framework originally developed in our earlier study on working time in industrialized countries (Messenger, ed., 2004). Because of the large 'gaps' in what is known about working hours and working time arrangements in these countries, this policy discussion will also suggest a number of areas for future research. Finally, it will offer some concluding remarks regarding the way forward towards decent working time around the world.

7.1 Summary of main findings

This first section of this concluding chapter summarizes the main findings from each of the earlier chapters of our study. Chapter 2 opened by examining one of the central areas of working time policy, the limitation of working hours. It focused on developments in the legal standards in this area, with the aim of assessing their development over the years in which fears about economic globalization and its impact on working conditions, including working time, have emerged. The chapter first reviewed the significance of the two primary standards for weekly hours limits, the 40-hour and 48-hour weeks, focusing on their presence in the international standards. It then drew on legal research carried out by the ILO over the last 50 years and a current research project, documenting and comparing the working time laws that do exist, that is being carried out by the ILO's Conditions of Work and Employment Programme to examine developments in weekly hours and their present status. A convergence of weekly hours limits can be identified across the world, moving towards a broad consensus that the 40-hour week is the appropriate level for weekly hours. Substantial regional differences are apparent, however, most notably the presence of long hours limits in Latin America and uneven progress in reducing hours in Asia and the Pacific. Chapter 2 concluded that any 'race to the bottom' in legal standards is not apparent, but noted that it is necessary to compare the legal standards with actual working hours for a more reliable picture of their influence.

Following the review of regulatory frameworks for working time, we examined actual working hours from a global perspective in Chapter 3. First, we noted that the history of working hours in industrialized countries indicated that the developments are very unequal, thus making it almost impossible to identify a general pattern. Second, from a comparative perspective, not much change appears to have occurred in the gaps between industrialized and developing countries in terms of average working hours in the manufacturing sector. However, this analysis does not explain much of the reality of working time in both groups of countries, as working hours tend to be diverse among individual workers: across these countries, some individuals are working very long hours while others are working short hours. In some cases, this leads to a situation where no 'standard hours' exist in practice. In Chapter 3, as a way of demonstrating where we stand now with regard to the century-long principle of a 48-hour working week, we estimated that about 22 per cent of workers globally are working more than 48 hours per week. Finally, considering that legal standards may not be well implemented in practice, we calculated 'observance rates' to assess the influence of the weekly working hours standards in practice, and found it to be below 50 per cent in some countries. Based on this finding, an 'effective working-hour regulation' index was established to capture both the *de jure* and the *de facto* aspects of working time law: the content of the legislation, and its influence on workplace practices. The result suggests that great caution should be exercised when applying existing labour regulation indicators that do not consider the *de facto* aspects of such regulation (e.g. the World Bank's Rigidity of Employment Index).

Chapter 4 reviewed a few of the significant changes in the dynamics of the global workforce, considering two key demographic factors that have important implications for working time – gender and age. First, gender is clearly a crucial factor differentiating working hours among workers. In particular, even though women are increasingly engaged in the paid workforce, their temporal availability for paid work appears to be significantly constrained by the time that they need to devote to their household/domestic responsibilities. Regarding the distribution of working hours, we see two distinct gender-based patterns. For men, there is a pattern of long hours working (49 hours per week or more) in many countries, although the proportion of employees affected varies quite substantially across countries. For women, we see a working time pattern that is essentially the reverse of that of men: high proportions of female employees who are working part-time hours that are, moreover, dramatically higher than the comparable proportions of male employees working part-time hours. The end result is that, despite women's increased participation in the paid workforce, there is a clear 'gender gap' in working hours in all regions of the world. Age, on the other hand, appears to be considerably less powerful but nonetheless important as a factor in shaping working hours. The very limited data available on working hours by age group in developing and transition countries suggest that hours of paid work tend to be slightly shorter for both younger and retirement-age workers than for prime-age workers. Nevertheless, the variability in working hours by age group is actually quite modest; it is only for the oldest age group – those workers 65 years or older – that there is a substantial reduction in their working hours, primarily in the form of a higher incidence of short-hours working.

Chapter 5 reviewed two significant aspects of the structure of the global economy and their implications for working time: first, hours of work and work schedules in the expanding service sector – often referred to as 'tertiarization' – and second, what is known about working hours in the informal economy. The results of this analysis show that average hours of work are particularly long in certain service subsectors, notably the wholesale and retail trade; hotels and restaurants; and transport, storage and communications. Likewise, both the governmental sector and particularly the education sector have relatively short hours. Finally, work schedules in the service sector indicate that shift work is quite common across all regions of the world, and that night and weekend work are often an integral part of such shift systems. In addition, Chapter 5 also examined working time in the informal economy, focusing primarily on self-employment – which represents at least three-fifths of informal employment in developing countries. The results indicate that dominant proportions of the self-employed in industrialized countries work very long hours; however, substantial proportions of self-employed women in some of these countries work short hours – most likely as a strategy for balancing their work and family responsibilities.[1] In contrast, the common pattern for the self-employed in developing countries is a diversification of working hours, with a relatively flat distribution of hours that includes substantial proportions of workers working very long hours (49 hours per week or more) and short hours (less than 35 hours per week). Gender appears to be a key variable affecting the working hours of the self-employed in developing countries, too. A higher proportion of self-employed men than wage-earning men in those developing countries responding to the survey are working long hours; yet, the proportions of self-employed men working short hours are also greater, suggesting that these men are more likely to be underemployed as well. For self-employed women in developing countries, short hours are clearly the rule, which suggests the possibility that many women are using self-employment as a means of obtaining part-time, or at least reduced, hours, in order to earn some money while handling their family responsibilities. Finally, while the pattern of self-employment in transition countries is quite diverse, the most common pattern is short hours for both men and women. The most likely explanation is the fact that self-employment is concentrated among 'extreme' age groups – youth under 20 years old and older workers over 60 years – both of whom use short-hours self-employment as a secondary source of income.

Chapter 6 outlined current policy directions on working time in developing countries, building on Chapters 4 and 5 by discussing the policy responses to a number of the trends they highlighted. The focus was on the broad themes that underlie the policy measures and the chapter also highlighted some of the deeper issues that influence their success. In reviewing the continuing trend towards preventing long hours, for example, two factors that can undermine attempts to reduce hours were explored: workers' need to work long hours to ensure that they have adequate earnings; and the widespread recourse by employers to overtime to attempt to increase productivity, rather than changing work organization or investing in training. The chapter explored in some detail the trend towards the promotion of working time flexibility in policy documents, but pointed out that, given the alternatives of long hours and informal work, these flexibility measures do not appear to be much used in practice. It also noted that working part-time is not a realistic option for most workers in these countries due to its impact on household income. Part-time work was also discussed as a measure that is beginning to be considered in developing countries to advance work–family reconciliation, and some questions were raised about its impact on gender equality. Finally, Chapter 6 noted that working time policies, and individual legal rights in particular, often have limited influence on actual working hours in developing economies, and singled out some of the reasons for this divergence between policy and practice.

7.2 Implications for policy in developing and transition countries

7.2.1 *Towards decent working time*

Our first volume on working time in industrialized countries (Messenger, ed., 2004) developed a broad framework for working time policies that was grounded in exploring the implications of the International Labour Organization's decent work agenda in the area of working time. Its conclusion (Anxo *et al.* 2004) was that decent working time arrangements need to fulfil five inter-connected criteria, in that they should:

- preserve health and safety;
- be 'family friendly';
- promote gender equality;
- enhance productivity; and
- facilitate worker choice and influence over working hours.

In this chapter, this framework is deployed in considering how these five dimensions of 'decent working time' are and can be further reflected in countries beyond the industrialized world.

A few preliminary points should be made. First, it should be stressed that, as the preceding chapters have conveyed, working hours is not a subject on which interest, firm-level change or state policies are confined to advanced economies. The vast majority of countries across all regions have demonstrated a concern that working hours be limited by enacting legal measures to this effect. And over the last few decades, governments and the social partners in developing and transition countries have devoted attention to the more recent approaches towards working time, including further hours reductions, flexibilization in favour of employers and, to a lesser extent, workers, as well as the promotion of part-time work. However, these policy measures are not yet as well developed as in industrialized countries, and it is our suggestion that a familiarity with the experience of these countries, and of European countries in particular, would be useful to policy actors in other regions. This experience not only offers a range of models and options for developing and transition countries to draw on, but can also alert them to some of the pitfalls that can be encountered.

It must also be stressed at the outset that research on actual working hours and policies in developing countries is very limited and that many issues have not yet been explored. As a result, it is not possible to offer the kind of detailed policy prescriptions that can be made for industrialized countries. Instead, although a number of specific measures are highlighted, our suggestions inevitably tend to be in the form of general principles that should be taken into account towards advancing decent working hours. Indeed, one of our primary suggestions is that more in-depth research on working hours in developing and transition economies must be conducted. Some important working time issues for future research in these countries include the following: tracking developments in actual hours; analysing policies and their potential impact; assessing the influence of legal norms; identifying workers' needs and preferences and the extent to which they are being realized; conducting case studies on innovative firm-level practices and examining their impact on both enterprise productivity and the well-being of workers and their families; and assessing the role of working hours in relation to gender equality.

Moreover, the existence of large informal economies in these countries, combined with a lack of available data on working hours in informal employment, has meant that the patterns of working hours have been at best only poorly understood for a large proportion of the world's workers. The employment relationship is often the 'pivot' on which working hours turn. This can be seen from the diverse and relatively flat (and unstable) distribution of working hours among the self-employed in developing countries, which stands in marked contrast to that of formal employees, for whom the dominant pattern in developing countries is one of standard to long hours working. Therefore, it will be important for future research to investigate working hours by employment status in these countries in much greater depth, particularly regarding the informal economy.

Finally, in attempting to develop decent working time arrangements, it is vital also to look beyond measures targeted directly at working hours. Most obviously, given the relationship between poverty and long hours across developing countries, wage policies are central to the success of initiatives to reduce excessively long working hours, and are discussed in this context in the following section. It is also evident from the remainder of this chapter that cutting across all of the dimensions that we suggest for working time policies is the need for continuing efforts to build and strengthen the institutions and mechanisms which can ensure that whatever policies are put in place are effective. This calls, then, for improvements in labour administration, courts and tribunals, and efforts towards developing strong and effective social dialogue mechanisms, not only to ensure that workers' needs and preferences can be identified, heard and taken into account, but also to allow employers and workers to develop the level of cooperation needed to craft measures that both protect workers and advance firms' productivity.

7.2.2 Healthy working time

Preserving workers' health and workplace safety is the most basic of the goals that underlie working time policies, and has from the outset been one of the central objectives of measures to address long hours. Indeed, weekly hours limits can be seen as the primary response to the caution in the health and safety literature against regular work beyond 50 hours a week, when in the form of either a 48-hour limit coupled with tight restrictions on overtime work or a lower limit (see, for example, Spurgeon 2003; Dembe *et al.* 2005). As we saw in Chapter 2, significant progress was made across the world in the enactment of statutory hours limits during the last century. As a result, the majority of countries now have statutory limits below 48 hours, and a 40-hour week is in place in around half of them.

However, as we saw in Chapter 3, the more extensive information on developing countries made available through the recent ILO data-collection exercise on the distribution of working hours has confirmed that deviations from weekly hours limits are widespread in many countries, and that they can be associated with very long hours. A compelling need, then, is to assess the influence of these limits in practice, and therefore the strength of the regulatory regimes in which they are found. Progress has been made towards systematizing and comparing these kinds of data, some of which were presented in the opening chapters of this report. Perhaps the most significant finding is that intervention in the form of regulation is needed to reduce hours: it cannot simply be assumed that hours reductions will be an inevitable by-product of economic growth. Moreover, in a number of industrialized countries, most notably Denmark, it has been possible to regulate working hours through collective bargaining, an achievement attributable to a highly sophisticated regulatory regime that involves a substantial degree of coordination between the social partners at the national level (Anxo and O'Reilly 2000; Lee 2004). In transition and developing economies, however, although efforts to facilitate bargaining are essential, as long as collective mechanisms remain poorly developed, statutory standards will continue to be of primary significance.

To this end, research is needed on the precise reasons for the level of observance of the statutory standards in individual countries: the particular mix of the range of relevant factors that determine whether they will be broadly observed or widely ignored, including the extent of overtime work, levels of enforcement or awareness of the law, union density, the coverage of the legislation, wage rates, etc. Further research is also essential to identify the factors which make working time laws and policies that address these issues more effective in certain countries than in others (even among countries with similar income levels). Also, research regarding the industrial relations frameworks in developing and transition countries (where such frameworks exist), and their relationship to working time patterns, would be helpful for a broader understanding of the forces shaping working hours in these countries. This research could include, for example, a review of the role of multi-national corporations (MNCs) and corporate social responsibility initiatives in shaping collective working time standards and practices. Finally, as working time policies in developing and transition countries have been debated in a developmental context, more systematic studies of the relationship between working time regulation (e.g. working hours limits, paid leave entitlements) and economic performance would be useful in bringing some substance to what has been a rather ideologically driven debate.

Also, as we saw in Chapter 5, the tertiarization of the global economy appears to be one factor contributing to the broader bifurcation of working hours, as these hours vary substantially across its component subsectors. Moreover, contrary to what might be expected from the experiences of industrialized countries, working hours are quite long in a number of the service subsectors, particularly the wholesale and retail trade, hotels and restaurants, and transport, storage and communications. When we add the fact that shift work, including night work, is extensively used in services – particularly in those subsectors in which working hours are already long, such as trade, and hotels and restaurants – the potential negative impacts on both workers' health and workplace safety are substantial and thus need to be a focus of policies to advance 'healthy working time'.

Although in-depth policy guidance must await the completion of further research (see above), some broad preliminary suggestions can already be made. The first is that an adherence to primary hours limits needs to be encouraged. Clearly, laws and regulations that establish limits on working hours, such as the 48-hour limits in the Hours of Work (Industry) Convention, 1919 (No. 1) and the Hours of Work (Commerce and Offices) Convention, 1930 (No. 30), and the 40-hour limit in the Forty-Hour Week

Convention, 1935 (No. 47), are a necessary minimum condition for restraining excessively long hours of work. Exceptions and exclusions in national laws that permit substantial deviations from hours limits are currently rare, and the principle of universality in worker protection should be upheld. Moreover, this principle extends beyond normal hours to efforts to deter frequent resort to overtime work. Obviously, work beyond normal or even overtime limits must be permitted in certain circumstances, as it is by both the international standards and national laws, to respond to circumstances such as unexpected or exceptional workloads, accidents or emergencies. But beyond these kinds of exceptions, if long hours are to be prevented, substantial regular overtime work must be avoided as part of a concerted effort to reduce hours across the economy or in sectors or occupations in which they are high. Legal limits alone, however, are unlikely to be sufficient for achieving this objective. There also needs to be both a credible enforcement mechanism, such as the labour inspectorate, as well as adherence to the established 'norms' among companies regarding the 'rules of the game'.

With respect to workers in the informal economy, some techniques that are being suggested and tested to improve the application of labour laws in the informal economy also have the potential to contribute towards addressing long hours. A number of these suggestions tend towards rein-forcing existing approaches, for example by allocating additional resources to traditional enforcement mechanisms such as labour administrations and courts, or addressing corruption (see, for example, Davidov 2005). Others focus on extending the coverage of existing legislation by ensuring that it reaches beyond traditional forms of employment or clarifies the party responsible for discharging workers' rights. More innovative techniques are also being aired; these include: conducting campaigns to educate workers and employers on the benefits of labour laws, improved job quality and formalization; developing awareness-raising initiatives on legal rights or designing organizing efforts around them; permitting informal workers to collectively bargain; and implementing codes of conduct (Fenwick *et al.* 2006). Moreover, these kinds of measures could be integrated into initiatives on formalizing the informal economy, thereby strengthening the potential of formalization to advance labour protection.

Finally, the influence of wage rates on working hours can be expected to play a particularly strong role in undermining statutory limits. The relation-ship between these central elements of working life is inevitably of profound significance in developing and transition economies, where long working hours and overtime work in particular are often used to compensate for low wages. Wages must therefore be placed at the core of attempts to reduce hours. In particular, it should be noted that workers cannot be expected to favour hours reductions that will prevent them from earning a decent wage, and that where the lowering of legal (normal) hours limits fuels an expanded recourse to overtime work, its impact will be negligible. Attention to wage policies, and in particular to introducing a minimum wage or maintaining it as a meaningful standard, can thus make an important contribution towards breaking the vicious cycle of low pay and long hours (see Eyraud and Saget 2005).

7.2.3 'Family-friendly' working time

It is evident that the recognition that hours of paid work must be amenable to family life is uneven across different regions of the world, having been translated into policies and concrete measures primarily in the industrialized world and particularly in Europe. The relationship between working hours and caring and domestic labour, however, is equally strong in other regions. Chapters 4 and 5 have highlighted the strength of this relationship and its outcomes in developing economies, in the shape of low female labour force participation rates and the concentration of short hours among women in informal jobs. These data confirm prior research findings that women's responsibility for childcare and domestic labour plays a large part in compelling them to withdraw from the labour market or work on a part-time or casual basis, and provide empirical support for previous anecdotal observations on the centrality of informal economy work as a default method of combining paid and domestic labour in the developing world.

It is our suggestion that the appropriate response to these trends is to make the reconciliation of work and family life a prominent concern of economic and social policies in countries at all levels of development, and that the need to preserve sufficient time to combine paid work with childcare, elder care and other family and domestic obligations should be an integral element of these policies. Work–family initiatives at both the national- and firm-level are essential for ensuring not only the well-being of workers, particularly women, and children, the elderly and the sick, but are also in the long-term productive interests of the economy, as is explored in more detail below. Moreover, it is apparent that time for caring is becoming ever more significant, as increasing numbers of households become responsible for the care of the elderly and those suffering from HIV/AIDS.

To this end, the whole range of policy measures so far developed to aid work–family balance are available to be drawn on and adapted to national circumstances. These offer an array of options, including collective hours reductions, flexi-time schemes, emergency family leave, part-time work, legal rights for individual workers to change their hours based on family needs, and efforts to synchronize various community time arrangements, such as working hours and school opening hours. Indeed, as we saw in Chapter 6, some of these initiatives have been adopted in developing countries, often as part of the broader objective of increasing the participation of women in paid work. These include, among the countries looked at in-depth for this report, the Republic of Korea, Malaysia and Jamaica (though in a less concrete form thus far). The experience of these countries' concerted efforts towards promoting work–family balance is particularly significant in the process of information-sharing over the available techniques, in that they offer highly valuable test cases of how lower-income countries can embark on working time oriented work–family policies. As such, they are of great value for those countries that have yet to take steps in this direction, and their experience should be carefully tracked and assessed and widely publicized.

At the same time, many countries, especially those at very low income levels (i.e. less developed countries), also need measures that are of a different kind from those prominent in the industrialized world, and such measures are not well integrated into debates on working time policy. It has been suggested that, for sub-Saharan Africa for example, reducing the substantial amounts of time that women spend on domestic work must involve measures towards ensuring accessible water supplies, improving their access to transport, and investing in labour-saving domestic technologies (see further Blackden and Wodon, eds, 2006). Moreover, working time policies and strategies for formalization of the informal economy can be tied together, to the benefit of both. This would involve, as a first step, recognizing the aspect of informal work that is so favoured by women: the flexibility it gives them to combine paid labour with their non-market work. The preservation of this aspect of informal jobs during the formalization process, then, would not only benefit workers, and women in particular, but may also play a part in facilitating formalization.

7.2.4 Gender equality through working time

Although further research on the household division of labour between men and women in developing and transition economies is needed, we saw in Chapter 4 that, where these data are available, it confirms that women are primarily responsible for domestic and care work. The measures outlined in the previous section, then, can also advance gender equality by alleviating some of the difficulties women face in engaging in paid work while caring for their families. These efforts are welcome, but, as we have seen, as yet underdeveloped; efforts to further extend them are needed in conjunction with other equality initiatives in areas such as hiring, wages and benefits, and career development.

Also, with respect to the informal economy, when we break down the distribution of working hours among the self-employed by sex, we see (as is so often the case) a split in paid working hours operating along gender lines: it is predominantly men who are working longer paid hours and largely women who are working shorter paid hours. Further study of this phenomenon is merited, particularly for the purpose of better understanding the key factors driving women into short-hours self-employment in the developing country context. For example, it might be expected that a strong traditional gender division of labour in a country would be a key factor pushing women into short-hours self-employment, as would rigid (inflexible) work schedules and a lack of affordable, accessible childcare (this latter phenomenon is already well documented in industrialized countries). In addition, research in relation to policy proposals that would provide incentives for the development of short-hours jobs in the formal economies of developing countries (e.g. policies that have been implemented in many EU countries), which might provide women with an alternative to informal self-employment, would also be useful.

In designing any work–family reconciliation measures, however, it is necessary to carry out the complex and sensitive task of analysing their impact on gender equality, in particular by taking into account women's disproportionate responsibility for caring and domestic obligations, while avoiding the assumption that these are solely a concern for women. Among working time-oriented techniques, particular concerns in this regard are raised by the promotion of part-time work as a work–family measure. In the formal sector of developing economies, work of less than full-time hours is currently relatively rare, to a large extent due to the low wage levels that render it infeasible. However, Chapter 6 has highlighted some early signs of part-time work being identified, at least in government policy documents, as a potential method of facilitating work–family reconciliation.

Reduced hours can play a valuable role in realizing this objective, especially in the early years of a child's life and as needed or desired in subsequent years, and this approach has been instrumental in increasing the labour force participation of women in many countries. The concern, however, is that part-time work would, as it has in most industrialized economies, be concentrated in low-skill/low-quality jobs – thus becoming a 'trap' from which it is difficult to be promoted or to move to full-time hours – or that this option would be taken up overwhelmingly by women alone, to the detriment of gender equality. And indeed, there are some signs of these problems in developing and transition economies, although the status of part-time work in these countries needs to be thoroughly investigated. To address these problems, the experience of industrialized countries can be drawn on to inform the design of policies in other regions. In particular, this experience suggests a need, from the outset, for efforts to ensure that part-time work is of high quality, is available across all jobs and occupations, and allows smooth transitions between shorter and longer hours. The measures used to attain these goals will be shaped by local institutions and traditions, but can be informed by the principles and measures found in the ILO's Part-Time Work Convention 1994 (No. 175) and the EU's Part-time Work Directive, as well as national-level policies (where these exist). Moreover, a broader approach towards work–family reconciliation will be needed that resists treating part-time work as the only or primary available measure, thus overshadowing or displacing other potential options.

7.2.5 Productive working time

Given the urgent need for productivity increases in developing economies, any contribution that working time policies can make towards this objective is of particular significance. As we have seen in Chapter 2, the potential of hours reductions towards this goal has been recognized in a number of the countries on which studies were conducted for this book. This role for working hours limits is more often overlooked, however, in both industrialized and developing countries (see World Bank 2004, 2005 and a response in Lee and McCann 2007). It is therefore incumbent to stress that regular long hours, and competition that is grounded in them, are both harmful to workers and unproductive. In contrast, statutory hours limits, when designed in conjunction with other labour market policies towards the same objective, can contribute towards enhancing productivity and therefore can be integrated into the social and economic policies of developing economies. Reasonable hours limits help to maintain workers' health and thereby their productive capacity. They also function as an incentive for firms to modernize their work organization, including their working time arrangements, and to invest in improving their technology and enhancing the skills of their management and workforces.

It is clear that the problem of long working hours is often linked with the problem of low wages (as was discussed earlier in Section 7.2.2). Moreover, both of these problems are closely linked with low productivity: enterprises with low hourly productivity often try to compensate by requiring their workers to work long hours to raise the total output; at the same time, of course, these companies cannot afford to pay their workers very much (even if they wish to do so) due to their limited output and, as a result, their often razor-thin profit margins. Thus, efforts to reduce working hours, if carried out in isolation from initiatives to address low wages, could easily result in either widespread avoidance of the law and/or an increase in multiple job holding among workers.

Under these circumstances, one important component of the way forward towards decent working time must be to encourage and assist enterprises to improve their unit or hourly productivity. Improved hourly productivity can and should go hand-in-hand with reduced hours of work and higher hourly wages. For example, we know that there is substantial evidence pointing to a link between reductions in long working hours and increased hourly productivity, including the ILO's own previous research (see White 1987 for a review of the relevant literature). Such productivity gains result not only from physiological factors such as reduced fatigue (as in the case of workers who are working long hours on a regular basis), but also from an improvement in employee attitudes and morale. The largest potential productivity gains can be expected from reductions in 'excessive' hours of work – i.e. more than 48 hours per week – which also helps to advance the other dimensions of decent working time as well. There is substantial empirical evidence that reductions in 'excessively' long hours of work – typically linked with changes in work organization, methods of production, and similar factors – have resulted in substantial productivity gains over the years (see, for example, White 1987; Bosch and Lehndorff 2001).[2]

Measures to assist enterprises to improve their hourly productivity include providing workplace training to both managers and workers on how to improve the planning and management of working time and workloads, including ensuring the provision of adequate rest periods, such as regular rest breaks during the working day, as well as minimum periods of daily and weekly rest. Another option is for attention to be directed towards substituting extensive reliance on overtime with productivity bonus schemes. This technique, however, requires high levels of dialogue and trust between workers and employers, to ensure that workers continue to benefit from increases in productivity, as well as careful monitoring to avoid the potential for damaging and unsustainable levels of work intensification. It is worth stressing that workers cannot be expected to forgo the direct and relatively transparent method of increasing their wages through overtime payments for opaque and unreliable systems of productivity bonuses. To the extent that pay-for-performance incentives are deployed by firms as a tool to increase unit productivity, it is important that such systems, their payment rates and workers' resulting earnings be made clear and easily understandable to workers.

The ILO's technical assistance efforts have also demonstrated that improvement in a variety of working conditions, including working time, is possible and practical, even for the smallest enterprises, because of its potential to increase productivity. Through the application of action-oriented programmes, such as Work Improvement in Small Enterprises (WISE), evidence has been gathered over the years that change is possible and cost-effective, and that it will be sought by those concerned once they become aware of their potential to achieve such improvements (Rinehart 2006).[3] In order to reach a larger scale, such workplace-level efforts clearly need to be complemented by changes in the regulatory framework for small enterprises/informal economy development and for working and employment conditions. Such regulatory changes should be aimed not only at upgrading conditions in the informal economy but also, most importantly, at helping companies and workers to make the transition towards formality.

To realize the goal of enhancing hourly productivity, hours reductions also need to form part of a broader package of measures to improve job quality and develop the skills and capacities of the workforce (Bosch and Lehndorff 2001). As part of this investment, a particular focus on women and their contribution to economic growth is needed, by embedding in social and economic policies a vision of gender equality not only as a valuable objective in itself, but also as an economic asset that is in the long-term productive interests of the economy. Under this kind of model, for example, the inability of women burdened with domestic and care obligations to work in the formal economy would be viewed not solely as a disadvantage for the women concerned and as a poor work–family outcome, but also as unproductive, in that it represents the loss of a valuable resource to the economy. In addition to measures to prevent discrimination in hiring, access to training and career development, working time measures could be tied to this goal, in particular those outlined in the previous sections that permit the combination of paid work and family life and reduce the time women spend on domestic labour.

Another important way in which working time measures are currently seen as contributing to advancing productivity, particularly in the context of industrialized countries, is through working time flexibility – for example, in the form of the capacity of firms to vary working hours over periods of longer than a week (i.e. hours averaging schemes). Chapter 6 outlined the response to calls for legal measures to permit flexibilization in this direction, by permitting the averaging of weekly hours limits over periods of up to a year. In countries that have higher hours limits, and in particular those at the 48-hour level, this approach has potential as part of the initiatives to reduce hours. Care is needed, however, in the design of both firm-level schedules and the laws that govern them. Indeed, any assumption that the highly sophisticated models of flexible hours regulation developed for countries in which collective agreements structure working hours can simply be transferred without amendment to developing and transition economies should be resisted. A preliminary question raised in Chapter 3, for example, which would have to be addressed as a part of an integrated skills/productivity agenda at the national level, is whether there is any incentive to introduce flexible working hours at firm-level in many developing countries, given the existence of the alternative conduits to flexibility of overtime and informal jobs. Where this is the case, measures to limit overtime and move towards formalization and labour law enforcement would contribute towards ensuring that the forms of flexibility in operation advance the interests of both the economy and society as a whole.

7.2.6 Choice and influence over working time

Workers in developing and transition countries are not often asked about how they would like to allocate their time (for an exception, see Heymann 2005). What would be their ideal working hours? Which starting or finishing times would they prefer? How much time do they need to care for their families? The need to find answers to these kinds of questions opens up avenues for future research in countries outside the industrialized world. However, the techniques that can be drawn on to increase the options currently available to workers are already available. Reductions in working hours, for example, can play a role in advancing the worker-influence dimension of 'decent working time' by allowing a greater degree of choice for workers over how they divide their time between their jobs and the other elements of their lives. Work–family measures can also broaden the range of available options, by allowing workers more time to devote to their families and making formal economy jobs a possibility for greater numbers of women.

However, there is a concern that in weakly regulated regimes, including those in industrialized countries such as Australia, the United Kingdom and the United States, some forms of flexible working time arrangements – even those that apparently provide a substantial degree of worker influence over their working hours – may not sufficiently protect workers who do not have the collective strength to realize their preferred hours. In the context of countries in which collective institutions are not well developed, and therefore in the vast majority of developing and transition economies, the relaxation of legislated standards on working hours in favour of flexibility, without parallel developments in collective bargaining, cannot help but raise concerns. This is especially the case in the absence of the data needed to adequately assess the impacts of such changes on the length and timing of working hours.

Working time flexibility measures, if poorly designed, can usher in long hours over substantial periods and prevent workers from fully engaging with the other aspects of their lives that depend on their work schedules being relatively predictable, or undermine periods traditionally reserved for the entire community for leisure, family life and domestic obligations. Careful consideration of these issues, then, together with the input not only of the social partners but also of community groups, religious communities and individual citizens, is suggested. And where working time flexibility measures are introduced, they should be tailored towards balancing flexibility with protection, through the use of techniques such as absolute maximums on the hours that can be worked in any given week, notice periods, and measures towards individual influence, such as the right to refuse to work on traditional rest days.

In addition to these primarily indirect measures, in recent decades industrialized countries have witnessed a growing recognition that working time arrangements should be made more flexible in ways that favour workers, including by enabling them to directly influence their working hours. This approach has crystallized in measures ranging from flexi-time schemes and time-banking accounts to legal rights for workers to change their hours (Messenger, ed., 2004). As we saw in Chapter 6, some individual choice measures are in operation in developing economies, although they appear to be in only a small number of countries and firms. It is our suggestion that these approaches should be built on where they exist and begin to be reflected where they are not yet present. The vast majority of governments and companies, for example, can require or introduce simple individual choice techniques, such as: rights to notice of when overtime will be required; choice regarding whether and when to work overtime hours; and consultation on starting and finishing times and flexi-time schemes. In certain countries, these measures will be a starting point for further developments, while in others they can be combined from the outset with more advanced measures that have been pioneered in the EU.

Although mechanisms that permit the exercise of genuine choice are to be valued, caution is needed regarding transplanting the notion of individual influence to developing and transition economies, given the higher levels of poverty in these countries. 'Individual opt-outs' from working time protections, for example, which recognize workers' consent as a valid reason to exempt them, raise the same type of concerns as in the handful of industrialized countries in which they have been enacted. It appears, however, that these kinds of opt-outs are currently found in the laws of only a small number of developing countries. Moreover, in order to make individual choice measures more effective, supporting measures can be taken in areas beyond the field of working time, including: initiatives that strengthen collective actors and institutions; introduce and strengthen minimum wages; increase childcare provision; and address the social and cultural norms that help to structure working hours at the firm-level (see further Lee and McCann 2006).

7.3 Concluding remarks

This final chapter has outlined the ways in which the notion of 'decent working time' and its various dimensions can be drawn on to guide working time policy in developing and transition countries. Underlying these suggestions has been the implicit contention that even where other policy objectives are more pressing, working conditions, including working hours, can be addressed by developing countries, with some urgency in the case of the rapidly industrializing economies. In line with the tenor of the international labour standards, our policy suggestions assume that individuals are entitled to share in the fruits of economic progress. Moreover, decent working conditions, including reasonable working hours, can form part of a foundation that can be sustained and built on to help guarantee future social and economic advances.

Thus, working time, the topic of the very first international labour standard, the Hours of Work (Industry) Convention, 1919 (No. 1), remains of great importance today. This is not to say, however, that making changes to working time arrangements in transition and developing economies is an uncomplicated endeavour. Working time is, as always, a challenging area – one that is both technically complex and highly polarized in terms of the viewpoints of different actors, not least those of workers, employers, and their organizations. Seen in this context, it is perhaps not surprising that it has been extraordinarily difficult to achieve a social consensus regarding working time in many countries, and that efforts to consider potential revisions to existing international labour standards on this subject (such as Convention No. 1 and its sister Convention covering working hours in the service sector, the Hours of Work (Commerce and Offices) Convention, 1930 (No. 30)) have likewise been fraught with difficulty.[4]

In crafting appropriate working time policies, the needs and circumstances of the country in which they will be implemented have to be taken into account, including its level of development, industrial relations and legal systems, and cultural and social traditions. These kinds of factors have long been highlighted by the governments of developing countries when discussing working hours, including within ILO forums, and a number of them are reflected in the international standards. Taking these considerations into account, the principles and measures that form part of progressive working time policies in industrialized countries are available to all regions; are already being introduced in some of them; and can be further developed by being drawn on and adapted to different national contexts.

Finally, although our suggestions have focused in turn on each of the dimensions of decent working time, they have shared common themes that are worth stressing. Most notably, we have highlighted a number of times throughout that the interaction of wages and working time is central to reducing working hours, and that they must be addressed in tandem if policies towards decent working hours are to be effective. Also, it is clear that rather than a deregulatory approach towards working hours, strong protective regulation, widely enforced and observed, is necessary as the basic framework within which working hours are arranged in transition and developing economies. Finally, we have emphasized the need for social dialogue to permit workers' needs and preferences to be heard and acted on; to enhance firms' productivity; and to allow workers and employers to work together towards realizing the kinds of high-skill/high-quality firms and economies in which unacceptable working hours have no role.

Notes

1 Introduction

1 Murray (2001) provides an excellent review of how Convention No. 1 was adopted. She notes that '[t]he issue which the ILO in fact tackled in 1919 was not how to avoid exhaustion or even death from overwork, but *what was the optimum balance between work and non-work to ensure that (standard) workers could lead satisfactory lives as citizens of civilized societies?*' (p. 43, emphasis original).
2 Apparently, the adoption of the 48-hour working week was intended to introduce flexibility to the eight-hour working day. 'The Workers considered that an eight-hour day meant just that: eight hours of work per day for everyone, six days a week, with the possible exception of Saturdays, when it might be a four-hour day ... The Employers were unconvinced of the practicability of installing the eight-hour day, and accepted the forty-eight-hour week only ... in principle ... The Convention, as it emerged, tended to embody the principle of the forty-eight-hour week rather than the eight-hour day. This allowed more elasticity in the arrangement of the hours of work, and facilitated the adoption of a half holiday, or even a whole holiday on Saturday or some other day of the week, by enabling a longer period than eight hours to be worked on other days' (Alcock 1971: 43).
3 www.ilo.org/travdatabase
4 This chapter is largely based on labour force survey data. For a study based on time-use surveys, see Blackden and Wodon (eds) (2006).

2 Legal progress towards reducing working hours

1 Murray also suggests as influential the view of the ILO's Director, Albert Thomas, that shorter hours would increase productivity (2001: 45–46).
2 Article 24.
3 Article 7(d).
4 Article 2.
5 Article 31(2).
6 Additional Protocol to the American Convention on Human Rights in the Area of Economic, Social and Cultural Rights 1988.
7 For example, Argentina, Costa Rica, Cuba, El Salvador, Guatemala, Mexico, Nicaragua, Panama, Paraguay, Peru, Venezuela.
8 For example, Bulgaria, Latvia, Lithuania, Slovakia.
9 The database also includes information on legislation on maternity protection and minimum wages.
10 In India, a 48-hour limit applies in specified sectors and occupations, including factories.
11 For purposes of comparability, the leave periods specified in Table 2.5 are those that apply to a five-day working week.

3   Global trends in actual working hours

1 As discussed in Chapter 2, in some countries workers do not use their statutory leave for various reasons. This is particularly the case in Asian countries such as Japan and the Republic of Korea, and the reasons are complex. See Japan Institute of Labour (2002).

2 Some countries such as Croatia, Slovakia and Ukraine are excluded due to apparent measurement errors in the reported figures.

3 A simple example would be helpful here: two countries with three workers have the same average hours at 40 hours per week, but in country A, all of these three workers are working 40 hours, whereas in country B, they are working 20, 40 and 60 hours per week, respectively. It is not difficult to imagine different welfare implications of the average of 40 hours in these countries.

4 As will be discussed later in Chapter 6, another factor is those occupations and sectors which are exempt from the coverage of the regulations.

5 The discussion in this subsection draws on Lee and McCann (2007).

6 In fact, this group refers primarily to 44 and 45 hours, as only two countries have other standards within this range.

7 The formula used for normalization is $[(10/13 * (48\text{-}SH_i)]$ and $[(1/10 * OR_i)]$ where SH_i is country i's statutory hours and OR_i refers to country i's observance rate.

8 Some caveats should be made to this comparison, as the Republic of Korea is still in the process of implementing the 40-hour working week. Nonetheless, it is predicted that even after the implementation process is completed, the extent of non-observance will be extraordinarily high.

9 For this, it is essential to better understand the relationship between statutory limits and their observance. Without such analysis, any index on working time regulation, including the one presented in this paper, will remain preliminary.

10 To avoid confusion, it needs to be said that the distinction between employee and self-employed in labour statistics is not necessarily in line with the legal definition (i.e. who technically *should* be considered an employee under labour legislation).

11 These figures are estimated for paid employees only, since they are more likely to be affected by the ratification of these Conventions. The self-employed are excluded from the figures.

4   Gender, age and working time

1 This is not to say, however, that women's participation in the global labour force has reached a level that is at or even near parity with men's labour force participation, although the 'gender gap' in this regard has been closing. In 2003, there were only 63 women who were active in the global labour force for every 100 active men (ILO 2004: 5).

2 More recent (2004) estimates of women's global labour force participation rate indicate a slight decline in this rate, due primarily to a decrease in labour force participation rates among young women. This is part of a broader decline in labour force participation among youth in all regions of the world over the past decade, which is largely due to their increased participation in education (ILO 2005a).

3 The gender analysis in this report is designed to explain the differences in working hours between men and women and covers the period from 1992 to 2001 – a period when men generally had longer hours of paid work than women in that country. Thus, the situation in Hungary is rather typical in nearly all countries around the world.

4 In other words, the Hungary analysis suggests that, if a way could be found to

equalize the hours of unpaid family-related work between men and women, it appears likely that women would increase their hours of paid work.

5 The definition of what constitutes part-time work varies by country. For purposes of this report, however, part-time hours are defined as paid work of less than 35 hours per week on average.

6 The ILO Workers with Family Responsibilities Recommendation, 1981 (No. 165) suggests a progressive reduction of hours of work and the introduction of more flexible working time arrangements in order to assist those workers with families.

7 Only correlation coefficients based on the merged data are provided and discussed. The overall results are valid even when analysis is done separately for individual countries.

8 Of course, in countries with a high incidence of child/youth labour, this first stage of the life course may be cut short prematurely. However, as noted earlier, there has in fact been a decrease in the labour force participation rate of youth in all regions of the world, and this decrease is due primarily to an increase in the proportion of youth who are participating in education (ILO 2005a).

9 See, for example, Naegele *et al.* 2003; Anxo and Boulin, eds, 2005; Anxo *et al.* 2006. These authors argue for a new organization of time over the life course, in response to the increasing diversity of individuals' personal circumstances and their preferences regarding working time.

10 Data on average working hours by age category were presented only in a small number of the country reports, and even in these instances, the precise age categories used varied across countries.

11 One study (Jolivet and Lee 2004) found evidence that older workers in the EU Member States exhibited a greater diversity in their hours of work, as they were more likely to work both longer and shorter hours.

12 The Spearman correlation coefficient = –0.156, which is statistically significant at the 0.01 level.

13 Given the differences in the datasets used in the various country studies, it was not possible to establish a common threshold for part-time hours across countries. The thresholds for calculating part-time hours vary from less than 30 hours per week up to less than 40 hours per week in one country (Chile). See the notes at the bottom of Figure 4.2 for details.

14 According to the Russian study, this occurred during the period between 1999–2000 and 2001–2.

15 Unfortunately, it was not possible to present age categories disaggregated by sex for most of the countries studied, given the limitations in the data provided in the various country reports.

5 Tertiarization, informalization and working time

1 It is recognized that comparisons based on average hours of work can be problematic for countries and industries in which there are substantial proportions of part-time workers. However, the incidence of part-time work is typically much lower in the formal economy of developing and transition countries than in developed countries, with some notable exceptions such as community, social and personal services (see Table 5.4 for some country examples of the incidence of part-time work in major service subsectors).

2 The ISIC-Revision 3 classification of economic activities is used here for the sake of convenience, as this is the most recent classification scheme (established by the UN in 1990), and also most ILO Member States report statistical data using this scheme. However, a number of countries continue to report their statistical data

using ISIC-Revision 2, which follows a similar (but not identical) structure. See also Note 1 above.

3 It should be noted that, in those countries still using ISIC-Revision 2, this subsector is combined together with the wholesale and retail trade into a single major industry group (Major Division 6).

4 It should be noted that, in those countries still using ISIC-Revision 2, this subsector is combined with public administration and defence, health and social work, and other community, social and personal services into a single major industry group (Major Division 9, Community, Social and Personal Services).

5 Tourism is a key component of this subsector in Jamaica, and it is an industry with a large proportion of part-timers in that country. Curiously enough, however, the rate of part-time work is relatively low in hotels and restaurants, which are obviously linked with tourism.

6 For the purposes of this discussion, part-time work is not considered to be a 'flexible' working time arrangement. Part-time work primarily involves a change (reduction) in the number of weekly hours, while the working time arrangements discussed here focus on alternative ways of arranging any given number of hours (e.g. alternative shift patterns).

7 The informal economy – which dominates African employment (particularly in Sub-Saharan Africa) – is another matter entirely, and it will be discussed in the next section.

8 Eight of the ten new Member States are transition economies; the two exceptions are Cyprus and Malta.

9 Separate figures for the tourism industry are provided in the Jamaica country study report (Taylor 2004) due to the importance of this industry in Jamaica.

10 Under the ILO conceptual framework of informal employment (ILO 2002a), both own-account workers and employers in informal sector enterprises are considered to be in informal employment because of the nature of their enterprises. Under the ICLS definitions, *informal sector enterprises* are 'private unincorporated enterprises (excluding quasi-corporations) i.e. enterprises owned by individuals or households that are not constituted as separate legal entities, and for which no complete accounts are available that would permit a financial separation of the production activities of the enterprise from that of the owners' (Hussmanns 2004: 3). It should also be noted that some proportion of those individuals considered to be in self-employment may in fact be employees who have not been properly classified; nonetheless, due to the nature of the business, they would still be considered to be in informal employment.

11 Data available from an ILO survey on the distribution of employed persons by their hours of work allow us to examine the extent of variations in working hours among the self-employed at one point in time (see the discussion below), but does not permit an examination of differences in the hours of individual workers across time.

12 In should be noted that, even in an industrialized country context, there will also be disadvantaged individuals who are 'pushed' into self-employment by a lack of available wage alternatives, and these workers could have short hours as well (if they are underemployed). Given the limited data available on the characteristics of self-employed workers in the survey (which would enable us to identify their relative levels of advantage/disadvantage), the intent in this discussion is simply to broadly characterize the phenomenon of self-employment and describe its relationship with working hours.

13 If the 48-hour category is added, then several additional countries would show one-half or more of all self-employed men working long hours: Bolivia, Mexico and Madagascar. It should also be noted that in Peru, for which sex-disaggregated

data were not provided, almost half (49.4 per cent) of all self-employed workers were working 49 hours a week or more.

14 Maloney (p. 1162) argues that 'the explanation for the disproportionate representation of women in informal self-employment may again be found in certain desirable characteristics of the sector, particularly, flexibility. Interview data from Goldstein (2000) for Argentina and Chant (1991) for Mexico suggest that women may more easily balance their productive (market) and reproductive (homecare) roles if they work for themselves than if they are employees.' While one can certainly argue whether such informal jobs are actually 'desirable', given the very limited range of alternatives for paid work available to these women, the informal self-employment option may indeed be the best one available to them.

15 Irregular occupations include temporary employment with an official contract, for example.

16 The high proportions of workers with 'unknown' hours in Bulgaria (29.9 per cent) and Hungary (32.4 per cent) makes the overall pattern of working hours for the self-employed in these countries very difficult to interpret.

17 As noted earlier in this chapter, it should be emphasized that the self-employed in industrialized countries are more likely to have formal, incorporated businesses and to be required to participate in national social security, retirement and health insurance schemes (ILO 2002a).

6 Working time issues in developing countries

1 The ILO's Reduction of Hours of Work Recommendation, 1962 (No. 116), for example, calls for a reduction in normal hours without any reduction in wages (Paragraph 4).

2 Unfortunately hourly wage data cannot be presented here. It is entirely plausible (and in fact often the case) that workers with long hours may have lower hourly rates and extend their hours to compensate for such low hourly wages.

3 Cyprus, the Czech Republic, Estonia, Hungary, Latvia, Lithuania, Malta, Poland, Slovakia and Slovenia.

4 Council Directive (EC) 93/104 concerning certain aspects of the organization of working time [1993] OJ L307/18.

5 Council Directive (EC) 97/81 concerning the Framework Agreement on part-time work concluded by UNICE, CEEP and the ETUC [1998] OJ L14/9.

7 Summary and implications for policy

1 As noted in Chapter 5, it should be emphasized that the self-employed in industrialized countries are more likely to have formal, incorporated businesses, and to be required to participate in national social security, retirement and health insurance schemes (ILO 2002a).

2 It should be noted that the productivity gains connected with reductions in working time tend to decrease as the length of working time decreases. More recent empirical studies of the productivity effects of reductions in working time have focused on the reduction of hours of work from a lower baseline level (i.e. 40 hours per week or fewer) and these studies generally show weak or no effects of working time reductions in countries in which hours of work are already relatively short (see, for example, Anxo and Bigsten 1989).

3 Towards this end, the ILO has developed a working time training module to help managers and workers to analyse the working time arrangements in their companies and to take practical actions to reduce regular long hours and improve the organization of working time.

4 Recently, however, the ILO's Governing Body approved a Tripartite Meeting of Experts on Working Time, which is expected to be convened in the near future. When this meeting is convened, it will be the first technical discussion of working time at the international level in over a decade. Therefore, at the very least, this meeting will offer an opportunity to look at the subject of working time in all of its multiple dimensions, review the existing evidence regarding a variety of important questions and discuss some possible approaches for addressing these issues.

Bibliography

ILO country study reports on working time and work organization

Azerbaijan: Maharramov, A. *Working time and the organization of working time in the Republic of Azerbaijan*. ILO Conditions of Work and Employment Programme unpublished report (draft), 2005.

Brazil: Saboia, J. *Survey report. Working week and organization of labour in Brazil*. ILO Conditions of Work and Employment Programme unpublished report, 2002.

Chile: Echeverría, M. *Labour organization and time in Chile*. ILO Conditions of Work and Employment Programme unpublished report, 2002.

China: Zeng, X.; Liang, L.U.; Idris, S.U. *Working time in transition: the dual task of standardization and flexibilization in China*, Conditions of Work and Employment Programme Series No. 11 (Geneva, ILO, 2005).

Czech Republic: Berkovsky, J.; Kolář, P.; Kotiková, J.; Řehák, J.; Spousta, J.; Tvrdy, L. *Working time and work organization in the Czech Republic. Final report*. ILO Conditions of Work and Employment Programme unpublished report, 2002.

Hungary: Galasi, P. *A WTWO country study: Hungary*. ILO Conditions of Work and Employment Programme unpublished report, 2002.

Jamaica: Taylor, O. *Working time and work organization (WTWO) in Jamaica*. ILO Conditions of Work and Employment Programme unpublished report, 2004.

Korea, Republic of: Yoon, J.H. *Working time and work organization in Korea*. ILO Conditions of Work and Employment Programme unpublished report, 2001.

Malaysia: Nagaraj, S. *Working time and work organization (WTWO) country study: Malaysia*. ILO Conditions of Work and Employment Programme unpublished report, 2004.

Mauritius: Richards, N. *Working time in Mauritius*. ILO Conditions of Work and Employment Programme unpublished report, 2005.

Mexico: Esponda (Espinosa), B.R. *Working hours in Mexico: 1995–2000*. ILO Conditions of Work and Employment Programme unpublished report, 2001.

Peru: Aparicio Valdez, L. *Working time and work organization in Peru*. ILO Conditions of Work and Employment Programme unpublished report, 2001.

Russian Federation: Chetvernina, T.; Kosmarski, V.; Belozorova, S.; Thode, N.; Sobolev, E.; Smirnov, P. *Working time and work organization: Russia country study*. ILO Conditions of Work and Employment Programme unpublished report, 2004.

Senegal: Ndiaye, A. *Étude sur le temps de travail et l'organisation du travail. Cas du Sénégal*. Conditions of Work and Employment Programme Series No. 13 (Geneva, ILO, 2005).

Tunisia: Alouane, Y.; Ben Salem, L.; Safi, A.; Negazi, A. *Organisation et temps du travail en Tunisie*. ILO Conditions of Work and Employment Programme unpublished report, 2003.

References

Alcock, A. 1971. *History of the International Labour Organisation* (London, Macmillan).

Altman, M.; Golden, L. 2005. 'Alternative economic approaches to analyzing hours of work determination and standards', in Oppenheimer, M. and Mercuro, N. (eds) *Law and Economics: Alternative economic approaches to legal and regulatory issues* (Armonk, NY, M.E. Sharpe).

Anxo, D. 1999. 'Working time: research and development', Employment & Social Affairs, Industrial Relations and Industrial Change (Brussels, European Commission).

——2004. 'Working time patterns among industrialized countries: a household perspective', in Messenger, J.C. (ed.) *Working Time and Workers' Preferences in Industrialized Countries: Finding the balance* (London, Routledge).

——; Bigsten, A. 1989. 'Working hours and productivity in Swedish manufacturing', *Scandanavian Journal of Economics*, Vol. 91, No. 3, pp. 613–19.

——; O'Reilly, J. 2000. 'Working time regimes and transitions in comparative perspective', in O'Reilly, J.; Cebrian, I. and Lallement, M. (eds) *Working Time Changes: Social integration through transitional labour markets* (Cheltenham, Edward Elgar Publishing).

——; Boulin, J.-Y. (eds) 2005. *Working Time Options over the Life Course: Changing social security structures* (European Foundation for the Improvement of Living and Working Conditions, Luxembourg, Office for Official Publications of the European Communities).

——; Boulin; J.-Y.; Fagan, C. 2006. 'Decent working time in a life course perspective', in Boulin, J.-Y., Lallement, M., Messenger, J.C. and Michon, F. (eds) *Decent Working Time: New trends, new issues* (Geneva, ILO).

Asian Development Bank 2005. *Labor Markets in Asia: Promoting full, productive, and decent employment* (Manila, ADB).

Bienefeld, M. 1972. *Working Hours in British Industry: An economic history* (London, Weidenfeld and Nicolson).

Blackden, M.; Wodon, Q. (eds) 2006. 'Gender, time use, and poverty in Sub-Saharan Africa, World Bank Working Paper No. 73 (Washington, DC, World Bank).

Bosch, G.; Lehndorff, S. 2001. 'Working-time reduction and employment: experiences in Europe and economic policy recommendations', *Cambridge Journal of Economics*, Vol. 25, pp. 209–43.

——; Dawkins, P.; Michon, F. (eds) 1993. *Times Are Changing: Working time in 14 industrialized countries* (Geneva, International Institute for Labour Studies).

Botero, J.; Djankov, S.; La Porta, R.; Lopez-de-Silanes, F.; Shleifer, A. 2004. 'The regulation of labor' *Quarterly Journal of Economics*, Vol. 119, No. 4, pp. 1339–82.

Boulin, J.-Y.; Lallement, M.; Messenger, J.C.; Michon, F. (eds) 2006. *Decent Working Time: New trends, new issues* (Geneva, ILO).

Bourdieu, J.; Reynaud, B. 2006. 'Factory discipline, health and externalities in the reduction of working time in nineteenth century France', *Socio-Economic Review*, Vol. 4, No. 1, pp. 93–118.

Browne, J.; Deakin, S.; Wilkinson, F. 2002. 'Capabilities, social rights and European market integration', ESRC Centre for Business Research Working Paper 253 (Cambridge, University of Cambridge).

Carr, D. 1996. 'Two paths to self-employment? Women's and men's self-employment in the United States', *Work and Occupations*, Vol. 23, pp. 26–53.

Chaney, E.; Castro, M.G. 1993. *Muchacha No More: Household workers in Latin America and the Caribbean* (Philadelphia, Temple University Press).

Davidov, G. 2005. 'Enforcement problems in "informal" labor markets: a view from Israel', *Comparative Labor Law and Policy Journal*, Vol. 27, pp. 3–25.

Dembe, A.E.; Erickson, J.B.; Delbos, R.G.; Banks, S.M. 2005. 'The impact of overtime and long work hours on occupational injuries and illnesses: new evidence from the United States', *Journal of Occupational and Environmental Medicine*, Vol. 62, pp. 588–97.

Devine, T.J. 1994. 'Characteristics of self-employed women in the United States', *Monthly Labor Review*, March, pp. 20–33.

Dhanani, S. 2004. *Unemployment and Underemployment in Indonesia, 1976–2000: Paradoxes and issues*, Socio-Economic Security Series (Geneva, ILO).

Esim, S.; Smith, M. 2004. *Gender and Migration in Arab States: The case of domestic workers* (Beirut, ILO Regional Office for Arab States).

European Commission and Eurostat. 2003. *Time Use at Different Stages of Life: Results from three European countries* (Brussels, European Commission and Eurostat).

European Foundation for the Improvement of Living and Working Conditions. 2006. *Working Time and Work–Life Balance in European Companies: Establishment survey on working time 2004–2005* (Luxembourg, Office for Official Publications of the European Communities).

Eurostat. 2005. *European Union Labour Force Survey* (Brussels, Eurostat).

Eyraud, F.; Saget, C. 2005. *The Fundamentals of Minimum Wage Fixing* (Geneva: ILO).

Fagan, C. 2004. 'Gender and working time in industrialized countries', in Messenger, J.C. (ed.) *Working Time and Workers' Preferences in Industrialized Countries: Finding the balance* (London, Routledge).

——; O'Reilly, J. (eds) 1998. *Part-Time Prospects: An international comparison of part-time work in Europe, North America and the Pacific Rim* (London, Routledge).

——; Burchell, B.J. 2002. *Gender, Jobs and Working Conditions in the European Union* (Dublin, European Foundation for the Improvement of Living and Working Conditions).

Fenwick, C.; Howe, J.; Marshall, S; Landau, I. 2006. 'Labour and labour-related laws in micro- and small enterprises: innovative regulatory approaches', unpublished working paper (Geneva, ILO).

Ford, H. 1926. 'Why do I favor five days' work with six days' pay?' (interview with S. Crowther), *World's Work*, October, pp. 613–16.

Frenkel, S.; Kuruvilla, S. 2002. 'Logics of action, globalization, and changing employment relations in China, India, Malaysia and the Philippines', *Industrial and Labor Relations Review*, Vol. 55, pp. 387–412.

Fridenson, P.; Reynaud, B. (eds) 2004. *La France et le Temps de Travail 1814–2004* (Paris, Odile Jacob).

Gadrey, N.; Jany-Catrice, F.; Pernod-Lemattre, M. 2006. 'The working conditions of blue-collar and white-collar workers in France compared: a question of time', in Boulin, J.-Y.; Lallement, M.; Messenger, J.C. and Michon, F. (eds) *Decent Working Time: New trends, new issues* (Geneva, ILO).

Ghosheh, N.; Lee, S.; McCann, D. 2006. *Conditions of Work and Employment for Older Workers: Understanding the issues*, Conditions of Work and Employment Programme Series No. 15. (Geneva, ILO).

Golden, L. 2001. Flexible work schedules: what are workers trading off to get them? *Monthly Labor Review*, Vol. 124, No. 3 March, pp. 50–67.

——; Figart, D. (eds) (2000) *Working Time: International trends, theory and policy perspectives* (London: Routledge).

Görg, H.; Strobl. E. 2003. 'The incidence of visible underemployment: evidence for Trinidad and Tobago', *Journal of Development Studies*, Vol. 39, No. 3, pp. 81–100.

Heymann, J. 2005. *Forgotten Families* (Cambridge, MA, Harvard University Press).

Houseman, S.; Nakamura, A. (eds) 2001. *Working Time in Comparative Perspective (II): Life-cycle working time and nonstandard work* (Kalamazoo, MI, W.E. Upjohn Institute for Employment Research).

Huberman, M. 2002. *Working Hours of the World Unite? New international evidence of worktime, 1870–2000*, CIRANO Scientific Series 2002s-77 (Montreal, CIRANO).

Hussmanns, R. 2004. 'Measuring the informal economy: from employment in the informal sector to informal employment', Working Paper No. 53 (Geneva, ILO Policy Integration Department, Bureau of Statistics).

Ilahi, N. 2001. *Gender and the Allocation of Adult Time: Evidence from the Peru LSMS Panel Data*, Policy Research Report on Gender, December (Washington, DC, World Bank).

Incomes Data Services (IDS) 2005. *The 24-Hour Workplace*, IDS HR Study 205, September, p. 2.

International Labour Office (ILO) 1958. *Hours of Work*, International Labour Conference Report VIII (Geneva, ILO).

——1967. *Hours of Work. A world survey of national law and practice* (Geneva, ILO).

——1984. *Working Time: Reduction of hours of work, weekly rest and holidays with pay* (Geneva, ILO).

——1995. *Working Time Around the World*, Conditions of Work Digest Vol. 14 (Geneva, ILO).

——2002a. *Women and Men in the Informal Economy: A statistical picture* (Geneva, ILO).

——2002b. *Decent Work and the Informal Economy*, Report of the Director-General, International Labour Conference, 90th Session, Report VI (Geneva, ILO).

——2003a. *Key Indicators of the Labour Market (KILM), third edition* (Geneva, ILO).

——2003b. 'Guidelines concerning a statistical definition of informal employment', endorsed by the Seventeenth International Conference of Labour Statisticians, *Seventeenth International Conference of Labour Statisticians*, Report of the Conference, Geneva, 24 Nov. to 3 Dec.

——2003c. *Equality, Labour and Social Protection for Women and Men in the Formal and Informal Economy in Viet Nam: Issues for advocacy and policy development* (Hanoi, ILO).

——2004. *Global Employment Trends for Women 2004* (Geneva, ILO).

——2005a. *Key Indicators of the Labour Market (KILM), fourth edition* (Geneva, ILO).

——2005b. *Labour and Social Trends in Asia and the Pacific 2005* (Geneva, ILO).

——2005c. *World Employment Report, 2004–2005* (Geneva, ILO).

——2005d. *Hours of Work: From fixed to flexible?* (Geneva, ILO).

ILO Bureau of Statistics. 2004. 'Employment in the informal economy in the Republic of Moldova, ILO Policy Integration Department Working Paper No. 41 (Geneva, ILO).

Japan Institute of Labour. 2002. *Research on Annual Paid Holidays*. JIL Research Report No. 152 (Tokyo).

Jolivet, A.; Lee, S. 2004. *Employment Conditions in an Ageing World: Meeting the working time challenge*, Conditions of Work and Employment Programme Series No. 9 (Geneva, ILO).

Kelly, E.L.; Kalev, A. 2006. 'Managing flexible work arrangements in US organizations: formalized discretion or "a right to ask"', *Socio-Economic Review*, Vol. 4, pp. 379–416.

Knight, F.H. 1933. *Risk, Uncertainty and Profit* (London, London School of Economics and Political Science).

Lee, S. 2003. 'Political economy of working time in Korea: tensions in the reduction of working hours', paper presented at 15th Annual Meeting on Socio-Economics, June.

——2004. 'Working-hour gaps: trends and issues', in Messenger, J.C. (ed.) *Working Time and Workers' Preferences in Industrialized Countries: Finding the balance* (London, Routledge), pp. 29–59.

——; Wood, A. 2005. 'Globalization, flexibilization, and changes in employment conditions in Asia and the Pacific: a review', ILO Conditions of Work and Employment Programme unpublished paper (draft), August (Geneva, ILO).

——; McCann, D. 2006. 'Working time capability: towards realizing individual choice', in Boulin, J-Y.; Lallement, M.; Messenger, J.C. and Michon, F. (eds) *Decent Working Time: New trends, new issues* (Geneva, ILO).

——; McCann, D. 2007.'Measuring labour market institutions: conceptual and methodological questions on "working hours rigidity"', in Berg, J. and Kucera, D. (eds) *Labour Institutions in the Developing World: Cultivating justice through labour law and policies* (Geneva, ILO and Basingstoke, Palgrave Macmillan).

——; Wood, A. 2007. 'Changing patterns in the world of work in Asia: an overview', in Burgess, J. and Connell, J. (eds) *Globalisation and Work in Asia* (Oxford, Chandos).

Lehndorff, S. 2000. 'Working time reduction in the European Union: a diversity of trends and approaches' in Golden, L. and Figart, D. (eds) *Working Time: International trends, theory and policy perspectives* (London, Routledge).

Leiva, S. 2000. *Part-time Work in Chile: Is it precarious employment? Reflections from a gender perspective* (Santiago, ECLAC–UN).

Lundall, P. 2002. *Special Problems in Securing a Reduction in Working Hours: The case of security workers* (Cape Town, University of Cape Town Development Policy Research Unit).

McCann, D. 2005. *Working Time Laws: A global perspective* (Geneva, ILO).

——2006. 'The role of work/family discourse in strengthening traditional working time laws: some lessons from the on-call work debate', in Murray, J. (ed.) *Work,*

Family and the Law, Law in Context, Vol. 23, No. 1, p. 127 (Annandale, NSW, The Federation Press).

——2008. 'Decent working hours as a human right: intersections in the regulation of working time', in Fenwick, C. and Novitz, T. (eds) *Legal Protection of Workers' Human Rights: Regulatory changes and challenges* (Oxford, Hart).

Maddison, A. 1995. *Monitoring the World Economy, 1820–1992* (Paris, OECD).

Maloney, W.F. 2004. 'Informality revisited', *World Development*, Vol. 32, No. 7, pp. 1159–78.

Mehran, F. 2005. 'Measuring excessive hours of work, low hourly pay, and informal employment through a Labour Force Survey: a pilot survey in the Philippines', presented at UNECE/ILO/Eurostat Seminar on the Quality of Work, Geneva, May.

Messenger, J.C. (ed.) 2004. *Working Time and Workers' Preferences in Industrialized Countries: Finding the balance* (London, Routledge).

——; Stettner, A. 2000. *Is the Outcome Desirable? The quality of work in self-employment* (Geneva, ILO Social Finance Programme).

Murray, J. 2001. *Transnational Labour Regulation: The ILO and EC compared* (The Hague, Kluwer Law International).

Mwatha Karega, R.G. 2002. *Work and Family Study in Kenya: Implications for combining work and family responsibilities.* ILO Conditions of Work and Employment Programme unpublished report.

Naegele, G.; Barkholdt, C.; DeVroom, B.; Goul Andersen, J.; Krämer, K. 2003. *A New Organization of Time over Working Life* (Dublin, European Foundation for the Improvement of Living and Working Conditions).

O'Reilly, J.; Bothfeld, S. 2002. 'What happens after working part-time? Integration, maintenance or exclusionary transitions in Britain and western Germany', *Cambridge Journal of Economics*, Vol. 26, pp. 409–39.

——; Cebrian, I.; Lallement, M. (eds) 2000. *Working Time Changes: Social integration through transitional labour markets* (Cheltenham, Edward Elgar Publishing).

Organization for Economic Co-operation and Development (OECD) 2000. Chapter 3. 'Employment in the service economy: a reassessment', in *OECD Employment Outlook 2000* (Paris, OECD).

——2001. Chapter 3. 'The characteristics and quality of service sector jobs', in *OECD Employment Outlook 2001* (Paris, OECD).

——2004. *OECD Employment Outlook 2004* (Paris, OECD).

Parker, S.; Belghitar, Y.; Barmby, T. 2005. 'Wage uncertainty and the labour supply of self-employed workers', *Economic Journal*, Vol. 115, March, C190–C207.

Phelps Brown, E.H.; Browne, M.H. 1968. 'Hours of work', in *International Encyclopedia of the Social Sciences*, Vol. 8 (New York, the Macmillan Company and the Free Press), pp. 487–91.

Purcell, K.; Hogarth, T.; Simm, C. 1999. *Whose Flexibility? The costs and benefits of 'non-standard' working arrangements and contractual relations* (York, York Publishing Services/Joseph Rowntree Foundation).

Rae, J. 1894. *Eight Hours for Work* (London, Macmillan).

Rees, H.; Shaw, A. 1986. 'An empirical analysis of self-employment in the UK', *Journal of Applied Econometrics*, Vol. 1, pp. 95–108.

Reich, R. 1992. *The Work of Nations* (New York, Vintage Books).

Rinehart, R. 2006. *Designing Programmes to Improve Working and Employment*

Conditions in the Informal Economy: A literature review. Conditions of Work and Employment Programme Series No. 10 (Geneva, ILO).

Rubery, J.; Grimshaw, D.; Ward, K. 2006. 'Time, work and pay: understanding the new relationships', in Boulin, J.-Y.; Lallement, M.; Messenger, J.C. and Michon, F. (eds) *Decent Working Time: New trends, new issues* (Geneva, ILO).

Schor, J. 1992. *The Overworked American: The unexpected decline of leisure* (New York, Basic Books).

Schumpeter, J. 1934. *The Theory of Economic Development: An inquiry into profits, capital, and credit* (Cambridge, MA, Harvard University Press).

Sorj, B. 2004. *Reconciling Work and Family: Issues and policies in Brazil*. Conditions of Work and Employment Programme Series No. 8 (Geneva, ILO).

South Africa Department of Labour. 2000. *South Africa Report on Working Time*, South Africa Department of Labour unpublished report.

Spurgeon, A. 2003. *Working Time: Its impact on safety and health* (ILO and Korean Occupational Safety and Health Research Institute).

Supiot, A. 2001. *Beyond Employment: Changes in work and the future of labour law in Europe* (Oxford, Oxford University Press).

Tang, N.; Cousins, C. 2005. 'Working time, gender and family: an East–West European comparison', *Gender, Work and Organization*, Vol. 12, No. 6, pp. 527–50.

Thompson, E. 1967. 'Time, work-discipline, and industrial capitalism', *Past and Present*, Vol. 38, pp. 56–97.

Tipple, G. 2006. 'Employment and work conditions in home-based enterprises in four developing countries: do they constitute decent work?', *Work, Employment, and Society*, Vol. 20, No. 1, March, pp. 167–79.

Torres, L. 1998. *Labour Markets in Southern Africa. Fafo-report 257* (Oslo, Fafo Institute for Applied Social Science).

Valodia, I. 2001. 'Economic policy and women's informal work in South Africa', *Development and Change*, Vol. 32, pp. 871–92.

Vaughan-Whitehead, D. (ed.) 2005. *Working and Employment Conditions in the New EU Member States: Convergence or diversity* (Geneva, ILO).

Vaughan-Whitehead, D. 2005. 'The world of work in the new EU Member States: diversity and convergence', in Vaughan-Whitehead, D. (ed.) *Working and Employment Conditions in the New EU Member States: Convergence or diversity?* (Geneva, ILO).

White, M. 1987. *Working Hours: Assessing the potential for reduction* (Geneva, ILO).

Wong, G.; Picot, G. (eds) 2001. *Working Time in Comparative Perspective (I): Patterns, trends, and the policy implications of earnings inequality and unemployment* (Kalamazoo, MI, W.E. Upjohn Institute for Employment Research).

World Bank. 2004. *The World Development Report: A better investment climate for everyone* (Washington, DC, World Bank).

——2005. *Doing Business 2006* (Washington, DC, World Bank).

Zeytinoglu, I.U.; Cooke, G. 2006. 'Who is working on weekends? Determinants of regular weekend work in Canada', in Boulin, J.-Y.; Lallement, M.; Messenger, J.C. and Michon, F. (eds) *Decent Working Time: New trends, new issues* (Geneva, ILO).

Statistical annex

The number of workers by hours of work

Notes

Different countries report different age ranges (for example for Albania, 15+, for Argentina, 25+)

PE – paid employees; SE – self-employed; TE – total employment

Some columns may not total 100.00 due to rounding errors.

Country	Gender and year						
Albania	Age: 15+	Female (%)			Male (%)		
Main job	Hours	1995	2001	2004	1995	2001	2004
PE	<15		0.96			1.07	
	15–24		13.48			11.31	
	25–34		17.94			19.36	
	35		1.80			2.09	
	36–39		6.15			7.15	
	40		40.92			35.53	
	41–47		1.82			1.27	
	48		13.27			14.79	
	49–59		2.81			5.13	
	60+		0.85			2.30	
	Total		100.00			100.00	
SE	<15		8.78			6.74	
	15–24		16.99			15.73	
	25–34		33.08			29.98	
	35		3.70			3.52	
	36–39		9.76			8.80	
	40		11.87			13.93	
	41–47		7.17			6.34	
	48		3.05			4.82	
	49–59		3.45			6.11	
	60+		2.15			4.05	
	Total		100.00			100.00	
TE	<15		6.22			5.00	
	15–24		15.84			14.37	
	25–34		28.11			26.71	
	35		3.08			3.08	
	36–39		8.57			8.29	
	40		21.40			20.57	
	41–47		5.41			4.78	
	48		6.40			7.88	
	49–59		3.24			5.81	
	60+		1.72			3.52	
	Total		100.00			100.00	

Country		Gender and year					
Argentina	*Age: 25+*	*Female (%)*			*Male (%)*		
Main job	*Hours*	*1995*	*2000*	*2004*	*1995*	*2000*	*2004*
PE	<15			15.16			3.01
	15–24			25.46			8.94
	25–34			15.38			8.32
	35			3.88			2.93
	36–39			2.58			2.71
	40			11.63			15.38
	41–47			9.21			14.52
	48			4.33			8.61
	49–59			6.60			15.27
	60+			5.44			19.99
	Unknown			0.33			0.33
	Total			100.00			100.00
SE	<15			20.14			9.34
	15–24			14.16			10.48
	25–34			11.33			8.91
	35			2.34			1.56
	36–39			3.41			2.75
	40			5.83			9.62
	41–47			6.76			8.71
	48			5.12			5.69
	49–59			11.11			16.07
	60+			18.58			26.01
	Unknown			1.23			0.85
	Total			100.00			100.00
TE	<15			16.28			5.03
	15–24			22.93			9.43
	25–34			14.47			8.51
	35			3.54			2.49
	36–39			2.76			2.72
	40			10.33			13.54
	41–47			8.66			12.67
	48			4.51			7.68
	49–59			7.61			15.52
	60+			8.39			21.91
	Unknown			0.53			0.49
	Total			100.00			100.00

Armenia	*Age: 25+*	*Female (%)*			*Male (%)*		
Main job	*Hours*	*1995*	*2001*	*2004*	*1995*	*2001*	*2004*
PE	<15		5.51	20.60		3.40	7.19
	15–24		16.02	7.80		3.10	2.80
	25–34		12.21	6.70		5.00	2.50
	35		3.60	1.20		1.90	1.00
	36–39		4.40	4.50		4.00	2.00

Country			Gender and year				
Armenia continued Main job	Age: 25+	*Female (%)*			*Male (%)*		
	Hours	1995	2001	2004	1995	2001	2004
	40		31.23	24.30		29.87	22.68
	41–47		6.51	11.10		6.89	10.19
	48		10.11	11.50		16.48	16.78
	49–59		4.20	5.60		11.69	8.19
	60+		6.21	6.70		17.68	26.67
	Unknown		0.00	0.00		0.00	0.00
	Total		100.00	100.00		100.00	100.00
SE	<15		4.00	16.70		5.39	11.11
	15–24		9.09	13.80		9.69	9.61
	25–34		16.68	21.70		12.79	12.01
	35		5.59	4.40		5.99	3.90
	36–39		4.00	1.00		3.10	1.10
	40		7.09	9.10		7.09	7.21
	41–47		6.09	5.20		8.49	5.01
	48		3.50	3.40		3.70	4.00
	49–59		17.18	12.60		13.39	16.52
	60+		26.77	12.10		30.37	29.53
	Unknown		0.00	0.00		0.00	0.00
	Total		100.00	100.00		100.00	100.00
TE	<15		5.20	19.10		4.20	9.00
	15–24		14.30	10.10		5.60	6.00
	25–34		13.30	12.50		7.90	7.00
	35		4.10	2.50		3.40	2.30
	36–39		4.30	3.10		3.60	1.60
	40		25.30	18.40		21.30	15.50
	41–47		6.40	8.80		7.50	7.70
	48		8.50	8.40		11.70	10.80
	49–59		7.40	8.30		12.30	12.10
	60+		11.20	8.80		22.50	28.00
	Unknown		0.00	0.00		0.00	0.00
	Total		100.00	100.00		100.00	100.00

Australia	Age: 25+	*Female (%)*			*Male (%)*		
All jobs	Hours	1995	2000	2004	1995	2000	2004
PE	<15	23.14	21.83	13.05	9.91	9.77	2.82
	16–24	14.67	14.58	14.82	4.33	4.54	2.82
	25–34	16.21	16.42	15.68	9.27	8.69	3.82
	35–39	16.99	16.98	22.71	16.10	15.89	22.13
	40	12.84	12.38	17.85	18.19	17.85	26.25
	41–44	3.69	3.98	2.68	5.93	5.68	4.61
	45–49	4.96	5.57	5.44	10.90	10.99	11.51
	50–59	4.64	5.13	5.38	13.42	14.00	15.20
	60+	2.87	3.12	2.37	11.96	12.59	10.85
	Total	100.00	100.00	100.00	100.00	100.00	100.00

Country	Gender and year						
Australia continued *All jobs*	*Age: 25+*	*Female (%)*			*Male (%)*		
	Hours	*1995*	*2000*	*2004*	*1995*	*2000*	*2004*
SE	<15	38.18	38.95	31.33	12.35	12.63	6.26
	16–24	10.89	11.04	12.09	5.78	5.99	4.95
	25–34	10.03	10.55	12.93	7.57	7.94	7.70
	35–39	5.99	6.18	7.11	5.75	6.56	7.31
	40	7.51	7.32	10.01	12.35	12.84	18.15
	41–44	2.01	1.91	1.57	2.62	2.61	2.05
	45–49	4.22	4.38	5.03	8.34	8.51	10.13
	50–59	7.91	7.77	9.38	16.60	16.23	19.51
	60+	13.25	11.89	10.55	28.64	26.71	23.95
	Total	100.00	100.00	100.00	100.00	100.00	100.00
TE	<15	25.26	23.95	15.17	10.39	10.30	3.43
	16–24	14.14	14.14	14.51	4.62	4.80	3.19
	25–34	15.34	15.70	15.36	8.93	8.55	4.51
	35–39	15.44	15.64	20.91	14.06	14.18	19.50
	40	12.09	11.76	16.95	17.04	16.93	24.81
	41–44	3.45	3.72	2.55	5.28	5.11	4.16
	45–49	4.86	5.42	5.40	10.39	10.54	11.27
	50–59	5.10	5.46	5.85	14.04	14.41	15.97
	60+	4.33	4.21	3.31	15.24	15.17	13.17
	Total	100.00	100.00	100.00	100.00	100.00	100.00
Azerbaijan *Main job*	*Age: 25+*	*Female (%)*			*Male (%)*		
	Hours	*1995*	*2000*	*2003*	*1995*	*2000*	*2003*
PE	<9			0.36			0.21
	9–15			4.30			1.43
	16–20			5.27			1.81
	21–30			10.08			4.59
	31–40			62.93			60.88
	41–50			13.62			18.60
	51+			3.45			12.46
	Total			100.00			100.00
SE	<9			0.21			0.10
	9–15			3.61			0.88
	16–20			6.15			3.45
	21–30			19.31			13.59
	31–40			44.24			37.58
	41–50			18.97			27.29
	51+			7.51			17.11
	Total			100.00			100.00
TE	<9			0.29			0.17
	9–15			3.99			1.20
	16–20			5.67			2.50
	21–30			14.27			8.38
	31–40			54.44			51.08

Country		Gender and year						
Azerbaijan continued Main job	*Age: 25+*	*Female (%)*			*Male (%)*			
	Hours	*1995*	*2000*	*2003*	*1995*	*2000*	*2003*	
	41–50			16.05			22.26	
	51+			5.29			14.42	
	Total			100.00			100.00	

Bolivia	*Age: 10+*	*Female (%)*			*Male (%)*			
	Hours	*1995*	*2000*	*2004*	*1995*	*2000*	*2004*	
PE	<15		6.36			3.25		
	15–24		19.60			7.92		
	25–34		10.45			4.99		
	35		0.83			0.92		
	36–39		4.35			2.16		
	40		16.87			12.17		
	41–47		5.24			4.11		
	48		15.93			19.07		
	49–59		6.89			14.49		
	60+		13.48			30.91		
	Total		100.00			100.00		
SE	<15		12.08			7.50		
	15–24		14.73			12.23		
	25–34		9.34			8.58		
	35		2.75			1.65		
	36–39		4.18			4.01		
	40		3.64			4.96		
	41–47		5.36			5.54		
	48		10.94			17.30		
	49–59		12.18			12.09		
	60+		24.81			26.16		
	Total		100.00			100.00		
TE	<15		10.92			5.92		
	15–24		15.71			10.63		
	25–34		9.56			7.25		
	35		2.36			1.38		
	36–39		4.22			3.32		
	40		6.31			7.63		
	41–47		5.33			5.01		
	48		11.95			17.96		
	49–59		11.11			12.98		
	60+		22.52			27.92		
	Total		100.00			100.00		

Country		Gender and year					
Bulgaria	*Age: 15+*	*Female (%)*			*Male (%)*		
Main job	*Hours*	*1995*	*2000*	*2004*	*1995*	*2000*	*2004*
PE	<15			0.13			0.07
	15–24			1.41			0.72
	25–34			1.85			0.77
	35			0.70			0.30
	36–39			0.31			0.20
	40			81.00			78.61
	41–47			1.90			1.78
	48			6.24			6.82
	49–59			2.45			2.83
	60+			0.85			1.59
	Unknown			3.15			6.31
	Total			100.00			100.00
SE	<15			1.81			0.74
	15–24			4.94			3.80
	25–34			9.57			6.02
	35			1.25			1.27
	36–39			0.19			0.28
	40			26.45			26.45
	41–47			2.94			2.99
	48			9.32			8.95
	49–59			10.19			11.69
	60+			5.38			6.69
	Unknown			27.96			31.12
	Total			100.00			100.00
TE	<15			0.32			0.19
	15–24			1.82			1.28
	25–34			2.75			1.72
	35			0.77			0.48
	36–39			0.30			0.21
	40			74.66			69.08
	41–47			2.02			2.00
	48			6.60			7.21
	49–59			3.35			4.45
	60+			1.38			2.53
	Unknown			6.03			10.83
	Total			100.00			100.00
Canada	*Age: 15+*	*Female (%)*			*Male (%)*		
Main job	*Hours*	*1995*	*2000*	*2004*	*1995*	*2000*	*2004*
PE	<15	5.56	4.39	4.30	1.35	1.13	1.30
	15–24	12.52	11.39	11.07	2.42	2.25	2.57
	25–34	12.23	14.16	14.87	3.35	3.95	4.32
	35	12.00	12.98	13.32	5.29	6.02	6.29
	36–39	17.65	20.50	20.64	9.88	12.88	13.72
	40	31.48	31.07	30.63	53.28	55.61	54.30

Country		Gender and year					
Canada continued	*Age: 15+*	*Female (%)*			*Male (%)*		
Main job	*Hours*	*1995*	*2000*	*2004*	*1995*	*2000*	*2004*
	41–47	3.61	2.97	2.87	9.13	8.57	8.57
	48	0.35	0.27	0.34	1.21	0.87	0.93
	49–59	3.14	1.54	1.30	8.63	5.34	5.02
	60+	1.45	0.75	0.65	5.46	3.38	2.98
	Total	100.00	100.00	100.00	100.00	100.00	100.00
SE	<15	16.71	14.36	13.44	3.73	3.59	3.48
	15–24	14.86	14.99	16.06	4.97	5.15	5.35
	25–34	14.61	16.62	15.91	7.84	8.15	8.54
	35	4.86	5.46	5.98	3.34	4.10	4.29
	36–39	1.46	1.51	1.64	1.09	1.44	1.53
	40	19.45	19.01	17.46	25.24	24.69	23.68
	41–47	4.51	5.56	5.83	5.83	7.53	8.43
	48	0.74	0.67	0.68	1.09	0.86	0.94
	49–59	10.76	10.84	12.31	19.14	19.46	19.60
	60+	12.03	10.96	10.69	27.73	25.02	24.15
	Total	100.00	100.00	100.00	100.00	100.00	100.00
TE	<15	6.97	5.77	5.46	1.85	1.66	1.77
	15–24	12.82	11.88	11.71	2.96	2.88	3.17
	25–34	12.53	14.50	15.01	4.30	4.86	5.22
	35	11.10	11.94	12.38	4.88	5.60	5.86
	36–39	15.61	17.87	18.22	8.02	10.38	11.10
	40	29.96	29.40	28.95	47.34	48.86	47.72
	41–47	3.72	3.33	3.25	8.43	8.35	8.54
	48	0.40	0.32	0.38	1.18	0.87	0.93
	49–59	4.10	2.82	2.70	10.86	8.42	8.16
	60+	2.79	2.17	1.93	10.18	8.11	7.53
	Total	100.00	100.00	100.00	100.00	100.00	100.00
Croatia	*Age: 15+*	*Female (%)*			*Male (%)*		
All jobs	*Hours*	*1995*	*2001*	*2004*	*1995*	*2001*	*2004*
PE	<15		11.22			6.82	
	15–24		1.63			0.70	
	25–34		0.61			0.00	
	35		0.00			0.00	
	36–39		0.00			0.00	
	40		54.90			49.65	
	41–47		27.55			30.42	
	48		2.04			0.00	
	49–59		0.00			6.64	
	60+		2.04			5.77	
	Unknown		0.00			0.00	
	Total		100.00			100.00	
SE	<15		0.00			0.00	
	15–24		0.00			0.00	

Country		Gender and year					
Croatia continued *All jobs*	*Age: 25+*	*Female (%)*			*Male (%)*		
	Hours	*1995*	*2001*	*2004*	*1995*	*2001*	*2004*
	25–34		0.00			0.00	
	35		25.00			3.95	
	36–39		0.00			0.00	
	40		0.00			28.95	
	41–47		0.00			24.34	
	48		0.00			2.63	
	49–59		75.00			17.76	
	60+		0.00			22.37	
	Unknown		0.00			0.00	
	Total		100.00			100.00	
TE	<15		11.25			7.32	
	15–24		5.07			3.41	
	25–34		3.65			3.03	
	35		0.63			0.76	
	36–39		0.00			0.00	
	40		46.28			41.79	
	41–47		24.41			26.77	
	48		0.00			0.00	
	49–59		4.44			8.46	
	60+		4.28			8.46	
	Unknown		0.00			0.00	
	Total		100.00			100.00	
Cyprus *Main job*	*Age: 25+*	*Female (%)*			*Male (%)*		
	Hours	*1995*	*2000*	*2004*	*1995*	*2000*	*2004*
PE	<15		0.84	1.06		0.48	0.38
	15–24		3.12	3.01		0.94	1.03
	25–34		6.86	6.49		1.64	1.58
	35		8.08	10.79		3.88	7.41
	36–39		37.94	33.30		40.08	40.01
	40		29.57	24.28		33.54	31.24
	41–47		4.99	15.13		5.74	6.45
	48		2.88	2.63		2.16	2.65
	49–59		3.70	2.15		7.35	5.19
	60+		1.87	1.17		3.87	3.81
	Variable hours		0.17	0.00		0.30	0.24
	Total		100.00	100.00		100.00	100.00
SE	<15		8.43	8.54		1.23	2.48
	15–24		22.56	16.27		4.55	4.92
	25–34		16.16	17.11		5.40	4.12
	35		3.88	5.24		2.94	2.71
	36–39		4.82	4.34		3.50	5.41
	40		16.55	18.56		26.18	20.46
	41–47		5.47	8.24		10.09	8.95
	48		1.01	1.48		1.50	2.75

Country		Gender and year					
Cyprus continued	Age: 25+	Female (%)			Male (%)		
Main job	Hours	1995	2000	2004	1995	2000	2004
	49–59		8.86	8.38		16.85	17.07
	60+		11.63	10.68		26.09	29.30
	Variable hours		0.63	1.15		1.67	1.83
	Total		100.00	100.00		100.00	100.00
TE	<15		2.19	2.34		0.72	1.05
	15–24		6.59	5.28		2.09	2.28
	25–34		8.53	8.31		2.84	2.40
	35		7.33	9.84		3.58	5.90
	36–39		32.02	28.33		28.42	28.91
	40		27.24	23.30		31.19	27.78
	41–47		5.07	13.95		7.13	7.25
	48		2.54	2.43		1.95	2.68
	49–59		4.62	3.22		10.38	9.00
	60+		3.61	2.80		10.96	11.99
	Variable hours		0.25	0.20		0.74	0.75
	Total		100.00	100.00		100.00	100.00
Czech Republic	Age: 25+	Female (%)			Male (%)		
Main job	Hours	1995	2000	2004	1995	2000	2004
PE	1.0–14.4	0.87	0.74	0.81	0.41	0.30	0.26
	14.5–24.4	3.63	3.27	3.12	0.82	0.82	0.86
	24.5–34.4	5.24	4.72	4.38	1.47	1.19	1.09
	34.5–35.4	1.88	1.64	1.04	0.29	0.26	0.35
	35.5–39.4	1.94	1.99	13.02	1.46	1.62	14.40
	39.5–40.4	27.71	29.06	68.74	30.10	32.08	62.01
	40.5–47.4	49.79	49.81	4.45	47.26	43.81	5.88
	47.5–48.4	1.24	1.38	0.47	2.44	2.49	0.80
	48.5–59.4	3.36	3.61	2.77	9.29	10.52	9.69
	59.5–99.9	1.36	1.38	1.09	5.12	5.75	4.38
	Unknown	2.97	2.34	0.10	1.34	1.05	0.26
	Variable hours	0.01	0.05	0.00	0.01	0.10	0.02
	Total	100.00	100.00	100.00	100.00	100.00	100.00
SE	1.0–14.4	2.40	2.24	1.82	1.03	0.66	0.73
	14.5–24.4	4.45	5.10	5.13	1.39	1.28	1.32
	24.5–34.4	6.70	8.93	8.61	1.96	1.97	1.57
	34.5–35.4	2.62	2.71	2.45	0.69	0.54	0.83
	35.5–39.4	1.06	0.55	1.17	0.12	0.19	0.48
	39.5–40.4	13.79	18.23	40.02	8.44	12.73	23.24
	40.5–47.4	16.97	16.62	5.40	10.66	12.11	5.64
	47.5–48.4	1.55	1.26	1.00	0.80	0.78	0.51
	48.5–59.4	21.23	25.52	19.90	24.74	30.45	31.67
	59.5–99.9	27.26	17.47	13.49	48.81	38.16	33.47
	Unknown	1.98	1.25	0.94	1.31	0.97	0.46
	Variable hours	0.00	0.13	0.07	0.05	0.16	0.07
	Total	100.00	100.00	100.00	100.00	100.00	100.00

Country		Gender and year					
Czech Rep. continued	*Age: 25+*	*Female (%)*			*Male (%)*		
Main job	*Hours*	*1995*	*2000*	*2004*	*1995*	*2000*	*2004*
TE	1.0–14.4	1.01	0.91	0.92	0.51	0.37	0.37
	14.5–24.4	3.70	3.47	3.35	0.91	0.91	0.96
	24.5–34.4	5.37	5.18	4.86	1.55	1.35	1.20
	34.5–35.4	1.95	1.76	1.20	0.35	0.32	0.46
	35.5–39.4	1.86	1.83	11.67	1.24	1.34	11.27
	39.5–40.4	26.48	27.88	65.47	26.55	28.18	53.28
	40.5–47.4	46.89	46.19	4.55	41.26	37.43	5.82
	47.5–48.4	1.27	1.37	0.53	2.17	2.15	0.74
	48.5–59.4	4.93	6.00	4.72	11.82	14.54	14.63
	59.5–99.9	3.65	3.13	2.50	12.28	12.27	10.92
	Unknown	2.89	2.22	0.21	1.34	1.04	0.31
	Variable hours	0.00	0.06	0.01	0.01	0.12	0.03
	Total	100.00	100.00	100.00	100.00	100.00	100.00

Estonia	*Age: 15–74*	*Female (%)*			*Male (%)*		
All jobs	*Hours*	*1995*	*2000*	*2003*	*1995*	*2000*	*2003*
PE	<15	1.93	1.60	1.93	0.98	0.74	1.09
	15–24	6.36	5.62	6.08	2.77	2.18	1.95
	25–34	5.69	4.82	4.04	2.50	1.67	1.57
	35	4.57	2.89	4.01	3.04	1.67	1.65
	36–39	3.15	1.67	0.95	1.66	0.70	0.67
	40	55.72	66.46	72.40	57.57	69.84	75.15
	41–47	7.99	5.66	3.17	7.20	4.70	2.89
	48	3.08	3.49	2.91	3.38	4.66	4.65
	49–59	6.80	4.33	2.66	9.73	7.73	5.36
	60+	4.71	3.46	1.86	11.18	6.10	4.91
	Unknown	0.00	0.00	0.00	0.00	0.00	0.00
	Total	100.00	100.00	100.00	100.00	100.00	100.00
SE	<15	0.00	0.00	0.00	0.00	0.00	0.00
	15–24	0.00	0.00	12.88	0.00	0.00	4.78
	25–34	18.10	7.38	0.00	7.47	5.82	0.00
	35	0.00	0.00	0.00	0.00	0.00	0.00
	36–39	0.00	0.00	0.00	0.00	0.00	0.00
	40	28.45	44.30	47.73	30.60	34.59	52.87
	41–47	0.00	7.38	0.00	0.00	5.82	0.00
	48	0.00	0.00	0.00	0.00	0.00	0.00
	49–59	21.55	16.78	24.24	26.33	24.32	24.20
	60+	31.90	24.16	15.15	35.59	29.45	18.15
	Unknown	0.00	0.00	0.00	0.00	0.00	0.00
	Total	100.00	100.00	100.00	100.00	100.00	100.00
TE	<15	2.17	1.67	1.92	1.17	0.96	1.29
	15–24	6.58	5.79	6.34	3.21	2.30	2.21
	25–34	6.03	4.90	4.22	2.85	2.06	1.65
	35	4.60	2.92	3.94	3.06	1.79	1.55

Country		Gender and year					

Estonia continued All jobs	*Age: 15–74*	*Female (%)*			*Male (%)*		
	Hours	*1995*	*2000*	*2003*	*1995*	*2000*	*2003*
	36–39	3.13	1.71	1.10	1.68	0.65	0.63
	40	53.61	64.56	70.29	53.75	65.20	71.87
	41–47	8.11	5.69	3.36	7.15	4.74	3.11
	48	2.94	3.31	2.84	3.30	4.71	4.23
	49–59	7.22	4.94	3.60	10.87	9.24	7.24
	60+	5.62	4.51	2.40	12.94	8.35	6.21
	Unknown	0.00	0.00	0.00	0.00	0.00	0.00
	Total	100.00	100.00	100.00	100.00	100.00	100.00

Ethiopia All jobs	*Age: 10+*	*Female (%)*			*Male (%)*		
	Hours	*1995*	*2000*	*2004*	*1995*	*2000*	*2004*
PE	<15			2.27			0.95
	15–24			5.05			3.55
	25–34			5.04			4.37
	35			2.46			1.34
	36–39			10.90			11.05
	40			13.89			13.87
	41–47			9.73			9.44
	48			7.25			12.14
	49–59			15.06			16.01
	60+			28.02			26.95
	Unknown			0.35			0.33
	Total			100.00			100.00
SE	<15			8.49			6.24
	15–24			18.24			9.10
	25–34			15.52			10.68
	35			4.08			3.81
	36–39			4.55			3.90
	40			6.08			6.32
	41–47			7.78			8.49
	48			2.71			5.97
	49–59			10.56			15.82
	60+			21.53			29.46
	Unknown			0.45			0.21
	Total			100.00			100.00
TE	<15			5.61			3.39
	15–24			12.15			6.11
	25–34			10.68			7.28
	35			3.33			2.48
	36–39			7.48			7.75
	40			9.69			10.38
	41–47			8.68			9.00
	48			4.81			9.29
	49–59			12.64			15.92
	60+			24.53			28.11
	Unknown			0.40			0.27
	Total			100.00			100.00

Country		Gender and year					
Finland	*Age: 25+*	*Female (%)*			*Male (%)*		
Main job	*Hours*	*1995*	*2000*	*2004*	*1995*	*2000*	*2004*
PE	<15	1.72	1.70	1.97	0.89	0.90	0.99
	15–24	4.42	6.14	6.55	1.27	2.49	2.97
	25–34	9.71	9.55	10.48	4.44	3.96	4.29
	35	4.05	3.18	3.17	2.28	2.38	2.09
	36–39	65.60	56.48	56.33	59.52	33.60	33.41
	40	9.21	16.48	15.28	21.45	42.31	42.31
	41–47	1.97	3.07	3.17	2.79	6.11	6.37
	48	0.25	0.23	0.22	0.25	0.45	0.66
	49–59	1.35	1.82	1.64	3.30	5.32	4.84
	60+	0.49	0.91	0.76	1.65	2.15	1.76
	Unknown	1.23	0.45	0.44	2.16	0.34	0.33
	Total	100.00	100.00	100.00	100.00	100.00	100.00
SE	<15	6.00	6.19	7.45	2.87	3.81	4.04
	15–24	9.00	6.19	7.45	4.31	4.29	6.57
	25–34	9.00	10.31	11.70	6.22	6.19	7.07
	35	6.00	4.12	5.32	3.35	3.33	3.03
	36–39	3.00	3.09	5.32	1.91	0.95	1.52
	40	12.00	16.49	15.96	15.31	16.67	19.70
	41–47	14.00	14.43	10.64	7.18	8.57	8.59
	48	0.00	0.00	2.13	1.44	0.95	1.52
	49–59	19.00	16.49	19.15	20.57	22.86	21.21
	60+	17.00	18.56	12.77	30.14	29.52	24.75
	Unknown	5.00	4.12	2.13	6.70	2.86	2.02
	Total	100.00	100.00	100.00	100.00	100.00	100.00
TE	<15	2.07	2.14	2.48	1.30	1.46	1.54
	15–24	4.91	6.12	6.63	2.00	2.93	3.62
	25–34	9.61	9.59	10.59	4.80	4.30	4.80
	35	4.26	3.37	3.27	2.50	2.47	2.26
	36–39	58.62	51.02	51.49	47.35	27.36	27.78
	40	9.50	16.43	15.35	20.22	37.33	38.37
	41–47	3.28	4.18	3.96	3.80	6.59	6.79
	48	0.44	0.31	0.40	0.50	0.64	0.72
	49–59	3.28	3.37	3.27	6.91	8.69	7.78
	60+	2.29	2.65	1.98	7.61	7.41	5.79
	Unknown	1.75	0.82	0.59	3.00	0.82	0.54
	Total	100.00	100.00	100.00	100.00	100.00	100.00
France	*Age: 25+*	*Female (%)*			*Male (%)*		
Main job	*Hours*	*1995*	*2000*	*2004*	*1995*	*2000*	*2004*
PE	<15	4.12	4.04	4.42	0.43	0.54	0.64
	15–24	13.84	13.33	12.38	3.58	3.16	2.91
	25–34	12.93	15.79	17.05	2.04	3.42	3.85
	35	3.00	14.95	27.21	1.45	18.55	31.83
	36–39	46.13	33.06	19.87	54.36	40.31	24.87
	40	5.91	4.99	7.45	8.09	6.10	11.34

Country		*Gender and year*					
France continued	*Age: 25+*	*Female (%)*			*Male (%)*		
Main job	*Hours*	*1995*	*2000*	*2004*	*1995*	*2000*	*2004*
	41–47	5.03	4.31	5.31	9.38	8.34	11.21
	48	0.24	0.16	0.28	0.65	0.38	0.65
	49–59	2.43	2.49	3.42	5.89	5.23	7.90
	60+	0.78	0.74	1.41	2.64	2.27	3.93
	Variable hours	5.57	6.15	0.00	11.11	11.52	0.00
	Unknown	0.01	0.00	1.19	0.40	0.19	0.87
	Total	100.00	100.00	100.00	100.00	100.00	100.00
SE	<15	3.57	2.58	3.90	0.47	0.46	0.90
	15–24	6.75	6.44	9.22	1.04	0.91	2.02
	25–34	7.62	6.56	10.40	1.40	1.37	1.96
	35	2.99	2.81	5.32	0.62	1.08	2.97
	36–39	5.11	3.75	2.96	2.81	2.05	1.85
	40	8.29	8.08	12.53	4.73	4.00	8.57
	41–47	7.33	7.49	10.64	6.14	5.54	10.53
	48	1.16	0.82	2.01	1.04	0.63	1.34
	49–59	10.99	11.48	16.43	15.61	15.07	24.02
	60+	15.24	13.58	24.94	25.44	25.23	45.13
	Variable hours	30.95	36.42	0.00	40.69	43.66	0.00
	Unknown	0.00	0.00	1.65	0.00	0.00	0.73
	Total	100.00	100.00	100.00	100.00	100.00	100.00
TE	<15	4.06	3.91	4.38	0.43	0.52	0.68
	15–24	13.03	12.72	12.13	3.16	2.83	2.78
	25–34	12.32	14.98	16.50	1.94	3.12	3.58
	35	3.00	13.88	25.43	1.31	15.97	27.63
	36–39	41.45	30.48	18.50	45.75	34.65	21.51
	40	6.18	5.26	7.86	7.53	5.78	10.93
	41–47	5.29	4.59	5.75	8.84	7.93	11.11
	48	0.34	0.22	0.42	0.71	0.41	0.75
	49–59	3.41	3.28	4.48	7.51	6.69	10.25
	60+	2.43	1.87	3.33	6.44	5.67	9.93
	Variable hours	8.47	8.82	0.00	16.04	16.27	0.00
	Unknown	0.01	0.00	1.23	0.33	0.16	0.85
	Total	100.00	100.00	100.00	100.00	100.00	100.00
Georgia	*Age: 25+*	*Female (%)*			*Male (%)*		
All jobs	*Hours*	*1995*	*2000*	*2004*	*1995*	*2000*	*2004*
PE	<20			10.31			3.11
	21–30			19.64			6.61
	31–35			16.08			12.26
	36–41			31.49			28.01
	42–50			13.65			27.23
	51–60			4.76			9.59

Country	Gender and year						
Georgia continued All jobs	Age: 25+	Female (%)			Male (%)		
	Hours	1995	2000	2004	1995	2000	2004
	60 or more			2.70			8.32
	Different in different seasons			1.36			4.86
	Total			100.00			100.00
SE	<20			21.10			13.49
	21–30			18.55			14.66
	31–35			12.11			14.37
	36–41			13.01			14.14
	42–50			8.38			12.23
	51–60			5.08			7.23
	60 or more			1.88			3.74
	Different in different seasons			19.89			20.14
	Total			100.00			100.00
TE	<20			17.26			9.95
	21–30			18.94			11.92
	31–35			13.53			13.65
	36–41			19.60			18.86
	42–50			10.26			17.34
	51–60			4.96			8.03
	60 or more			2.17			5.30
	Different in different seasons			13.28			14.94
	Total			100.00			100.00
Greece Main job	Age: 25+	Female (%)			Male (%)		
	Hours	1995	2000	2005	1995	2000	2005
PE	<15	1.20	1.29	1.30	0.35	0.21	0.32
	15–24	6.94	6.70	7.48	2.31	2.08	2.39
	25–34	11.56	11.63	10.93	5.15	5.22	4.95
	35	2.59	2.92	2.15	2.24	2.01	1.77
	36–39	18.44	13.20	10.40	16.57	11.59	9.11
	40	45.24	48.01	49.89	51.50	53.64	56.17
	41–47	4.43	4.10	4.02	4.44	4.19	3.84
	48	6.41	7.96	9.33	9.17	12.79	13.06
	49–59	2.04	2.41	2.62	4.58	4.62	4.43
	60+	1.02	1.62	1.88	3.46	3.47	3.97
	Unknown	0.11	0.15	0.00	0.24	0.19	0.00
	Total	100.00	100.00	100.00	100.00	100.00	100.00
SE	<15	1.64	1.23	2.22	0.70	0.35	0.85
	15–24	7.95	4.70	6.45	2.26	1.19	1.15

Country		Gender and year					

Greece continued	Age: 25+	Female (%)			Male (%)		
Main job	Hours	1995	2000	2005	1995	2000	2005
	25–34	11.35	14.71	13.38	3.46	5.31	3.73
	35	4.54	3.96	3.50	2.16	1.83	1.46
	36–39	3.87	2.82	1.95	1.69	1.77	0.92
	40	13.92	19.21	21.13	14.21	16.48	17.36
	41–47	12.22	9.03	7.49	10.97	7.72	7.26
	48	13.74	14.83	14.80	18.80	21.19	19.80
	49–59	14.35	14.11	14.56	16.48	17.07	17.57
	60+	15.83	14.24	14.53	28.58	26.13	29.91
	Unknown	0.57	1.16	0.00	0.69	0.97	0.00
	Total	100.00	100.00	100.00	100.00	100.00	100.00
TE	<15	1.40	1.27	1.61	0.52	0.27	0.53
	15–24	7.40	5.88	7.14	2.29	1.68	1.89
	25–34	11.47	12.89	11.75	4.34	5.26	4.46
	35	3.49	3.35	2.60	2.20	1.93	1.64
	36–39	11.78	8.96	7.59	9.41	7.22	5.82
	40	30.92	36.23	40.32	33.56	37.10	40.58
	41–47	8.00	6.12	5.17	7.58	5.76	5.21
	48	9.76	10.77	11.15	13.81	16.53	15.77
	49–59	7.67	7.19	6.59	10.31	10.16	9.70
	60+	7.80	6.78	6.09	15.55	13.55	14.39
	Unknown	0.32	0.56	0.00	0.45	0.54	0.00
	Total	100.00	100.00	100.00	100.00	100.00	100.00

Guatemala	Age: 25–60	Female (%)			Male (%)		
Main job	Hours	1995	2000	2004	1995	2000	2004
PE	<15			5.81			0.38
	15–24			6.80			3.94
	25–34			19.43			6.91
	35			3.30			2.00
	36–39			2.35			3.25
	40			16.12			15.74
	41–47			15.99			19.96
	48			7.14			14.33
	49–59			9.85			14.55
	60+			13.23			18.94
	Total			100.00			100.00
SE	<15			27.52			2.78
	15–24			21.08			6.54
	25–34			13.15			9.68
	35			2.70			2.65
	36–39			2.33			5.87
	40			1.67			8.90
	41–47			4.60			15.99
	48			4.05			18.48
	49–59			7.59			14.95

Country		Gender and year					
Guatemala continued	*Age: 25–60*	*Female (%)*			*Male (%)*		
Main job	*Hours*	*1995*	*2000*	*2004*	*1995*	*2000*	*2004*
	60+			15.30			14.15
	Total			100.00			100.00
TE	<15			17.90			1.51
	15–24			14.76			5.16
	25–34			15.93			8.21
	35			2.97			2.30
	36–39			2.34			4.47
	40			8.07			12.53
	41–47			9.64			18.10
	48			5.42			16.27
	49–59			8.59			14.74
	60+			14.38			16.70
	Total			100.00			100.00

Honduras	*Age: 10+*	*Female (%)*			*Male (%)*		
All jobs	*Hours*	*1996S*	*2001S*	*2004*	*1996S*	*2001S*	*2004*
PE	<15	2.21	2.75		1.47	1.66	
	15–24	3.53	3.25		3.87	3.31	
	25–34	6.56	9.16		4.33	4.82	
	35	1.96	1.52		1.06	1.15	
	36–39	2.94	2.55		3.55	4.91	
	40	17.86	15.74		13.74	10.34	
	41–47	25.97	29.58		32.48	37.55	
	49–59	14.14	12.04		14.37	13.67	
	60+	24.84	23.41		25.13	22.59	
	Unknown	0.00	0.00		0.00	0.00	
	Total	100.00	100.00		100.00	100.00	
SE	<15	23.28	20.88		3.53	3.44	
	15–24	17.48	15.33		6.99	6.19	
	25–34	11.87	10.61		8.60	8.51	
	35	3.13	3.43		1.71	2.20	
	36–39	3.05	3.85		8.42	7.36	
	40	3.32	3.87		8.73	6.45	
	41–47	7.44	9.65		25.76	31.90	
	49–59	7.39	7.85		11.60	11.39	
	60+	23.05	24.55		24.65	22.57	
	Unknown	0.00	0.00		0.00	0.00	
	Total	100.00	100.00		100.00	100.00	
TE	<15	12.86	11.97		3.10	3.85	
	15–24	10.73	10.15		6.15	5.59	
	25–34	10.18	10.20		7.27	7.21	
	35	2.78	2.61		1.58	1.81	
	36–39	3.18	3.08		6.57	6.52	
	40	10.44	9.84		11.17	8.68	

Country		Gender and year					

Honduras continued All jobs	Age: 10+	Female (%)			Male (%)		
	Hours	1996S	2001S	2004	1996S	2001S	2004
	41–47	16.18	19.77		28.48	34.11	
	49–59	10.47	9.60		12.80	11.63	
	60+	23.17	22.78		22.87	20.59	
	Unknown	0.00	0.00		0.00	0.00	
	Total	100.00	100.00		100.00	100.00	

Hungary Main job	Age: 25+	Female (%)			Male (%)		
	Hours	1995	2000	2004	1996	2001	2004
PE	<15	0.67	0.39	0.43	0.45	0.28	0.26
	15–24	3.24	3.48	3.70	0.98	1.09	1.40
	25–34	3.52	3.97	3.69	0.88	0.97	1.25
	35	0.51	0.43	0.65	0.18	0.14	0.23
	36–39	1.17	1.15	1.18	0.80	0.61	0.58
	40	71.30	75.82	81.82	62.71	67.49	75.97
	41–47	11.53	7.53	2.77	11.87	7.50	3.40
	49–59	2.23	2.33	1.39	6.40	6.04	4.34
	48	1.33	1.29	0.94	2.86	2.57	1.89
	60+	1.08	0.77	0.82	3.71	3.97	2.89
	Unknown	3.42	2.84	2.61	9.16	9.34	7.79
	Total	100.00	100.00	100.00	100.00	100.00	100.00
SE	<15	1.18	1.05	1.25	0.76	0.42	0.66
	15–24	3.26	3.84	5.04	1.25	0.88	1.63
	25–34	2.81	3.69	2.78	0.88	1.52	1.01
	35	0.63	0.26	0.13	0.23	0.10	0.15
	36–39	0.28	0.55	0.41	0.15	0.31	0.32
	40	44.16	42.28	48.38	32.81	33.31	37.80
	41–47	7.64	5.31	3.24	7.17	3.69	2.58
	49–59	9.77	8.06	5.60	13.42	10.83	9.48
	48	2.65	1.69	0.85	2.59	1.56	1.10
	60+	6.72	7.55	5.39	13.47	12.78	10.29
	Unknown	20.91	25.73	26.93	27.27	34.59	34.99
	Total	100.00	100.00	100.00	100.00	100.00	100.00
TE	<15	0.74	0.46	0.52	0.52	0.31	0.33
	15–24	3.25	3.52	3.84	1.04	1.05	1.44
	25–34	3.42	3.94	3.59	0.88	1.08	1.20
	35	0.53	0.41	0.59	0.19	0.13	0.22
	36–39	1.05	1.08	1.10	0.65	0.55	0.53
	40	67.52	72.06	78.29	55.78	60.48	68.83
	41–47	10.99	7.28	2.82	10.78	6.72	3.25
	49–59	3.28	2.97	1.84	8.03	7.02	5.31
	48	1.52	1.33	0.93	2.80	2.36	1.74
	60+	1.86	1.53	1.30	5.97	5.78	4.28
	Unknown	5.85	5.40	5.18	13.35	14.52	12.87
	Total	100.00	100.00	100.00	100.00	100.00	100.00

Country		Gender and year					
Indonesia	*Age: 15+*	*Female (%)*			*Male (%)*		
All jobs	*Hours*	*1996*	*2000*	*2003*	*1996*	*2000*	*2003*
PE	1–4	0.18	0.16	0.09	0.05	0.05	0.02
	5–9	1.09	1.00	0.71	0.38	0.25	0.16
	10–14	2.26	2.26	2.11	0.59	0.56	0.58
	15–19	3.53	2.65	3.42	1.06	0.84	1.09
	20–24	5.29	5.09	6.66	2.24	2.13	2.51
	25–34	14.51	14.11	13.32	8.49	8.18	8.61
	35–44	30.20	29.46	28.98	30.40	30.57	30.41
	45–54	26.34	29.90	30.85	35.66	39.89	40.51
	55–59	6.10	5.15	5.55	9.60	7.79	7.81
	60–74	6.71	7.28	5.92	9.30	8.13	6.96
	75+	3.80	2.92	2.40	2.23	1.61	1.35
	Total	100.00	100.00	100.00	100.00	100.00	100.00
SE	1–4	0.72	0.56	0.32	0.33	0.16	0.14
	5–9	3.67	1.91	1.62	1.18	0.78	0.70
	10–14	7.71	4.84	3.20	2.69	2.43	1.45
	15–19	7.95	6.07	4.53	3.49	2.88	2.24
	20–24	11.00	11.07	9.00	6.12	5.66	4.47
	25–34	18.76	18.51	18.01	16.18	14.51	12.30
	35–44	23.82	25.16	26.73	26.10	25.66	26.55
	45–54	10.15	11.68	12.96	21.24	22.92	24.65
	55–59	5.16	7.38	7.36	9.35	9.72	9.90
	60–74	7.61	8.67	11.62	10.73	12.66	14.39
	75+	3.45	4.16	4.66	2.58	2.62	3.22
	Total	100.00	100.00	100.00	100.00	100.00	100.00
TE	1–4	0.40	0.32	0.17	0.16	0.10	0.06
	5–9	2.16	1.36	1.02	0.68	0.46	0.35
	10–14	4.53	3.27	2.48	1.37	1.31	0.88
	15–19	5.37	3.99	3.80	1.97	1.65	1.49
	20–24	7.66	7.43	7.45	3.68	3.53	3.19
	25–34	16.28	15.83	14.92	11.35	10.71	9.89
	35–44	27.55	27.78	28.21	28.80	28.61	29.07
	45–54	19.61	22.77	24.76	30.29	33.12	35.01
	55–59	5.71	6.02	6.17	9.51	8.56	8.53
	60–74	7.08	7.82	7.86	9.83	9.94	9.53
	75+	3.65	3.40	3.17	2.36	2.02	2.00
	Total	100.00	100.00	100.00	100.00	100.00	100.00
Ireland	*Age: 25+*	*Female (%)*			*Male (%)*		
Main job	*Hours*	*1995*	*2000*	*2004*	*1995*	*2000*	*2004*
PE	<15		5.49	5.99		0.52	0.59
	15–24		21.85	22.72		4.19	3.19
	25–34		10.06	12.79		2.93	2.81
	35		5.24	5.77		2.83	3.42
	36–39		32.78	33.50		35.19	41.79
	40		14.50	11.65		26.58	25.14

Country		Gender and year					
Ireland continued Main job	Age: 25+	Female (%)			Male (%)		
	Hours	1995	2000	2004	1995	2000	2004
	41–47		2.80	2.09		6.54	6.45
	48		0.25	0.15		1.10	1.05
	49–59		1.62	1.08		6.38	5.31
	60+		0.91	0.65		3.91	2.93
	Variable hours/ not stated		4.51	3.60		9.84	7.33
	Total		100.00	100.00		100.00	100.00
SE	<15		4.23	6.23		0.41	0.74
	15–24		10.57	12.06		1.72	1.79
	25–34		7.40	10.51		2.42	2.64
	35		2.75	2.53		0.82	1.09
	36–39		3.81	6.81		2.33	3.69
	40		13.53	15.37		10.81	13.18
	41–47		4.65	4.47		4.18	4.04
	48		0.00	0.00		0.78	0.58
	49–59		8.88	7.39		12.00	12.67
	60+		12.90	7.59		24.20	20.83
	Variable hours/ not stated		31.29	27.04		40.34	38.75
	Total		100.00	100.00		100.00	100.00
TE	<15		5.38	6.01		0.49	0.63
	15–24		20.84	21.86		3.45	2.79
	25–34		9.83	12.60		2.78	2.76
	35		5.02	5.50		2.23	2.76
	36–39		30.20	31.34		25.38	30.96
	40		14.41	11.95		21.87	21.74
	41–47		2.96	2.29		5.83	5.76
	48		0.23	0.14		1.00	0.92
	49–59		2.26	1.59		8.06	7.40
	60+		1.98	1.21		9.97	8.02
	Variable hours/ not stated		6.90	5.50		18.95	16.25
	Total		100.00	100.00		100.00	100.00
Israel	Age: 25+	Female (%)			Male (%)		
	Hours	1995	2000	2004	1995	2000	2004
PE	<15	4.57	4.81	5.21	0.97	1.14	1.50
	15–24	14.25	13.31	12.87	3.18	3.25	3.99
	25–29	6.81	5.99	5.92	1.27	1.47	1.37
	30	8.88	7.82	7.56	1.64	1.72	1.74
	31–34	2.82	2.30	2.56	0.49	0.48	0.57
	35	6.34	6.15	6.00	1.31	1.32	1.54
	36–39	4.83	4.46	4.50	1.30	1.24	0.94

Country	Gender and year					
Israel continued	Age: 25+	Female (%)			Male (%)		
	Hours	1995	2000	2004	1995	2000	2004
	40	18.71	20.38	20.77	12.64	14.56	15.28
	41–44	6.67	8.54	8.40	5.72	6.99	6.91
	45	12.66	12.27	11.89	22.75	19.96	19.66
	46–49	4.33	3.93	4.11	12.25	11.17	11.09
	50	3.90	4.82	5.26	10.81	12.35	13.79
	51–59	2.46	2.06	2.00	9.02	7.82	7.53
	60	1.48	1.65	1.71	7.50	8.79	7.21
	61+	1.15	1.24	1.15	9.01	7.43	6.71
	Unknown	0.14	0.26	0.10	0.14	0.31	0.16
	Total	100.00	100.00	100.00	100.00	100.00	100.00
SE	<15	7.24	7.00	8.70	1.80	1.93	2.52
	15–24	15.39	13.91	16.05	4.50	3.79	5.65
	25–29	5.24	4.54	5.49	1.21	1.24	2.01
	30	9.01	7.88	5.98	2.58	2.49	3.08
	31–34	1.36	0.55	0.73	0.41	0.31	0.38
	35	4.22	4.82	4.99	1.36	1.73	1.99
	36–39	5.23	3.55	2.35	1.60	1.08	0.94
	40	10.34	15.86	16.80	6.87	9.10	11.20
	41–44	8.85	6.48	4.33	2.03	1.93	1.85
	45	6.53	9.37	8.69	10.23	10.93	11.31
	46–49	10.04	7.30	4.44	10.25	9.22	7.21
	50	5.08	5.97	7.02	9.48	12.62	13.14
	51–59	4.87	3.79	5.14	13.98	12.30	10.02
	60	2.75	3.90	3.38	13.90	12.59	11.08
	61+	3.62	3.70	5.38	19.21	17.71	16.86
	Unknown	0.24	1.37	0.54	0.59	1.02	0.75
	Total	100.00	100.00	100.00	100.00	100.00	100.00
TE	<15	4.84	5.00	5.48	1.12	1.28	1.66
	15–24	14.37	13.37	13.12	3.42	3.34	4.24
	25–29	6.65	5.86	5.89	1.26	1.43	1.47
	30	8.89	7.82	7.44	1.81	1.85	1.94
	31–34	2.68	2.15	2.42	0.48	0.45	0.54
	35	6.12	6.03	5.92	1.32	1.39	1.61
	36–39	4.87	4.38	4.33	1.36	1.21	0.94
	40	17.87	19.98	20.46	11.57	13.64	14.66
	41–44	6.89	8.35	8.08	5.03	6.13	6.15
	45	12.04	12.01	11.63	20.41	18.43	18.40
	46–49	4.90	4.23	4.14	11.88	10.84	10.50
	50	4.02	4.92	5.40	10.56	12.40	13.69
	51–59	2.70	2.22	2.25	9.95	8.58	7.90
	60	1.61	1.85	1.84	8.69	9.43	7.80
	61+	1.40	1.46	1.48	10.91	9.17	8.24
	Unknown	0.15	0.36	0.13	0.22	0.43	0.25
	Total	100.00	100.00	100.00	100.00	100.00	100.00

Country		Gender and year					
Japan*	Age: 15+	Female (%)			Male (%)		
All jobs	Hours	1995	2000	2004	1995	2000	2004
PE	<15	5.36	6.51	7.31	1.29	1.60	2.02
	15–29	0.00	20.30	22.29	0.00	4.09	5.17
	15–34	26.32	29.67	32.65	7.10	7.83	10.30
	30–34	0.00	9.37	10.36	0.00	3.77	5.13
	35–39	0.00	10.41	9.81	0.00	5.28	5.39
	35–42	34.91	34.66	33.07	28.42	28.44	28.36
	40–48	0.00	40.70	37.05	0.00	46.92	42.86
	43–48	20.31	16.45	13.78	26.94	23.73	19.89
	49–59	9.29	8.70	8.93	20.87	20.87	21.33
	60+	3.77	3.90	4.02	15.25	17.32	17.77
	Unknown	0.05	0.10	0.23	0.13	0.16	0.29
	Total	100.00	100.00	100.00	100.00	100.00	100.00
SE	<15	14.03	16.14	17.17	4.51	5.81	6.87
	15–29	0.00	23.06	22.73	0.00	11.09	11.26
	15–34	32.19	32.91	32.32	14.69	17.25	18.13
	30–34	0.00	9.85	9.60	0.00	6.16	6.87
	35–39	0.00	8.18	7.58	0.00	6.87	6.11
	35–42	18.17	18.45	17.93	17.86	19.72	19.47
	40–48	0.00	19.08	18.69	0.00	29.05	27.48
	43–48	9.71	8.60	8.33	17.86	16.20	14.12
	49–59	12.05	11.32	11.62	20.37	17.96	19.08
	60+	13.85	12.58	12.12	24.71	22.54	22.52
	Unknown	0.00	0.00	0.51	0.00	0.18	0.38
	Total	100.00	100.00	100.00	100.00	100.00	100.00
TE	<15	7.23	8.28	8.84	1.80	2.23	2.71
	15–29	0.00	20.77	22.31	0.00	5.11	6.02
	15–34	27.57	30.20	32.52	8.29	9.26	11.38
	30–34	0.00	9.44	10.24	0.00	4.15	5.34
	35–39	0.00	9.98	9.46	0.00	5.51	5.50
	35–42	31.26	31.59	30.65	26.70	27.06	26.98
	40–48	0.00	36.62	34.07	0.00	44.11	40.53
	43–48	17.96	15.00	12.89	25.46	22.56	19.02
	49–59	9.88	9.20	9.31	20.76	20.40	20.94
	60+	5.91	5.49	5.30	16.75	18.09	18.39
	Unknown	0.19	0.27	0.51	0.24	0.37	0.57
	Total	100.00	100.00	100.00	100.00	100.00	100.00
Korea, Republic of	Age: 25+	Female (%)			Male (%)		
All jobs	Hours	1995	2000	2004	1995	2000	2004
PE	<15		2.79	3.07		0.81	0.89
	15–24		4.37	5.51		1.67	2.03
	25–34		5.19	5.70		1.88	2.36
	35		0.75	0.85		0.22	0.17
	36–39		5.89	6.37		3.25	3.45
	40		7.57	11.47		5.09	10.17

* Two different sets of hour band categories are reported by Japan (however, <15, 60+ and unknown are common to both).

Country		Gender and year					
Korea, Rep. of continued	*Age: 25+*	*Female (%)*			*Male (%)*		
All jobs	Hours	1995	2000	2004	1995	2000	2004
	41–47		20.33	22.19		17.33	20.18
	48		9.35	8.48		9.76	9.17
	49–59		26.22	21.09		33.68	28.03
	60+		17.54	15.27		26.31	23.55
	Unknown		0.00	0.00		0.00	0.00
	Total		100.00	100.00		100.00	100.00
SE	<15		2.78	3.31		2.22	2.76
	15–24		6.42	7.19		3.94	4.47
	25–34		5.81	6.84		3.83	4.45
	35		0.58	0.70		0.33	0.41
	36–39		6.91	8.48		5.11	5.95
	40		6.49	6.31		4.74	6.26
	41–47		11.90	10.20		11.64	11.58
	48		3.98	3.99		5.20	5.76
	49–59		20.68	18.79		26.64	23.85
	60+		34.44	34.19		36.37	34.50
	Unknown		0.00	0.00		0.00	0.00
	Total		100.00	100.00		100.00	100.00
TE	<15		2.79	3.16		1.33	1.56
	15–24		5.28	6.15		2.52	2.91
	25–34		5.48	6.13		2.60	3.11
	35		0.67	0.79		0.26	0.25
	36–39		6.34	7.17		3.95	4.35
	40		7.11	9.52		4.97	8.77
	41–47		16.61	17.66		15.20	17.09
	48		6.99	6.79		8.06	7.94
	49–59		23.78	20.22		31.05	26.53
	60+		24.97	22.41		30.06	27.48
	Unknown		0.00	0.00		0.00	0.00
	Total		100.00	100.00		100.00	100.00
Lithuania	*Age: 25+*	*Female (%)*			*Male (%)*		
Main job	Hours	1998	2000	2004	1998	2000	2004
PE	<15	0.81	0.80	0.87	0.79	0.56	0.36
	15–24	8.23	9.68	8.70	4.05	5.24	3.76
	25–34	7.20	7.04	10.10	3.59	3.73	6.37
	35	1.37	1.52	0.76	0.84	0.40	0.60
	36–39	3.14	4.29	6.59	2.29	1.82	3.15
	40	59.97	60.37	58.15	69.42	70.67	70.88
	41–47	2.48	1.87	1.88	2.24	2.55	3.35
	48	4.18	2.88	2.61	5.25	4.70	4.38
	49–59	1.54	1.53	1.11	2.74	3.82	2.32
	60+	2.05	2.22	0.78	4.73	3.44	1.94
	Unknown	9.02	7.81	8.46	4.05	3.08	2.90
	Total	100.00	100.00	100.00	100.00	100.00	100.00

Country		Gender and year					
Lithuania continued	*Age: 25+*	*Female (%)*			*Male (%)*		
Main job	*Hours*	*1998*	*2000*	*2004*	*1998*	*2000*	*2004*
SE	<15	3.95	4.37	2.55	3.37	4.32	1.32
	15–24	12.48	12.83	17.90	8.79	10.76	14.46
	25–34	17.46	21.36	25.83	11.52	19.19	22.57
	35	11.22	8.23	5.78	10.07	9.23	4.24
	36–39	1.01	3.71	3.28	1.87	4.50	2.86
	40	13.89	21.25	22.24	20.42	20.64	27.13
	41–47	7.67	6.35	11.37	6.33	6.90	12.02
	48	3.50	2.81	1.64	3.14	3.91	3.15
	49–59	12.35	10.90	5.80	13.47	12.59	9.19
	60+	12.12	4.18	2.11	18.15	5.96	1.95
	Unknown	4.35	4.02	1.50	2.87	1.99	1.10
	Total	100.00	100.00	100.00	100.00	100.00	100.00
TE	<15	1.33	1.42	1.15	1.38	1.43	0.57
	15–24	8.95	10.24	10.22	5.15	6.52	6.06
	25–34	8.92	9.56	12.70	5.42	7.32	9.85
	35	3.02	2.70	1.59	2.98	2.45	1.38
	36–39	2.78	4.19	6.04	2.19	2.44	3.09
	40	52.25	53.49	52.20	58.10	59.06	61.47
	41–47	3.35	2.66	3.45	3.19	3.56	5.21
	48	4.07	2.87	2.45	4.76	4.52	4.11
	49–59	3.35	3.18	1.89	5.22	5.85	3.80
	60+	3.74	2.56	1.00	7.83	4.02	1.94
	Unknown	8.23	7.14	7.31	3.78	2.83	2.51
	Total	100.00	100.00	100.00	100.00	100.00	100.00
Luxembourg	*Age: 15+*	*Female (%)*			*Male (%)*		
Main job	*Hours*	*1995*	*2000*	*2004*	*1995*	*2000*	*2004*
PE	<15	4.72	4.30	5.42	0.23	0.08	0.15
	15–24	19.05	22.69	25.07	1.53	1.46	1.18
	25–34	6.93	8.70	10.45	1.05	1.19	0.70
	35	0.54	0.88	0.96	0.27	0.38	0.20
	36–39	5.04	4.21	4.12	2.65	2.73	2.56
	40	58.77	56.11	52.68	86.05	86.59	92.67
	41–47	1.48	1.45	0.36	2.30	1.91	0.53
	48	0.89	0.54	0.51	1.12	0.70	0.84
	49–59	1.57	0.68	0.37	2.80	3.05	0.66
	60+	1.02	0.43	0.05	2.01	1.91	0.51
	Total	100.00	100.00	100.00	100.00	100.00	100.00
SE	<15	5.31	2.40	4.49	0.76	0.74	0.46
	15–24	10.57	9.75	17.44	0.75	1.61	2.79
	25–34	8.45	9.78	6.73	1.33	4.27	2.49
	35	2.15	3.22	1.45	0.19	0.27	0.24
	36–39	0.68	3.66	0.55	0.00	1.99	0.00
	40	22.39	30.67	27.26	25.15	19.34	24.23
	41–47	4.99	4.85	4.00	4.93	3.78	4.92

Country	Gender and year						
Luxembourg continued	*Age: 15+*	*Female (%)*			*Male (%)*		
Main job	*Hours*	*1995*	*2000*	*2004*	*1995*	*2000*	*2004*
	48	1.49	4.64	3.14	2.76	3.33	3.99
	49–59	13.33	14.34	17.70	16.59	21.54	25.17
	60+	30.64	16.69	17.25	47.54	43.11	35.70
	Total	100.00	100.00	100.00	100.00	100.00	100.00
TE	<15	4.78	4.20	5.37	0.29	0.12	0.18
	15–24	18.25	21.95	24.64	1.44	1.47	1.29
	25–34	7.07	8.76	10.24	1.08	1.42	0.83
	35	0.69	1.02	0.99	0.26	0.37	0.20
	36–39	4.63	4.18	3.92	2.37	2.68	2.37
	40	55.36	54.66	51.25	79.68	81.66	87.69
	41–47	1.81	1.64	0.57	2.58	2.05	0.85
	48	0.95	0.77	0.65	1.29	0.89	1.07
	49–59	2.67	1.46	1.34	4.24	4.41	2.44
	60+	3.79	1.36	1.02	6.78	4.93	3.07
	Total	100.00	100.00	100.00	100.00	100.00	100.00
Macau, China	*Age: 14+*	*Female (%)*			*Male (%)*		
Usual job	*Hours*	*1996*	*2000*	*2004*	*1996*	*2000*	*2004*
PE	<35						
	35–39						
	40–44						
	45–49						
	50–54						
	55–59						
	60+						
	Unknown						
	Total						
SE	<35						
	35–39						
	40–44						
	45–49						
	50–54						
	55–59						
	60+						
	Unknown						
	Total						
TE	<35	5.74	6.25	5.96	3.78	3.43	3.65
	35–39	9.19	8.88	7.99	10.74	9.60	8.15
	40–44	12.37	12.84	13.69	13.10	14.15	12.84
	45–49	34.51	31.80	36.99	28.98	29.41	32.98
	50–54	8.15	9.72	7.28	7.99	8.50	7.39
	55–59	11.39	11.47	11.91	14.02	12.70	14.42
	60+	18.64	19.03	16.20	21.28	22.21	20.58
	Unknown	0.00	0.00	0.00	0.11	0.00	0.00
	Total	100.00	100.00	100.00	100.00	100.00	100.00

Country		Gender and year					
Macedonia, FYR	*Age: 15+*	*Female (%)*			*Male (%)*		
Main job	*Hours*	*1998*	*2000*	*2003*	*1998*	*2000*	*2003*
PE	<15	0.25	0.19	0.37	0.58	0.16	0.55
	15–24	1.07	0.88	1.30	0.81	0.68	0.64
	25–34	3.15	2.01	1.80	2.50	1.12	1.70
	35	2.71	2.82	1.55	1.93	2.00	0.81
	36–39	1.58	1.13	0.93	1.04	0.68	0.51
	40	72.70	68.84	62.44	73.87	69.61	63.57
	41–47	8.32	8.17	7.86	7.24	6.26	7.62
	48	7.38	10.68	19.12	5.70	9.90	15.83
	49–59	2.27	4.15	3.59	2.85	5.65	4.60
	60+	0.57	1.13	1.05	3.47	3.93	4.21
	Total	100.00	100.00	100.00	100.00	100.00	100.00
SE	<15	5.82	6.67	4.09	5.46	3.22	1.52
	15–24	16.71	6.86	6.23	12.14	5.33	6.72
	25–34	12.91	7.84	10.85	11.65	6.33	6.72
	35	2.53	1.96	3.02	3.03	4.99	1.63
	36–39	0.76	1.37	0.36	0.61	1.22	0.54
	40	27.59	23.14	20.82	31.31	24.97	15.62
	41–47	4.30	3.14	2.67	4.13	4.66	5.64
	48	2.78	6.47	8.01	3.88	8.21	8.24
	49–59	11.90	20.20	15.30	12.01	14.32	14.75
	60+	14.68	22.35	28.65	15.78	26.75	38.61
	Total	100.00	100.00	100.00	100.00	100.00	100.00
TE	<15	1.36	1.76	1.33	1.75	0.97	0.82
	15–24	4.19	2.28	2.57	3.51	1.91	2.35
	25–34	5.15	3.47	4.13	4.68	2.50	3.12
	35	2.68	2.61	1.93	2.19	2.80	1.04
	36–39	1.41	1.19	0.78	0.94	0.82	0.52
	40	63.77	57.70	51.72	63.64	57.76	50.05
	41–47	7.48	6.94	6.52	6.49	5.80	7.06
	48	6.42	9.70	16.25	5.29	9.48	13.69
	49–59	4.14	8.03	6.61	5.06	7.95	7.45
	60+	3.39	6.32	8.17	6.43	9.99	13.90
	Total	100.00	100.00	100.00	100.00	100.00	100.00
Madagascar	*Age: 15+*	*Female (%)*			*Male (%)*		
Main job	*Hours*	*1995*	*2001*	*2004*	*1995*	*2001*	*2004*
PE	<15		1.51			0.84	
	15–24		7.78			4.21	
	25–34		21.81			11.67	
	35		7.13			7.58	
	36–39		0.00			0.00	
	40		40.17			42.48	
	41–47		5.62			6.86	
	48		0.00			0.00	
	49–59		9.29			12.76	

Country	Gender and year						
Madagascar continued	*Age: 25+*	*Female (%)*			*Male (%)*		
Main job	*Hours*	*1995*	*2001*	*2004*	*1995*	*2001*	*2004*
	60+		6.70			13.60	
	Unknown		0.00			0.00	
	Total		100.00			100.00	
SE	<15		2.94			1.48	
	15–24		11.77			7.12	
	25–34		11.67			9.07	
	35		0.07			0.07	
	36–39		22.04			18.19	
	40		0.17			0.07	
	41–47		10.47			13.16	
	48		26.11			34.92	
	49–59		2.67			2.86	
	60+		12.08			13.05	
	Unknown		0.00			0.00	
	Total		100.00			100.00	
TE	<15		2.75			1.33	
	15–24		11.23			6.45	
	25–34		13.06			9.67	
	35		1.03			1.81	
	36–39		19.03			13.98	
	40		5.64			9.87	
	41–47		9.81			11.70	
	48		22.54			26.86	
	49–59		3.57			5.14	
	60+		11.34			13.18	
	Unknown		0.00			0.00	
	Total		100.00			100.00	
Malta	*Age: 15+*	*Female (%)*			*Male (%)*		
Main job	*Hours*	*1995*	*2000*	*2004*	*1995*	*2000*	*2004*
PE	<15		0.00	2.73		0.00	0.00
	15–24		9.22	11.67		1.97	2.65
	25–35		14.96	20.41		3.99	5.34
	36–39		0.00	1.21		0.00	0.68
	40		69.32	57.38		73.61	73.22
	41–48		6.50	5.19		10.01	8.96
	49–59		0.00	0.00		6.19	3.46
	60+		0.00	0.00		4.23	3.60
	Variable hours		0.00	1.42		0.00	2.09
	Total		100.00	100.00		100.00	100.00
SE	<15		0.00	0.00		0.00	0.00
	15–24		0.00	0.00		0.00	3.56
	25–35		0.00	0.00		9.59	7.28
	36–39		0.00	0.00		0.00	0.91

Country		*Gender and year*					
Malta continued	*Age: 15+*	*Female (%)*			*Male (%)*		
Main job	*Hours*	*1995*	*2000*	*2004*	*1995*	*2000*	*2004*
	40		100.00	100.00		42.82	30.40
	41–48		0.00	0.00		13.23	12.12
	49–59		0.00	0.00		15.64	18.21
	60+		0.00	0.00		18.71	17.06
	Variable hours		0.00	0.00		0.00	10.46
	Total		100.00	100.00		100.00	100.00
TE	<15		2.37	2.83		0.00	0.50
	15–24		9.52	11.69		2.19	2.79
	25–35		14.83	19.65		4.75	5.65
	36–39		0.00	1.42		0.85	0.72
	40		66.94	54.61		68.06	65.41
	41–48		6.33	5.61		10.35	9.46
	49–59		0.00	1.31		7.50	6.01
	60+		0.00	1.14		6.30	5.93
	Variable hours		0.00	1.75		0.00	3.54
	Total		100.00	100.00		100.00	100.00

Mauritius	*Age: 25+*	*Female (%)*			*Male (%)*		
Main job	*Hours*	*1995*	*1999*	*2004*	*1995*	*1999*	*2004*
PE	1–14		4.62	4.43		0.84	1.25
	15–24		9.54	7.84		4.13	2.40
	25–34		21.23	23.34		15.09	14.33
	35		5.85	5.54		4.49	4.74
	36–39		6.97	7.47		7.47	9.30
	40		10.05	10.70		19.22	14.81
	41–47		21.85	20.94		21.98	23.62
	48		3.49	3.78		5.17	6.56
	49–59		13.44	13.38		13.32	15.24
	60+		2.97	2.58		8.30	7.76
	Unknown		0.00	0.00		0.00	0.00
	Total		100.00	100.00		100.00	100.00
SE	1–14		27.09	15.60		6.55	4.99
	15–24		20.69	23.39		11.39	9.67
	25–34		14.78	20.18		13.57	18.88
	35		2.96	3.21		3.74	2.96
	36–39		4.43	4.59		7.18	7.33
	40		1.48	2.75		5.15	4.68
	41–47		7.39	9.63		15.76	16.22
	48		1.48	2.29		3.90	4.68
	49–59		10.34	8.72		19.19	17.32
	60+		9.36	9.63		13.57	13.26
	Unknown		0.00	0.00		0.00	0.00
	Total		100.00	100.00		100.00	100.00
TE	1–14		8.49	6.30		2.27	2.12

Country	Gender and year						
Mauritius continued *Main job*	*Age: 25+*	*Female (%)*			*Male (%)*		
	Hours	*1995*	*1999*	*2004*	*1995*	*1999*	*2004*
	15–24		11.46	10.45		5.95	4.09
	25–34		20.12	22.81		14.71	15.34
	35		5.35	5.15		4.30	4.31
	36–39		6.54	6.99		7.39	8.80
	40		8.57	9.37		15.69	12.38
	41–47		19.35	19.05		20.42	21.80
	48		3.14	3.53		4.85	6.10
	49–59		12.90	12.60		14.79	15.67
	60+		4.07	3.76		9.62	9.02
	Unknown		0.00	0.00		0.00	0.37
	Total		100.00	100.00		100.00	100.00
Mexico	*Age: 25+*	*Female (%)*			*Male (%)*		
Main job	*Hours*	*1995*	*2000*	*2004*	*1995*	*2000*	*2004*
PE	<15	5.54	4.57	5.43	0.62	0.41	0.58
	15–24	8.97	7.52	7.84	2.25	1.64	1.87
	25–34	15.65	12.47	12.89	5.13	4.00	4.22
	35	6.55	6.08	5.57	2.77	2.20	2.23
	36–39	2.95	3.25	3.04	2.21	2.14	2.47
	40	20.58	22.97	21.82	14.37	15.74	14.97
	41–47	12.40	13.44	13.26	15.98	17.91	17.58
	48	13.78	17.66	17.98	21.13	26.04	25.23
	49–59	8.21	7.19	7.33	17.18	13.30	14.50
	60+	5.29	4.83	4.82	17.86	16.40	16.33
	Unknown	0.08	0.05	0.03	0.51	0.21	0.03
	Total	100.00	100.00	100.00	100.00	100.00	100.00
SE	<15	19.53	16.31	16.71	2.70	2.01	2.38
	15–24	19.13	18.73	19.24	5.99	4.47	5.47
	25–34	13.25	11.39	12.31	6.63	5.49	5.87
	35	4.77	4.64	4.48	2.25	2.52	2.27
	36–39	4.25	5.96	6.83	7.04	6.55	7.79
	40	2.95	3.52	2.95	4.80	5.20	5.22
	41–47	7.35	10.09	9.15	13.02	15.62	16.27
	48	4.92	7.80	6.43	18.62	22.08	21.43
	49–59	10.19	8.79	9.59	17.14	16.16	15.55
	60+	13.02	12.36	12.31	21.40	19.74	17.72
	Unknown	0.64	0.43	0.00	0.42	0.16	0.04
	Total	100.00	100.00	100.00	100.00	100.00	100.00
TE	<15	12.04	9.32	10.07	1.55	1.05	1.29
	15–24	13.70	12.06	12.53	3.93	2.78	3.30
	25–34	14.53	12.03	12.66	5.81	4.60	4.87
	35	5.72	5.49	5.13	2.54	2.33	2.25
	36–39	3.56	4.35	4.59	4.38	3.91	4.58
	40	12.38	15.09	14.04	10.06	11.50	11.09
	41–47	10.05	12.08	11.57	14.65	17.00	17.06

Country	Gender and year						
Mexico continued	Age: 25+	Female (%)			Male (%)		
Main job	Hours	1995	2000	2004	1995	2000	2004
	48	9.66	13.65	13.22	20.00	24.45	23.72
	49–59	9.13	7.84	8.25	17.16	14.45	14.92
	60+	8.89	7.88	7.91	19.45	17.75	16.88
	Unknown	0.34	0.22	0.03	0.47	0.19	0.03
	Total	100.00	100.00	100.00	100.00	100.00	100.00
Moldova	Age: 25+	Female (%)			Male (%)		
Main job	Hours	1995	2000	2004	1995	2000	2004
PE	<15		0.19	0.15		0.05	0.03
	15–24		4.35	5.43		1.39	1.47
	25–34		2.77	3.43		1.66	1.44
	35		1.57	1.25		0.38	0.82
	36–39		3.31	2.43		1.46	0.99
	40		63.96	66.60		64.36	65.80
	41–47		8.83	5.01		9.29	5.39
	48		7.26	6.31		9.89	9.28
	49–59		1.69	1.73		2.86	3.10
	60+		0.87	0.88		1.90	1.50
	Unknown		5.19	6.79		6.77	10.19
	Total		100.00	100.00		100.00	100.00
SE	<15		2.27	0.18		0.80	0.24
	15–24		5.29	2.92		3.44	1.52
	25–34		6.08	12.08		4.47	7.41
	35		1.15	4.42		1.38	3.42
	36–39		2.58	5.58		2.68	4.85
	40		19.13	15.44		19.83	18.53
	41–47		3.46	2.74		4.11	3.94
	48		4.17	2.08		5.90	4.13
	49–59		2.86	2.48		5.45	3.90
	60+		1.75	0.35		3.31	1.19
	Unknown		51.25	51.73		48.64	50.88
	Total		100.00	100.00		100.00	100.00
TE	<15		0.95	0.16		0.31	0.11
	15–24		4.70	4.52		2.09	1.49
	25–34		3.99	6.54		2.64	3.67
	35		1.42	2.40		0.73	1.79
	36–39		3.04	3.56		1.90	2.43
	40		47.32	48.11		48.81	48.19
	41–47		6.85	4.19		7.48	4.85
	48		6.12	4.79		8.48	7.37
	49–59		2.11	2.01		3.76	3.38
	60+		1.18	0.69		2.39	1.38
	Unknown		22.32	23.03		21.41	25.35
	Total		100.00	100.00		100.00	100.00

Country		Gender and year					
Netherlands	*Age: 15+*	*Female (%)*			*Male (%)*		
All jobs	*Hours*	*1996*	*2000*	*2004*	*1996*	*2000*	*2004*
PE	<15	0.00	0.46	0.37	0.00	0.49	0.47
	15–24	20.69	19.34	18.26	15.57	16.10	15.74
	25–34	32.44	29.16	25.37	29.80	26.81	23.65
	35	2.69	2.75	2.92	3.08	2.96	2.70
	36–39	10.46	10.78	10.34	10.99	10.97	10.63
	40	2.62	2.59	2.70	2.49	2.60	2.57
	41–47	16.08	17.02	17.92	17.25	16.40	17.55
	48	2.03	1.92	2.14	2.57	2.29	2.36
	49–59	12.14	14.96	18.26	17.03	19.44	21.48
	60+	0.82	0.96	1.71	1.20	1.91	2.78
	Unknown	0.04	0.03	0.00	0.03	0.03	0.08
	Total	100.00	100.00	100.00	100.00	100.00	100.00
SE	<15	0.00	0.59	0.30	0.00	0.50	0.31
	15–24	4.98	4.69	4.17	5.24	3.52	4.25
	25–34	20.60	16.42	14.29	19.41	18.62	16.22
	35	2.66	2.93	2.98	2.62	2.35	2.99
	36–39	11.30	12.61	13.39	10.66	11.91	11.50
	40	2.99	4.11	2.98	2.45	3.02	3.46
	41–47	21.93	18.48	21.43	19.58	18.29	20.00
	48	2.99	2.93	2.68	2.97	3.19	2.36
	49–59	26.58	29.03	27.98	24.48	27.18	26.14
	60+	5.65	7.92	9.23	11.54	10.91	11.65
	Unknown	0.33	0.29	0.60	1.05	0.50	1.10
	Total	100.00	100.00	100.00	100.00	100.00	100.00
TE	<15	0.00	0.48	0.37	0.00	0.49	0.45
	15–24	19.04	17.88	16.93	14.17	14.42	14.13
	25–34	31.19	27.83	24.33	28.37	25.71	22.61
	35	2.72	2.77	2.90	3.04	2.88	2.74
	36–39	10.55	11.00	10.63	10.94	11.09	10.76
	40	2.65	2.77	2.73	2.48	2.66	2.70
	41–47	16.70	17.16	18.26	17.57	16.65	17.89
	48	2.13	2.00	2.19	2.60	2.41	2.34
	49–59	13.66	16.39	19.18	18.05	20.49	22.16
	60+	1.29	1.67	2.39	2.60	3.10	4.02
	Unknown	0.07	0.06	0.08	0.17	0.09	0.20
	Total	100.00	100.00	100.00	100.00	100.00	100.00
New Zealand	*Age: 15+*	*Female (%)*			*Male (%)*		
Main job	*Hours*	*1995*	*2000*	*2004*	*1995*	*2000*	*2004*
PE	<15	13.94	12.92	11.44	2.42	3.96	2.79
	15–24	16.17	15.89	15.80	2.66	2.71	3.03
	25–29	5.11	5.44	5.45	0.75	1.08	0.89
	30–34	7.87	8.09	8.85	1.90	2.17	2.41
	35	2.45	2.91	2.67	0.95	0.80	1.14
	36–39	8.59	6.99	6.75	3.95	3.16	3.41

Country		Gender and year					
New Zealand continued	Age: 15+	Female (%)			Male (%)		
Main job	Hours	1995	2000	2004	1995	2000	2004
	40	31.04	30.70	32.32	42.47	39.03	40.26
	41–47	7.06	7.27	8.06	16.22	16.71	18.18
	48	0.95	0.99	0.85	3.11	3.36	2.97
	49–59	4.82	5.90	5.45	16.56	17.03	16.64
	60+	1.85	2.58	2.35	8.90	9.74	8.26
	Unknown	0.14	0.32	0.02	0.11	0.26	0.02
	Total	100.00	100.00	100.00	100.00	100.00	100.00
SE	<15	24.37	22.43	22.43	3.58	6.10	6.10
	15–24	16.97	18.90	18.90	5.03	5.52	5.52
	25–29	6.22	5.36	5.36	2.44	2.14	2.14
	30–34	8.07	9.31	9.31	5.26	6.42	6.42
	35	3.70	3.67	3.67	2.36	3.11	3.11
	36–39	2.18	1.97	1.97	1.52	1.04	1.04
	40	12.44	12.27	12.27	22.10	19.14	19.14
	41–47	6.05	5.92	5.92	11.97	11.49	11.49
	48	1.01	1.27	1.27	2.90	1.49	1.49
	49–59	9.41	9.87	9.87	20.58	20.64	20.64
	60+	9.24	8.89	8.89	22.03	22.78	22.78
	Unknown	0.34	0.14	0.14	0.23	0.13	0.13
	Total	100.00	100.00	100.00	100.00	100.00	100.00
TE	<15	15.54	14.43	14.43	2.58	4.28	4.28
	15–24	16.02	16.13	16.13	2.99	3.14	3.14
	25–29	5.21	5.30	5.30	1.10	1.23	1.23
	30–34	7.85	8.29	8.29	2.50	2.95	2.95
	35	2.65	3.02	3.02	1.22	1.29	1.29
	36–39	7.40	6.06	6.06	3.15	2.50	2.50
	40	27.67	27.66	27.66	35.35	32.60	32.60
	41–47	7.08	7.08	7.08	15.15	15.06	15.06
	48	1.00	1.02	1.02	3.01	2.80	2.80
	49–59	5.78	6.73	6.73	18.67	18.94	18.94
	60+	3.62	4.00	4.00	14.15	15.00	15.00
	Unknown	0.18	0.29	0.29	0.13	0.23	0.23
	Total	100.00	100.00	100.00	100.00	100.00	100.00
Norway	Age: 16+	Female (%)			Male (%)		
All jobs	Hours	1996	2000	2004	1996	2000	2004
PE	<15	10.41	9.46	10.20	3.90	4.38	4.93
	15–24	19.63	16.83	16.13	2.83	3.29	3.90
	25–34	15.73	16.73	16.91	4.48	3.93	4.46
	35	6.07	6.18	5.83	3.80	3.47	3.16
	36–39	41.21	43.73	44.41	64.72	67.49	67.01
	40	2.60	2.59	2.24	5.85	5.57	5.11
	41–47	2.49	2.79	2.53	6.04	5.39	5.39
	48	0.11	0.10	0.10	0.29	0.27	0.28
	49–59	0.98	0.90	0.78	4.58	3.74	3.53

Country	Gender and year						
Norway continued *All jobs*	*Age: 16+*	*Female (%)*			*Male (%)*		
	Hours	*1996*	*2000*	*2004*	*1996*	*2000*	*2004*
	60+	0.33	0.30	0.39	2.73	2.10	1.86
	Unknown	0.43	0.40	0.49	0.78	0.37	0.37
	Total	100.00	100.00	100.00	100.00	100.00	100.00
SE	<15	11.36	10.64	9.09	2.46	3.54	5.00
	15–24	13.64	12.77	13.64	3.28	3.54	5.00
	25–34	15.91	12.77	13.64	5.74	4.42	5.83
	35	4.55	4.26	4.55	2.46	2.65	2.50
	36–39	11.36	14.89	15.91	8.20	11.50	12.50
	40	13.64	12.77	13.64	15.57	15.04	19.17
	41–47	11.36	12.77	11.36	13.11	13.27	13.33
	48	0.00	2.13	0.00	1.64	0.88	0.83
	49–59	9.09	10.64	9.09	22.95	21.24	19.17
	60+	6.82	6.38	6.82	22.95	23.01	15.83
	Unknown	2.27	0.00	2.27	1.64	0.88	0.83
	Total	100.00	100.00	100.00	100.00	100.00	100.00
TE	<15	10.66	9.75	10.34	3.98	4.45	5.16
	15–24	19.36	16.67	16.03	2.94	3.30	3.99
	25–34	15.68	16.57	16.78	4.58	4.04	4.58
	35	6.05	6.06	5.68	3.63	3.38	3.16
	36–39	39.55	42.23	43.24	58.39	62.08	61.31
	40	3.07	3.03	2.70	6.92	6.43	6.49
	41–47	2.87	3.22	2.89	6.83	6.10	6.16
	48	0.10	0.19	0.09	0.43	0.33	0.33
	49–59	1.43	1.33	1.12	6.49	5.36	5.07
	60+	0.72	0.57	0.65	4.93	4.12	3.24
	Unknown	0.51	0.38	0.47	0.87	0.41	0.50
	Total	100.00	100.00	100.00	100.00	100.00	100.00
Pakistan *All jobs*	*Age: 10+*	*Female (%)*			*Male (%)*		
	Hours	*1995*	*2000*	*2003*	*1995*	*2000*	*2003*
PE	<15			2.52			0.36
	15–24			7.28			1.45
	25–34			20.55			4.40
	35–41			22.56			12.76
	42–48			25.03			38.55
	49–55			8.70			10.75
	56+			13.36			31.73
	Total			100.00			100.00
SE	<15			6.53			0.46
	15–24			15.14			1.94
	25–34			25.11			4.12
	35–41			25.39			12.04
	42–48			15.96			19.50
	49–55			6.07			18.93

Country		Gender and year					
Pakistan continued	*Age: 10+*	*Female (%)*			*Male (%)*		
All jobs	*Hours*	*1995*	*2000*	*2003*	*1995*	*2000*	*2003*
	56+			5.80			43.01
	Total			100.00			100.00
TE	<15			4.62			0.64
	15–24			13.63			2.30
	25–34			26.54			4.91
	35–41			23.15			13.48
	42–48			17.70			27.75
	49–55			6.62			15.16
	56+			7.75			35.76
	Total			100.00			100.00
Panama	*Age: 15+*	*Female (%)*			*Male (%)*		
	Hours	*1995*	*2000*	*2004*	*1995*	*2000*	*2004*
PE	<15	2.50	2.69	4.59	1.86	2.19	2.51
	15–24	4.09	4.15	5.35	4.61	4.14	5.50
	25–34	5.83	5.70	4.31	4.19	3.50	3.27
	35	1.51	1.36	0.82	0.72	0.70	0.49
	36–39	1.16	0.98	1.28	1.05	1.12	1.08
	40	43.76	41.27	41.28	31.60	29.37	27.07
	41–47	9.64	8.86	11.59	10.24	9.88	14.21
	48	19.57	24.96	18.60	31.15	35.58	29.48
	49–59	5.70	4.99	6.20	6.63	6.04	7.62
	60+	6.24	4.81	5.87	7.92	7.23	8.71
	Unknown	0.00	0.22	0.11	0.03	0.26	0.06
	Total	100.00	100.00	100.00	100.00	100.00	100.00
SE	<15	27.45	28.85	35.68	8.05	10.14	12.28
	15–24	22.64	17.97	19.48	14.34	11.53	15.57
	25–34	11.60	10.55	9.08	9.87	6.94	8.66
	35	2.42	1.43	2.83	1.67	1.91	1.47
	36–39	1.57	0.94	1.38	2.16	2.11	2.41
	40	7.41	7.26	7.29	15.13	15.23	10.61
	41–47	1.71	3.12	3.71	4.68	4.56	6.83
	48	6.44	8.89	4.43	18.64	19.34	13.31
	49–59	5.57	7.41	4.75	9.43	9.34	9.28
	60+	13.14	13.21	11.28	16.00	18.22	19.59
	Unknown	0.06	0.37	0.09	0.03	0.67	0.00
	Total	100.00	100.00	100.00	100.00	100.00	100.00
TE	<15	6.89	7.88	11.82	3.38	4.37	5.31
	15–24	7.35	6.89	8.64	7.00	6.17	8.38
	25–34	6.84	6.66	5.42	5.59	4.44	4.81
	35	1.67	1.37	1.28	0.95	1.03	0.77
	36–39	1.23	0.98	1.30	1.32	1.39	1.46
	40	37.36	34.52	33.38	27.55	25.50	22.37
	41–47	8.25	7.72	9.76	8.88	8.42	12.10

Country		Gender and year						
Panama continued	Age: 15+	Female (%)			Male (%)			
	Hours	1995	2000	2004	1995	2000	2004	
	48	17.26	21.78	15.31	28.07	31.13	24.86	
	49–59	5.67	5.47	5.86	7.32	6.94	8.09	
	60+	7.46	6.48	7.13	9.91	10.23	11.82	
	Unknown	0.01	0.25	0.10	0.03	0.37	0.04	
	Total	100.00	100.00	100.00	100.00	100.00	100.00	
Peru	Age: 14+	Female (%)			Male (%)			
All jobs	Hours	1995	2001	2004	1995	2001	2004	
PE	<15		7.21	5.84		6.68	3.66	
	15–24		6.73	7.01		5.99	5.76	
	25–34		10.82	11.21		7.02	5.76	
	35		2.16	1.87		1.37	0.87	
	36–39		4.57	4.21		3.60	2.79	
	40		7.21	8.64		6.51	7.33	
	41–47		9.86	7.94		10.96	8.55	
	48		7.93	9.58		9.25	12.57	
	49–59		15.38	13.32		17.98	17.10	
	60+		28.13	30.37		30.65	35.60	
	Total		100.00	100.00		100.00	100.00	
SE	<15		21.32	16.52		8.81	6.58	
	15–24		13.63	13.88		10.83	8.78	
	25–34		10.11	10.13		8.81	7.68	
	35		2.86	3.52		1.65	1.65	
	36–39		3.52	3.52		3.49	3.29	
	40		1.54	1.98		2.39	2.74	
	41–47		6.81	7.05		8.07	5.85	
	48		2.64	3.08		4.95	6.58	
	49–59		9.89	10.13		14.50	12.43	
	60+		27.91	30.18		36.51	44.42	
	Total		100.00	100.00		100.00	100.00	
TE	<15		13.43	10.30		7.58	4.80	
	15–24		9.72	10.07		7.94	6.93	
	25–34		10.42	10.76		7.76	6.57	
	35		2.55	2.52		1.41	1.24	
	36–39		4.17	3.89		3.53	3.02	
	40		4.63	5.72		4.76	5.51	
	41–47		8.56	7.78		9.88	7.46	
	48		5.56	6.64		7.58	10.12	
	49–59		12.96	11.90		16.58	15.28	
	60+		28.01	30.43		32.98	39.08	
	Total		100.00	100.00		100.00	100.00	

Country		Gender and year					
Poland	*Age: 15+*	*Female (%)*			*Male (%)*		
Main job	*Hours*	*1995*	*2000*	*2004*	*1995*	*2000*	*2004*
PE	<19	3.67	3.56	4.49	1.39	1.62	2.15
	20–29	9.03	10.38	10.52	3.40	4.59	3.70
	30–39	5.57	6.76	10.19	3.32	4.47	7.70
	40–49	70.43	67.23	63.71	70.97	68.71	64.51
	50–59	4.32	4.21	4.52	9.28	9.18	10.10
	60+	2.15	2.61	2.67	7.76	8.04	9.16
	Did not work but had a job	4.83	5.24	3.91	3.88	3.39	2.69
	Total	100.00	100.00	100.00	100.00	100.00	100.00
SE	<19	16.51	14.97	15.34	7.78	6.97	9.32
	20–29	16.90	15.96	15.14	9.86	9.54	9.28
	30–39	12.73	14.22	14.95	9.38	9.12	10.35
	40–49	36.46	32.73	28.66	37.25	33.70	28.51
	50–59	8.00	10.50	11.62	14.76	17.61	17.21
	60+	6.34	8.39	9.86	17.88	19.96	22.23
	Did not work but had a job	3.06	3.23	4.44	3.09	3.11	3.09
	Total	100.00	100.00	100.00	100.00	100.00	100.00
TE	<19	7.15	6.38	7.04	3.35	3.20	4.08
	20–29	11.15	11.79	11.64	5.39	6.05	5.25
	30–39	7.48	8.62	11.33	5.19	5.84	8.46
	40–49	61.28	58.65	55.19	60.58	58.38	54.13
	50–59	5.30	5.78	6.23	10.98	11.68	12.14
	60+	3.28	4.05	4.40	10.88	11.54	12.92
	Did not work but had a job	4.35	4.74	4.16	3.63	3.31	3.02
	Total	100.00	100.00	100.00	100.00	100.00	100.00
Portugal	*Age: 15+*	*Female (%)*			*Male (%)*		
Main job	*Hours*	*1998*	*2000*	*2004*	*1998*	*2000*	*2004*
PE	<15	2.43	1.68	1.78	0.39	0.32	0.37
	15–24	6.15	5.91	5.18	1.23	1.06	1.19
	25–34	5.41	4.55	4.42	1.42	1.63	1.35
	35	15.33	18.84	22.35	8.09	10.39	11.49
	36–39	6.12	4.96	4.12	4.37	3.93	2.91
	40	49.90	53.31	53.02	59.56	64.27	65.71
	41–47	9.61	5.93	5.01	12.48	8.69	7.29
	48	1.45	1.09	1.09	2.32	1.92	1.79
	49–59	2.07	2.09	1.86	5.61	4.43	4.78
	60+	1.50	1.52	0.94	4.35	3.10	2.54
	Unknown	0.03	0.11	0.24	0.18	0.26	0.58
	Total	100.00	100.00	100.00	100.00	100.00	100.00
SE	<15	9.92	8.34	11.66	3.74	3.25	5.15
	15–24	15.37	16.13	16.38	6.90	7.04	8.84
	25–34	13.87	16.32	13.78	6.96	8.82	7.80

Country	Gender and year						
Portugal continued *Main job*	Age: 15+	*Female (%)*			*Male (%)*		
	Hours	*1998*	*2000*	*2004*	*1998*	*2000*	*2004*
	35	2.80	2.12	2.76	1.67	1.20	1.56
	36–39	1.13	2.26	0.91	0.65	1.40	0.44
	40	16.47	19.64	20.93	25.47	29.55	31.29
	41–47	10.21	8.93	7.91	13.73	12.96	9.73
	48	3.31	3.37	2.76	5.11	4.26	3.64
	49–59	10.99	10.06	9.62	15.88	15.05	14.16
	60+	15.51	11.33	10.76	19.16	15.22	15.13
	Unknown	0.42	1.48	2.54	0.74	1.25	2.26
	Total	100.00	100.00	100.00	100.00	100.00	100.00
TE	<15	4.50	3.43	4.16	1.38	1.15	1.71
	15–24	8.69	8.60	7.87	2.91	2.74	3.33
	25–34	7.75	7.64	6.67	3.07	3.65	3.15
	35	11.88	14.45	17.64	6.19	7.80	8.71
	36–39	4.74	4.25	3.35	3.27	3.21	2.22
	40	40.69	44.45	45.30	49.45	54.51	56.08
	41–47	9.77	6.73	5.70	12.85	9.89	7.97
	48	1.96	1.69	1.49	3.15	2.58	2.31
	49–59	4.52	4.19	3.73	8.65	7.42	7.40
	60+	5.36	4.10	3.30	8.74	6.51	6.06
	Unknown	0.14	0.47	0.79	0.35	0.54	1.05
	Total	100.00	100.00	100.00	100.00	100.00	100.00

Country	Gender and year						
Romania	Age: 15+	*Female (%)*			*Male (%)*		
All jobs	Hours	*1996*	*2000*	*2004*	*1996*	*2000*	*2004*
PE	1–35	3.35	3.25	2.50	2.96	2.35	1.47
	36–39	0.21	0.19	0.18	0.10	0.12	0.15
	40	83.77	80.40	80.51	79.80	77.43	75.93
	41–45	0.67	0.78	0.94	0.63	0.60	0.76
	46+	9.56	12.73	13.98	12.34	15.22	17.84
	Unknown	2.43	2.65	1.88	4.16	4.29	3.85
	Total	100.00	100.00	100.00	100.00	100.00	100.00
SE	1–35	24.36	25.77	27.82	17.00	17.11	18.17
	36–39	1.84	2.25	2.19	1.35	1.62	1.41
	40	9.47	8.43	15.96	10.83	11.47	16.82
	41–45	3.06	2.55	2.26	3.41	3.07	3.28
	46+	13.76	6.61	9.32	22.42	14.29	16.82
	Unknown	47.50	54.39	42.44	44.98	52.44	43.49
	Total	100.00	100.00	100.00	100.00	100.00	100.00
TE	1–35	12.35	13.68	11.08	7.64	8.52	7.19
	36–39	0.91	1.16	0.86	0.52	0.73	0.60
	40	51.96	47.06	58.62	56.82	49.84	55.68
	41–45	1.69	1.58	1.39	1.56	1.65	1.63
	46+	11.36	9.88	12.42	15.70	14.85	17.47
	Unknown	21.73	26.64	15.63	17.76	24.41	17.43
	Total	100.00	100.00	100.00	100.00	100.00	100.00

Country		Gender and year					
Russia	Age: 25+	Female (%)			Male (%)		
Main job	Hours	1995	2001	2004	1995	2001	2004
PE	<9	0.00	0.20	0.14	0.00	0.18	0.11
	9–15	0.00	0.34	0.34	0.00	0.21	0.18
	<16	7.92	0.00	0.00	4.52	0.00	0.00
	16–20	3.22	2.21	2.15	0.98	0.79	0.78
	21–30	5.00	3.67	3.36	2.34	1.36	1.20
	31–40	80.08	84.36	85.37	85.15	84.94	86.30
	41–50	3.10	3.67	3.87	5.01	6.00	5.86
	51+	0.68	1.41	1.32	2.00	3.77	3.53
	Temporal absence	0.00	4.14	3.45	0.00	2.75	2.04
	Total	100.00	100.00	100.00	100.00	100.00	100.00
SE	<9	0.00	5.63	4.95	0.00	3.04	3.40
	9–15	0.00	11.60	11.06	0.00	7.08	7.20
	<16	8.41	0.00	0.00	5.72	0.00	0.00
	16–20	2.18	8.19	8.50	1.68	5.58	6.51
	21–30	4.57	14.02	15.61	2.71	9.35	10.03
	31–40	75.78	36.65	38.47	74.31	40.11	41.59
	41–50	6.09	13.30	12.86	8.82	17.44	15.80
	51+	2.98	8.76	7.45	6.76	15.62	14.00
	Temporal absence	0.00	1.85	1.10	0.00	1.78	1.47
	Total	100.00	100.00	100.00	100.00	100.00	100.00
TE	<9	0.00	0.61	0.47	0.00	0.42	0.38
	9–15	0.00	1.20	1.06	0.00	0.80	0.76
	<16	7.95	0.00	0.00	4.61	0.00	0.00
	16–20	3.17	2.67	2.58	1.04	1.20	1.25
	21–30	4.97	4.45	4.19	2.37	2.04	1.93
	31–40	79.84	80.74	82.21	84.28	81.14	82.63
	41–50	3.27	4.40	4.47	5.31	6.97	6.67
	51+	0.81	1.97	1.73	2.38	4.77	4.39
	Temporal absence	0.00	3.97	3.30	0.00	2.67	1.99
	Total	100.00	100.00	100.00	100.00	100.00	100.00
Slovakia	Age: 15+	Female (%)			Male (%)		
Main job	Hours	1995	2000	2004	1995	2000	2004
PE	1–19			0.76			0.26
	20–29			3.12			1.25
	30–34			1.57			0.55
	35–39			22.56			17.84
	40–44			64.64			66.06
	45–49			2.82			6.33
	50+			2.80			7.39
	Not more than 4 weeks			1.73			0.32
	Total			100.00			100.00

Country		Gender and year					
Slovakia continued	*Age: 15+*	*Female (%)*			*Male (%)*		
Main job	*Hours*	*1995*	*2000*	*2004*	*1995*	*2000*	*2004*
SE	1–19			1.31			0.37
	20–29			3.78			0.73
	30–34			4.65			0.89
	35–39			5.96			2.82
	40–44			54.22			40.18
	45–49			10.03			10.24
	50+			19.33			44.46
	Not more than 4 weeks			0.73			0.31
	Total			100.00			100.00
TE	1–19			0.79			0.29
	20–29			3.16			1.16
	30–34			1.78			0.60
	35–39			21.33			15.41
	40–44			63.95			61.86
	45–49			3.33			7.00
	50+			4.01			13.34
	Not more than 4 weeks			1.65			0.32
	Total			100.00			100.00
Slovenia	*Age: 25+*	*Female (%)*			*Male (%)*		
Main job	*Hours*	*1995*	*2000*	*2004*	*1995*	*2000*	*2004*
PE	<15	1.00	0.00	0.00	0.61	0.00	0.00
	15–39	5.67	5.06	5.36	3.64	2.90	3.49
	40	73.33	81.01	82.44	70.91	79.42	77.96
	40+	20.00	13.92	12.20	24.85	17.68	18.55
	Total	100.00	100.00	100.00	100.00	100.00	100.00
SE	<15	4.00	3.85	0.00	1.27	1.19	0.00
	15–39	0.00	17.31	22.92	0.00	9.52	14.81
	40	20.00	25.00	31.25	27.85	30.95	32.10
	40+	76.00	53.85	45.83	70.89	58.33	53.09
	Total	100.00	100.00	100.00	100.00	100.00	100.00
TE	<15	0.00	1.35	1.79	0.72	0.70	1.31
	15–39	6.13	6.47	7.42	4.35	4.18	5.24
	40	66.57	72.51	74.68	61.84	69.61	69.00
	40+	27.30	19.68	16.11	33.09	25.52	24.45
	Total	100.00	100.00	100.00	100.00	100.00	100.00
Spain	*Age: 25+*	*Female (%)*			*Male (%)*		
	Hours	*1995*	*2000*	*2004*	*1995*	*2000*	*2004*
PE	<15	4.27	4.29	3.55	0.36	0.31	0.41
	15–24	8.61	9.00	10.97	0.93	1.17	1.13

Country		Gender and year					
Spain continued	Age: 25+	Female (%)			Male (%)		
	Hours	1995	2000	2004	1995	2000	2004
	25–34	8.43	8.35	8.58	2.03	2.07	1.95
	35	5.18	5.91	7.80	2.23	2.87	3.97
	36–39	15.21	14.05	11.75	8.85	9.03	7.68
	40	50.31	50.65	49.85	70.46	69.00	70.05
	41–47	4.20	3.70	3.39	5.88	5.54	5.36
	48	1.28	1.11	1.15	2.17	1.52	1.43
	49–59	1.60	2.10	1.93	4.30	5.85	5.90
	60+	0.92	0.83	1.02	2.75	2.65	2.13
	Unknown	0.03	0.00	0.00	0.06	0.00	0.00
	Total	100.00	100.00	100.00	100.00	100.00	100.00
SE	<15	3.75	3.74	3.11	0.88	0.70	0.70
	15–24	8.83	8.92	8.75	1.99	1.57	1.64
	25–34	7.65	7.30	8.09	2.42	2.04	2.24
	35	2.58	2.77	2.43	1.16	1.11	0.94
	36–39	1.69	1.17	1.22	0.84	0.42	0.45
	40	33.26	34.26	36.10	38.06	35.40	35.83
	41–47	10.74	10.92	11.37	11.89	11.13	11.35
	48	6.12	4.05	3.40	5.84	3.72	3.51
	49–59	12.51	14.96	14.54	18.79	23.94	26.64
	60+	12.87	11.91	11.00	18.12	19.98	16.68
	Unknown	0.00	0.00	0.00	0.00	0.00	0.00
	Total	100.00	100.00	100.00	100.00	100.00	100.00
TE	<15	4.13	4.19	3.48	0.50	0.40	0.47
	15–24	8.66	8.99	10.63	1.22	1.26	1.24
	25–34	8.23	8.16	8.51	2.14	2.06	2.02
	35	4.51	5.34	6.97	1.93	2.45	3.31
	36–39	11.74	11.70	10.12	6.65	6.99	6.11
	40	45.94	47.66	47.73	61.57	61.03	62.61
	41–47	5.87	5.02	4.63	7.53	6.87	6.66
	48	2.52	1.65	1.50	3.18	2.04	1.88
	49–59	4.39	4.45	3.88	8.27	10.14	10.41
	60+	3.98	2.86	2.56	6.97	6.76	5.29
	Unknown	0.02	0.00	0.00	0.05	0.00	0.00
	Total	100.00	100.00	100.00	100.00	100.00	100.00
Sri Lanka	Age: 25+	Female (%)			Male (%)		
	Hours	1996	1999	2003	1996	1999	2003
PE	<15	6.33	8.19	10.17	5.79	7.71	9.88
	15–24	9.17	9.55	11.06	8.60	9.49	11.24
	25–34	16.58	13.69	14.99	10.87	10.92	10.30
	35	2.19	2.24	2.40	1.88	1.08	1.38
	36–39	1.75	1.82	2.78	2.36	1.65	2.10
	40	21.75	20.78	19.76	21.59	19.90	17.01
	41–47	9.73	9.27	8.80	8.06	8.47	6.95
	48	17.51	18.55	12.48	14.48	14.17	12.49

Country	Gender and year						
Sri Lanka continued	*Age: 25+*	*Female (%)*			*Male (%)*		
	Hours	*1996*	*1999*	*2003*	*1996*	*1999*	*2003*
	49–59	9.15	9.00	9.23	13.33	12.14	11.91
	60+	5.85	6.93	8.34	13.04	14.48	16.74
	Total	100.00	100.00	100.00	100.00	100.00	100.00
SE	<15	21.50	18.48	19.36	11.57	11.40	12.24
	15–24	20.22	20.17	19.90	12.73	11.01	11.29
	25–34	19.05	17.48	19.47	13.89	12.22	13.18
	35	5.66	6.37	5.69	6.37	4.37	4.23
	36–39	1.56	2.71	1.68	2.03	2.12	2.26
	40	8.49	11.53	8.87	10.82	12.41	11.73
	41–47	5.25	3.87	4.86	6.80	6.62	5.26
	48	3.25	3.17	3.54	6.08	6.50	6.21
	49–59	6.28	6.82	6.52	12.58	13.33	12.46
	60+	8.74	9.40	10.12	17.14	20.01	21.13
	Total	100.00	100.00	100.00	100.00	100.00	100.00
TE	<15	12.33	12.83	14.23	8.20	9.30	10.92
	15–24	13.54	14.34	14.97	10.32	10.15	11.26
	25–34	17.56	15.40	16.97	12.12	11.48	11.57
	35	3.56	4.10	3.85	3.75	2.50	2.63
	36–39	1.67	2.22	2.29	2.22	1.85	2.17
	40	16.50	16.60	14.95	17.11	16.66	14.68
	41–47	7.95	6.84	7.06	7.53	7.67	6.21
	48	11.86	11.61	8.53	10.98	10.86	9.72
	49–59	8.02	8.02	8.03	13.02	12.66	12.16
	60+	7.00	8.04	9.13	14.74	16.87	18.68
	Total	100.00	100.00	100.00	100.00	100.00	100.00

Switzerland	*Age: 25+*	*Female (%)*			*Male (%)*		
Main job	*Hours*	*1996*	*2000*	*2004*	*1996*	*2000*	*2004*
PE	<15	23.11	21.63	20.37	3.66	3.67	3.60
	15–24	20.58	19.42	20.39	3.59	3.53	3.49
	25–34	15.71	16.12	17.27	8.88	6.40	5.74
	35	2.54	3.06	2.68	2.06	1.68	1.68
	36–39	4.55	4.58	4.90	4.35	3.35	3.42
	40	6.14	6.67	6.84	8.61	9.87	9.89
	41–47	20.48	21.62	20.23	44.80	44.12	44.80
	48	1.32	0.91	0.95	2.46	3.33	2.42
	49–59	4.16	4.14	4.63	16.02	16.82	18.00
	60+	1.42	1.84	1.74	5.55	7.23	6.96
	Total	100.00	100.00	100.00	100.00	100.00	100.00
SE	<15	35.88	34.89	31.82	7.04	8.22	7.52
	15–24	14.42	14.91	18.13	5.13	4.92	5.82
	25–34	10.37	11.47	11.65	6.26	5.76	7.79
	35	1.48	2.95	2.60	2.02	2.65	2.51
	36–39	2.47	2.95	2.08	3.36	1.99	1.52
	40	4.73	6.18	6.32	5.77	6.72	8.80

Country		Gender and year					
Switzerland continued	*Age: 25+*	*Female (%)*			*Male (%)*		
Main job	*Hours*	*1996*	*2000*	*2004*	*1996*	*2000*	*2004*
	41–47	9.29	7.55	9.89	17.05	15.06	14.58
	48	0.00	0.00	0.00	1.68	1.65	1.52
	49–59	11.02	7.59	7.08	20.41	20.39	19.85
	60+	10.33	11.50	10.43	31.27	32.65	30.08
	Total	100.00	100.00	100.00	100.00	100.00	100.00
TE	<15	24.93	23.48	21.80	4.20	4.40	4.14
	15–24	19.64	18.78	20.10	3.84	3.75	3.81
	25–34	14.89	15.46	16.55	8.46	6.30	6.02
	35	2.35	3.05	2.65	2.07	1.83	1.79
	36–39	4.26	4.32	4.54	4.20	3.11	3.18
	40	5.92	6.60	6.78	8.16	9.38	9.74
	41–47	18.81	19.64	18.92	40.36	39.50	40.61
	48	1.33	0.85	0.89	2.33	3.04	2.28
	49–59	5.15	4.63	4.93	16.72	17.40	18.26
	60+	2.72	3.20	2.83	9.66	11.30	10.17
	Total	100.00	100.00	100.00	100.00	100.00	100.00

Country		Gender and year		
Tanzania	*Age: 10+*	*Both (%)*		
Main job	*Hours*	*1995*	*2000*	*2004*
PE	1–9		0.36	
	10–19		0.99	
	20–29		2.43	
	30–39		2.97	
	40–49		26.35	
	50–59		22.93	
	60–69		16.28	
	70+		27.70	
	Total		100.00	
SE	1–9		3.68	
	10–19		10.47	
	20–29		13.74	
	30–39		17.20	
	40–49		28.05	
	50–59		11.23	
	60–69		7.17	
	70+		8.46	
	Total		100.00	
TE	1–9		3.42	
	10–19		9.74	
	20–29		12.86	
	30–39		16.10	
	40–49		27.91	
	50–59		12.31	
	60–69		7.88	
	70+		9.95	
	Total		100.00	

Country	Gender and year						
Thailand	Age: 15+	Female (%)			Male (%)		
All jobs	Hours	1995	2000	2004	1995	2000	2004
PE	1–9	0.13	0.38		0.04	0.16	
	10–19	0.73	1.13		0.55	1.07	
	20–29	2.12	2.73		1.46	2.88	
	30–34	1.85	1.98		1.57	2.53	
	35–39	12.88	14.68		11.48	13.10	
	40–49	42.44	47.90		38.53	42.99	
	50+	39.84	31.20		46.36	37.27	
	Total	100.00	100.00		100.00	100.00	
SE	1–9	0.51	0.67		0.29	0.41	
	10–19	2.27	2.94		1.64	2.71	
	20–29	6.64	7.11		5.88	5.64	
	30–34	2.61	2.80		2.22	2.36	
	35–39	10.87	9.59		7.12	6.56	
	40–49	23.47	25.63		20.63	21.26	
	50+	53.63	51.25		62.21	61.06	
	Total	100.00	100.00		100.00	100.00	
TE	1–9	0.35	0.54		0.17	0.30	
	10–19	1.63	2.14		1.11	1.95	
	20–29	4.77	5.16		3.76	4.37	
	30–34	2.30	2.44		1.91	2.44	
	35–39	11.70	11.86		9.22	9.58	
	40–49	31.32	35.55		29.25	31.31	
	50+	47.93	42.32		54.58	50.07	
	Total	100.00	100.00		100.00	100.00	
UK	Age: 25+	Female (%)			Male (%)		
	Hours	1995	2000	2003	1995	2000	2003
PE	<15		6.01	6.20		1.12	1.66
	15–24		17.03	14.61		1.90	1.63
	25–34		16.01	18.15		4.22	4.38
	35		2.98	3.01		1.49	1.53
	36–39		16.19	14.86		13.46	12.53
	40		6.54	6.48		7.71	8.32
	41–47		21.50	22.75		32.85	35.90
	48		1.29	1.09		3.77	2.74
	49–59		8.51	9.62		22.46	22.49
	60+		2.66	2.10		9.11	7.02
	Unknown		1.29	1.13		1.90	1.78
	Total		100.00	100.00		100.00	100.00
SE	<15		13.46	8.44		2.29	2.69
	15–24		13.72	13.93		2.76	3.28
	25–34		13.62	16.10		4.28	5.53
	35		2.81	3.10		1.68	1.47
	36–39		5.45	7.84		4.98	4.78

Country	Gender and year							
UK continued	Age: 25+	Female (%)			Male (%)			
	Hours	1995	2000	2003	1995	2000	2003	
	40		5.92	6.01		6.76	7.77	
	41–47		13.98	16.14		20.15	22.18	
	48		1.04	1.44		3.20	1.78	
	49–59		12.14	15.75		25.21	29.11	
	60+		12.52	8.83		24.66	18.79	
	Unknown		5.34	2.43		4.03	2.63	
	Total		100.00	100.00		100.00	100.00	
TE	<15		6.19	6.26		1.17	1.71	
	15–24		16.95	14.59		1.95	1.71	
	25–34		15.95	18.10		4.22	4.44	
	35		2.98	3.01		1.50	1.52	
	36–39		15.92	14.69		13.05	12.15	
	40		6.52	6.47		7.66	8.30	
	41–47		21.32	22.59		32.24	35.24	
	48		1.28	1.10		3.75	2.69	
	49–59		8.60	9.77		22.59	22.81	
	60+		2.90	2.26		9.87	7.59	
	Unknown		1.39	1.16		2.01	1.82	
	Total		100.00	100.00		100.00	100.00	

Ukraine	Age: 15–70	Female (%)			Male (%)			
Main job	Hours	1995	2000	2003	1995	2000	2003	
PE	<20		5.19	3.57		1.74	1.03	
	20–29		3.79	3.23		1.74	0.98	
	30–39		8.05	7.09		9.25	7.17	
	40		68.33	73.17		75.49	78.49	
	Not specified		6.64	6.97		9.21	10.67	
	Unknown		8.00	5.98		2.57	1.66	
	Total		100.00	100.00		100.00	100.00	
SE	<20		0.24	0.01		0.11	0.03	
	20–29		0.95	0.13		0.93	0.17	
	30–39		3.48	0.61		4.30	0.62	
	40		42.04	5.51		56.02	9.79	
	Not specified		11.60	18.99		16.38	33.31	
	Unknown		41.70	74.75		22.26	56.08	
	Total		100.00	100.00		100.00	100.00	
TE	<20		3.97	3.12		1.26	0.91	
	20–29		3.09	2.84		1.50	0.88	
	30–39		6.93	6.27		7.78	6.37	
	40		61.89	64.63		69.71	70.09	
	Not specified		7.86	8.48		11.34	13.43	
	Unknown		16.26	14.65		8.42	8.32	
	Total		100.00	100.00		100.00	100.00	

Country		Gender and year					
Uruguay	*Age: 25+*	*Female (%)*			*Male (%)*		
Main job	*Hours*	*1995*	*2000*	*2004*	*1995*	*2000*	*2004*
PE	<15	7.24	7.13	8.23	1.12	1.40	1.64
	15–24	14.66	15.24	15.30	2.94	3.64	4.28
	25–34	16.68	17.70	14.72	6.43	7.76	6.73
	35	3.61	3.48	3.13	2.50	2.14	1.93
	36–39	7.29	6.75	6.82	2.99	2.84	2.88
	40	13.07	17.57	20.96	16.37	18.19	21.19
	41–47	7.68	7.40	8.39	9.26	7.96	10.03
	48	12.20	13.75	12.68	25.09	26.89	25.41
	49–59	4.46	4.90	4.49	9.00	9.20	9.77
	60+	4.98	6.09	5.28	17.34	19.98	16.14
	Unknown	8.14	0.00	0.00	6.97	0.00	0.00
	Total	100.00	100.00	100.00	100.00	100.00	100.00
SE	<15	11.95	15.48	19.10	3.36	6.12	7.99
	15–24	16.64	18.86	17.17	8.04	8.66	12.94
	25–34	12.54	12.43	11.03	8.23	8.88	9.62
	35	1.08	1.82	1.23	1.21	1.37	0.89
	36–39	3.44	3.13	1.99	2.22	1.80	1.77
	40	9.44	11.41	13.28	12.45	14.04	18.04
	41–47	3.21	3.09	3.90	5.51	4.53	4.48
	48	6.54	7.37	6.99	12.31	12.56	10.51
	49–59	7.51	6.20	7.29	11.31	10.26	10.15
	60+	21.79	20.21	18.01	31.44	31.79	23.62
	Unknown	5.84	0.00	0.00	3.90	0.00	0.00
	Total	100.00	100.00	100.00	100.00	100.00	100.00
TE	<15	8.55	9.19	11.11	1.85	2.99	3.88
	15–24	15.22	16.19	15.83	4.61	5.34	7.33
	25–34	15.53	16.46	13.78	7.02	8.17	7.76
	35	2.91	3.08	2.64	2.08	1.89	1.57
	36–39	6.22	5.89	5.58	2.74	2.50	2.50
	40	12.06	16.05	18.93	15.09	16.83	20.10
	41–47	6.43	6.34	7.21	8.04	6.83	8.10
	48	10.62	12.15	11.15	20.91	22.09	20.18
	49–59	5.31	5.19	5.20	9.76	9.53	9.88
	60+	9.65	9.46	8.56	21.95	23.82	18.70
	Unknown	7.50	0.00	0.00	5.97	0.00	0.00
	Total	100.00	100.00	100.00	100.00	100.00	100.00
USA	*Age: 16+*	*Female (%)*			*Male (%)*		
All jobs	*Hours*	*1995*	*2000*	*2004*	*1995*	*2000*	*2004*
PE	1–4	1.17	1.07	1.16	0.68	0.55	0.65
	5–14	5.30	4.60	4.78	2.45	2.19	2.33
	15–29	17.20	15.41	16.01	8.25	7.37	7.85
	30–34	10.00	8.75	9.38	5.95	5.07	5.68
	35–39	10.10	9.04	9.19	5.27	4.65	4.89
	40	35.82	40.12	40.78	37.77	41.36	43.59

Country		Gender and year					
USA continued	Age: 16+	Female (%)			Male (%)		
All jobs	Hours	1995	2000	2004	1995	2000	2004
	41–48	10.00	9.84	8.52	13.93	13.11	11.54
	49–59	6.79	7.31	6.57	14.82	14.94	13.61
	60+	3.63	3.85	3.60	10.87	10.75	9.88
	Total	100.00	100.00	100.00	100.00	100.00	100.00
SE	1–4	4.94	4.54	4.71	2.07	1.63	1.98
	5–14	13.22	11.78	11.47	5.61	4.18	4.81
	15–29	21.13	21.14	21.64	11.89	10.40	11.91
	30–34	8.81	8.26	9.42	6.70	6.50	6.97
	35–39	6.58	6.46	6.11	5.30	5.28	5.66
	40	16.16	19.59	20.58	20.94	26.11	28.22
	41–48	6.33	5.90	5.66	7.68	7.76	7.23
	49–59	11.21	10.83	10.18	16.70	16.87	15.10
	60+	11.61	11.50	10.23	23.10	21.27	18.12
	Total	100.00	100.00	100.00	100.00	100.00	100.00
TE	1–4	1.41	1.28	1.37	0.82	0.64	0.76
	5–14	5.80	5.02	5.16	2.75	2.36	2.54
	15–29	17.52	15.80	16.38	8.62	7.65	8.21
	30–34	9.92	8.72	9.39	6.02	5.19	5.79
	35–39	9.86	8.88	9.01	5.27	4.71	4.96
	40	34.49	38.86	39.58	36.14	40.06	42.26
	41–48	9.75	9.60	8.35	13.33	12.66	11.16
	49–59	7.08	7.52	6.78	15.00	15.10	13.73
	60+	4.16	4.31	3.99	12.05	11.63	10.59
	Total	100.00	100.00	100.00	100.00	100.00	100.00
Zimbabwe	Age: 15+	Female (%)			Male (%)		
Main job	Hours	1995	1999	2004	1995	1999	2004
PE	<15		0.90			0.75	
	15–24		2.44			1.28	
	25–34		3.50			1.77	
	35		1.49			0.98	
	36–39		1.54			0.81	
	40		20.27			20.53	
	41–47		10.71			15.96	
	48		14.76			16.76	
	49–59		21.44			21.38	
	60+		19.70			17.60	
	Not stated		3.24			2.17	
	Total		100.00			100.00	
SE	<15		7.68			6.26	
	15–24		14.63			13.22	
	25–34		16.68			14.09	
	35		5.61			4.90	
	36–39		4.61			3.81	

Country	Gender and year						
Zimbabwe continued	*Age: 15+*	*Female (%)*			*Male (%)*		
Main job	*Hours*	*1995*	*1999*	*2004*	*1995*	*1999*	*2004*
	40		10.95			13.16	
	41–47		10.58			11.63	
	48		7.03			7.91	
	49–59		8.36			10.38	
	60+		7.62			11.86	
	Not stated		6.24			2.78	
	Total		100.00			100.00	
TE	<15		5.81			2.76	
	15–24		11.28			5.63	
	25–34		13.05			6.26	
	35		4.47			2.41	
	36–39		3.77			1.90	
	40		13.51			17.84	
	41–47		10.62			14.38	
	48		9.16			13.54	
	49–59		11.96			17.37	
	60+		10.95			15.51	
	Not stated		5.42			2.39	
	Total		100.00			100.00	

Index

actual working hours: economic factors 22; impact of regulations 22, 139; textile industry 26, 26; *see also* effective regulation index; observance rates

age of workers: informal economy 116, 118, 119; labour market participation 64, 79; long hours 83; patterns of working hours 79–80, 80, 81, 84, 140; short hours 81, 82, 84; *see also* life course

Albania: distribution of working hours 168

Alouane, Y. 97

Altman, M. 37

annual leave: actual leave taken 20; entitlement to 18, 20; flexibility 76, 78; international comparison 19, 26, 26; other leave for family matters 76, 84; reduction of working hours 20

annual working hours 25, 26; historical trends 25, 26

annualized hours schemes 100

Anxo, D. 22, 33, 55, 66, 141, 144

Aparicio Valdez, L. 32, 67, 94, 99

Argentina: distribution of working hours 169

Armenia: bifurcation of hours 62; distribution of working hours 169–70

Asian Development Bank 60

Australia: distribution of working hours 170–71; flexible working time 75; reported feelings of overwork 75

average working hours: limitations of figures 33, 62; manufacturing sector 27, 28–31, 32, 62, 89, 90; service sector 89, 90, 91–2, 93, 94, 95, 118, 140

Azerbaijan: distribution of working hours 171–2

Berkovsky, J. 69, 93, 95, 98, 121, 130, 131, 132, 135

Bienefeld, M. 22

bifurcation of hours 35, 61, 62, 63

Blackden, M. 58, 147

Bolivia: bifurcation of hours 61, 62; distribution of working hours 172

Bosch, G. 2, 123, 150

Botero, J. 10

Bothfeld, S. 60

Boulin, J.-Y. 2, 66

Bourdieu, J. 24

Brazil: irregular occupations 114; patterns of working hours by age groups 79, 80; reduction of hours 17–18; women's responsibility for domestic tasks 65, 66

Browne, J. 38

Browne, M. 24

Bulgaria: distribution of working hours 173

Burchell, B. 66, 75

Canada: distribution of working hours 173–4

Carr, D. 105, 112, 114

Castro, M. 115

Chaney, E. 115

Charter of Fundamental Rights of the European Union 9

Chetvernina, T. 81, 97, 118, 124, 126, 130, 132, 135, 136

children: laws to reduce working hours 8

Chile: part-time workers 55, 58; reduction of hours 12, 17; working hours over life course 81, 82

China: patterns of working hours by age groups 80, 80

collective agreements 10, 34, 35
commitment: long hours as indication of 136
compressed working weeks 130
Cooke, G. 99
country-specific circumstances: working time policies 154
country studies 4
Cousins, C. 125, 128, 132, 133
Croatia: distribution of working hours 174–5
Cyprus: distribution of working hours 175–6
Czech Republic: distribution of working hours 176–7

daily hours limits: preventing workplace accidents 10; regular time for non-work activities 10
Davidov, G. 145
decent working time arrangements 153, 154; criteria for 141, 142, 143; family-friendly working time 146–7; gender equality initiatives 147–8; healthy working time 143–6; productivity enhancing 149–51; workers' choice and influence over working time 151, 152, 153
Dembe, A. 143
developing countries: distribution of working hours for self-employed by gender 108–9, 113–14, 119, 140; short hours 55
Devine, T. 105
Dhanani, S. 58
disguised employment 136
distribution of working hours 33; bifurcation of hours 35, 61, 62, 63; data collection 36; diversification of hours worked 64, 88–9; individual country analysis 168–213; lack of data 36; non-observance of regulations 34, 35; overtime hours 34, 35, 35; part-time work 33, 34, 35; working time regimes 33–4, 35, 60, 61; *see also* long hours; short hours
domestic workers 115, 136

Echeverría, M. 81, 93, 95, 98, 115, 123, 128, 133, 135, 136
economic development and income levels: determining working hours 27, 32, 33, 43, 62; effective regulation index 44, 44; reduction of hours 22–3;

short hours 55, 58; statutory hours limits 38, 42
economic performance and working time regulation 144
economic value of leisure 24
effective regulation index (ERI) 43, 44, 45, 61, 63, 139; association with economic development 44, 44; international comparison 40–41, 43–4; *see also* observance rates
eight-hour day 1, 8, 24; productivity impacts 24
employment levels 66
employment promotion 9, 12, 17
employment relationship 142
ERI *see* effective regulation index
Esim, S. 115
Esponda, B. 83, 93, 121, 122, 123
Estonia: distribution of working hours 177–8
Ethiopia: distribution of working hours 178
EU Member States: working hours of older workers 80
EU Part-time Work Directive 125, 148
EU Working Time Directive 45, 125, 126
European Commission 65
European Foundation 2
Eurostat 65, 89, 98
excessive hours *see* long hours
extended opening hours 97
extension of working hours 24
Eyraud, F. 146

Fagan, C. 37, 55, 66, 69, 75, 128, 132
family-friendly working time 146–7; *see also* work–life balance
Fenwick, C. 137, 145
Figart, D. 2, 124
Finland: distribution of working hours 179
five-day week 18
flexible working time 74, 75, 84, 100, 124–5, 130; annualized hours schemes 100; availability of 84, 131; awareness and knowledge of 132; balancing the needs of employers and workers 130–31; compressed working weeks 130; daily schedule 76; effectiveness of policies 137, 141; employer support for 130; flexi-time schemes 129, 130; holidays 76, 78; hours averaging 100, 125–7, 132; lack of research on 124;

longer working hours 78, 84;
modulation schemes 100; night work
98, 129; non-standard work 131–2;
on-call work 130; other leave for
family matters 76, 84; part-time work
128; productivity 151; protection of
workers 152; shift work 96–8, 99, 129;
time-banking schemes 129; weekend
working 99–100; weekly rest periods
127–8; work–life balance 75, 76, 77, 78
Ford, H. 24
40-hour week 1, 9, 11–12, 17, 20, 138–9;
as social standard 9
48-hour week 1, 8, 9, 12, 17, 20, 24, 52,
139
Forty-Hour Week Convention, 1935
(No. 47) 1, 9, 144–5
France: distribution of working hours
179–80
Frenkel, S. 123, 124
future research requirements 142, 143,
144

Gadrey, N. 99
Galasi, P. 67, 81, 93, 94, 95, 98, 99, 121,
128, 129, 130, 133, 135
gender: distribution of working hours
168–213; equality initiatives 147–8,
150–51; gaps in working hours 74–5,
76, 84, 139–40
Georgia: distribution of working hours
180–81
Ghosheh, N. 80, 81
globalization 7
Golden, L. 2, 37, 78, 124
Görg, H. 60
Greece: distribution of working hours
181–2
Guatemala: distribution of working
hours 182–3

health and safety 143–6; daily hours
limits 10; incidence of long hours 45,
46–51, 52, 53, 54, 63; limiting hours
8–9
Heymann, J. 133
holidays *see* annual leave
Holidays with Pay Convention
(Revised), 1970 (No. 132) 18
Honduras: distribution of working hours
183–4
hours averaging 100, 125–7; extent of
use 132; protection from long hours
126–7

Hours of Work (Industry) Convention,
1919 (No. 1) 1, 8, 9, 24, 45, 52, 53, 144,
153
Hours of Work (Commerce and
Offices) Convention, 1930 (No. 30) 1,
8, 52, 53, 144, 154
Houseman, S. 2
Huberman, M. 25
human rights instruments 9
Hungary: distribution of working hours
184; reported feelings of overwork 75;
temporal constraints on women's
availability 67
Hussmans, R. 101

ICLS 37, 58, 102
IDS 98
Ilahi, N. 65
ILO *see* International Labour Office
inadequate employment 37
Incomes Data Service (IDS) 98
Indonesia: distribution of working hours
185
industrial relations frameworks 144
industrialization 24
industrialized countries: distribution of
working hours for self-employed by
gender 105, 106–7, 112–13, 118–19,
140; short hours 55
informal economy 101, 140, 142, 143,
145; age of workers 116, 118, 119;
conceptual framework 101, 102;
definition of 101; domestic workers
115; rights of workers 136–7;
secondary source of income 118, 119;
short hours 55, 58; size of 102, 102;
wage employment 103; women,
employment of 102; work schedules
dependent on volume of work 117;
see also self-employment
information sources 4–5
institutional framework 143;
determining working hours 27
intermittent work 94, 136
International Conference of Labour
Statisticians (ICLS) 37, 58, 102
International Covenant on
Economic, Social and Cultural
Rights 9
International Labour Office (ILO) 1, 2,
8, 9, 10, 12, 13, 14, 15, 26, 27, 31, 33, 33,
45, 53, 53, 54, 59, 60, 64, 65, 66, 67, 68,
74, 77, 80, 82, 86, 87, 88, 88, 90, 92, 96,
101, 102, 103, 103, 105, 112, 113, 116,

123, 138, 141, 143, 149, 150, 154;
Committee of Experts on the
Application of Conventions and
Recommendations 18; Constitution 8;
data collection on distribution of
working hours 36; Database of
Working Time Laws 4, 11, 16, 19, 120,
124
International Standard Industrial
Classification (ISIC) 89, 95
international standards 1, 7, 8, 9;
revisions to 153–4
Ireland: distribution of working hours
185–6
ISIC 89, 95
Israel: distribution of working hours
186–7

Japan: distribution of working hours 188
Jolivet, A. 81

Kalev, A. 78
Kelly, E. 78
Kenya: plantation work and family
responsibilities 73
Knight, F. 104
knowledge workers: working hours 104
Kuruvilla, S. 123, 124
Kuwait: domestic migrant workers 115

labour market participation: age of
workers 79; men 65, 66; women 64, 65,
66, 133
leave *see* annual leave
Lee, S. 2, 3, 7, 17, 24, 33, 34, 37, 38, 43,
44, 53, 55, 61, 78, 81, 114, 133, 134, 136,
144, 149, 153
Lehndorff, S. 27, 32, 123, 150
Leiva, S. 58
life course: tripartite division 79;
working hours of men and women 81,
82; *see also* age of workers
literature on working time 2
Lithuania: distribution of working hours
189–90
living standards 23
long hours 2, 36, 61; compensating for
lower wages 121, 122, 123, 141, 145–6,
154; concept of 37; earnings
advantages and benefit entitlements
121, 122, 122, 123; flexible working 78,
84; health and safety risks 45, 46–51;
52, 53, 54, 63; inadequate employment
37; as indication of commitment 136;

men 68, 69, 70, 71, 84; older workers
83; paid employees 52, 70, 71;
ratification of standards 52–3, 53;
self-employment 52; women 68, 70,
71; *see also* bifurcation of hours;
observance rates
Lundall, P. 94
Luxembourg: distribution of working
hours 190–91

Macau: distribution of working hours
191
McCann, D. 2, 3, 7, 9, 24, 37, 38, 43, 53,
78, 134, 136, 149, 153
Macedonia: distribution of working
hours 192
Madagascar: distribution of working
hours 192–3
Maddison, A. 24
Malaysia: commitment to women's
labour participation 133; extended
opening hours in retail sector 97;
flexible working time 75; promoting
productivity 124; temporal constraints
on women's availability 67; weekly
rest periods 127
Maloney, W. 114
Malta: distribution of working hours
193–4
manufacturing sector: average weekly
working hours 27, 28–31, 89, 90;
historical trends in weekly working
hours 27, 32, 62
Mauritius: bifurcation of hours 62;
distribution of working hours 194–5
Mehran, F. 37, 123
men: distribution of working hours
168–213; employment levels 66;
labour force participation 65, 66;
long hours 68, 69, 70, 71, 84; short
hours 68, 69, 72, 73; unemployment
levels 66
Messenger, J. 2, 6, 64, 69, 86, 88, 94, 112,
124, 138, 141, 152
Mexico: distribution of working hours
195–6; long hours of older workers 83;
working hours, earnings and benefits
122, 122
minimum working hours 24
modulation schemes 100
mothers: consent to work on rest days
and overtime 131
Murray, J. 8, 123
Mwatha Karega, R. 73

Nagaraj, S. 93, 94, 97, 124, 127, 131, 132, 133
Nakamura, A. 2
national legal standards 7
national statistics 4–5, 36
Ndiaye, A. 97, 98, 117, 121, 124, 126, 129, 130, 131, 135
Netherlands: distribution of working hours 197
New Zealand: distribution of working hours 197–8
night work 98, 129
Norway: distribution of working hours 198–9

observance rates 20–21, 22, 34, 35, 38, 39, 40–41, 42, 43, 61, 63, 134, 135, 136, 139, 144; *see also* effective regulation index
OECD 64, 87, 88
older workers *see* age of workers
on-call work 130
O'Reilly, J. 2, 33, 60, 128, 144
Organization for Economic Co-operation and Development (OECD) 64, 87, 88
overtime 34, 35, 35; as effective limit on weekly hours 18; importance of payments 121; increasing productivity 141; limits on 18, 45, 131; mothers of young children's consent 131; payments for 134–5; pregnant workers' right to refuse 131; resistance towards reducing 121; voluntary 135
overwork: reported feelings of 75, 76, 78

paid employees: distribution of working hours 168–213; long hours 52, 70, 71; short hours 56–7, 72, 73
Pakistan: distribution of working hours 199–200
Panama: distribution of working hours 200–01
Parker, S. 52
part-time work 128; distribution of working hours 33, 34, 35; extent of use in formal economy 132; gender equality 148; impact on household income 141; promotion of 133, 137; service sector 88–9, 95, 96, 96; terms and conditions of employment 134; work–family reconciliation 133, 141; *see also* short hours

Part-Time Work Convention, 1999 (No. 175) 148
pay-for-performance incentives 150
Perseu Abramo Foundation 65
Peru: distribution of working hours 201; fragmented shift systems 99; temporal constraints on women's availability 67
Phelps Brown, E. 24
Philippines: men and women's working hours 67, 68
Picot, G. 2
Poland: distribution of working hours 202
Portugal: distribution of working hours 202–3
pregnant workers: consent to work on rest days 131; right to refuse overtime 131
productivity: effect of working time 123–4, 141; eight-hour day 24; enhancing 149–51; flexible working time 151; gender equality 150–51
protective regulation 154
Protocol of San Salvador 9
Purcell, K. 69

ratification of standards: impact on long hours 52–3, 53
Rea, J. 24
reduction of hours 17, 18, 24, 25; application of modern practices 23; capabilities of workers and employers in maximizing net benefits 22; economic development, level of 22–3; factors to consider 22–3; lack of data on 24; living standards 23; phased introduction of statutory limits 17; political pressure for 24; potential to promote employment 9, 12, 17; preferences of employers and workers 23
Reduction of Hours of Work Recommendation, 1962 (No. 116) 9, 22
Rees, H. 104
regulations: globalization effects 7; impact on labour market in developing countries 3; *see also* effective regulation index; observance rates
Reich, R. 104
reported feelings of overwork 75, 76, 78
Republic of Korea: distribution of working hours 61, 61, 188–9; five-day

week 18; patterns of working hours by age groups 80, 80, 81; reduction of hours 12, 17, 18; responsibility for domestic tasks 66; weekly rest periods 127

Republic of Moldova: distribution of working hours 196; informal economy 116, 116

rest days 18, 127, 128; consent to work on 131; 18, 127, 128; flexible working 127–8; liberalizing prohibition of work on rest days 127, 128; longer rest periods 127; one-day weekly rest 1–2; reduction of working hours 18; religious groups contributing to debate on Sunday as rest day 128; weekly rest periods 18

retirement: timing of 79

Revised European Social Charter (1996) 9

Reynaud, B. 24

Richards, N. 97

rigidity of working time laws 43

Rinehart, R. 150

Romania: distribution of working hours 203

Rubery, J. 99

Russia: distribution of working hours 204

Saboia, J. 58, 64, 93, 98, 100, 115, 126, 130

Saget, C. 146

Schor, J. 24

Schumpeter, J. 104

scope of legislation 136

security industry: hours of work 94, 136

self-employment 103, 103; career/'pull' theory 104; default/'push' theory 104, 105; distribution of working hours 52, 69, 104, 105, 106–11, 112–17, 118, 119, 140, 168–213; long hours 52; short hours 56–7, 72, 73; temporal constraints on women 74

Senegal: informal economy 117; promoting productivity 124

service sector: average weekly working hours 89, 90, 91–2, 93, 94, 95, 118, 140; diversification of working hours 88–9; fragmentation of working time 99; healthy working time 144; implications for employment growth 87, 88; part-time work 88–9, 95, 96, 96; share of total employment 87, 88;

source of female employment 87; work schedules 96–100, 118, 140

Shah, A. 104

shift work 129; manufacturing sector 97; service sector 96–8, 99

short hours 61, 63; age of workers 81, 82, 84; developing countries 55; factors determining 58; industrialized countries 55; informal economy 55, 58; men 68, 69, 72, 73; national income, association with 55, 58; paid employees 56–7, 72, 73; proportion of workers 55, 56–7; self-employment 56–7, 72, 73; time-related underemployment 35, 35, 58–9, 59, 60, 61; women 68, 69, 72, 73, 81, 84; work–family constraints 58; *see also* bifurcation of hours; part-time work

Slovakia: distribution of working hours 204–5

Slovenia: distribution of working hours 205

small-scale surveys 4

Smith, M. 115

social consensus of working time 153

social dialogue 124, 154

social intervention 62

social protection systems 83;

Sorj, B. 66, 114

South Africa Department of Labour 94

Spain: distribution of working hours 205–6

Spurgeon, A. 8, 45, 143

Sri Lanka: bifurcation of hours 62; distribution of working hours 206–7

Stettner, A. 112

Strobl, E. 60

Supiot, A. 127

Switzerland: distribution of working hours 207–8

Tang, N. 125, 128, 132, 133

Tanzania: distribution of working hours 208

Taylor, O. 93, 94, 98, 100, 125, 128, 129, 130, 131, 132, 134, 135

temporal constraints on women 66, 67, 84; encouraging self-employment 74; work schedules 69, 73, 74; working when partners at home 74

ten-hour daily limit 8

tertiarization *see* service sector

textile industry: actual weekly hours 26, 26

Thailand: distribution of working hours 209

Thompson, E. 24

time-banking schemes 129

time-related underemployment 35, 35, 58–9, 59, 60, 61

Tipple, G. 117

Torres, L. 104

trade unions: determining working hours 27; flexible working time 130; observance of regulations 22; reduction of hours 24; *see also* collective agreements

transition countries: distribution of working hours for self-employed by gender 110–11, 114–18, 119, 140–41

Ukraine: distribution of working hours 210

unemployment levels 66

United Kingdom: distribution of working hours 209–10

United States: distribution of working hours 211–12

Universal Declaration of Human Rights 9

Uruguay: distribution of working hours 211

Valodia, I. 103

Vaughan-Whitehead, D. 69, 121, 123, 126, 128, 129, 132, 133, 134

wages: longer hours to compensate for lower wages 121, 122, 123, 141, 145–6, 154

weekend working: service sector 99–100

weekly hours limits 7–8, 11–12, 17–18, 20; deregulation 20; embodying a national aspiration 8; evolution of 13–16

Weekly Rest (Industry) Convention, 1921 (No. 14) 1, 18

Weekly Rest (Commerce and Offices) Convention, 1957 (No. 106) 1–2, 18

weekly rest periods *see* rest days

White, M. 22, 149, 150

Wodon, Q. 58, 147

women: childbearing and childrearing years 82; distribution of working hours 168–213; employment levels 66; informal economy 102; labour force participation 64, 65, 66, 133; long hours 68, 70, 71; part-time self-employment 69, 105; part-time work 133; service sector 87; short hours 68, 69, 72, 73, 81, 84; unemployment levels 66; *see also* self-employment; temporal constraints on women; work–life balance

Wong, G. 2

Wood, A. 114, 134

Work Improvement in Small Enterprises (WISE) 150

work–life balance 76: absence of work–family policies 133; daily hours limits 10; family-friendly working time 69, 146–7; flexible working time 75, 76, 77, 78; gender equality initiatives 148; hours reductions 9, 17; part-time work 133, 141; responsibility for domestic work 65, 66; self-employment for women 105, 112–13, 114; short hours 58; work–family policies 132, 133, 134; workers with children 75, 77, 78

work schedules: family-friendly 69; informal economy 117; service sector 96–100, 118, 140; temporal constraints of women 69, 73, 74

workers' choice and influence over working time 23, 151, 152, 153

working time flexibility *see* flexible working time

working time regimes 44, 45; distribution of working hours 33–4, 35, 60, 61

World Bank 3, 33, 38, 43, 44, 54, 58, 63, 139, 149

Yoon, J. 17, 20, 66, 81, 98, 121, 126, 127, 130, 132, 135

Zeng, X. 20, 54, 80, 93, 94, 97, 98, 99, 100, 121, 125, 126, 135

Zeytinoglu, I. 99

Zimbabwe: distribution of working hours 212–13